THE CHRONICLE OF A CONTINENT

IN THE 2ND REVISED EDITION, DISCOVER

* The origins of myths and stereotypes about Africa—and the truths about its place in world history

*The evolution of early African societies, kingdoms, and city-states

*The struggle for independence and the pan-African movement

*The rise of Islamic fundamentalism

*And much more

JOSEPH E. HARRIS, a noted black scholar, studied for his B.A. and M.A. degrees at Howard University and obtained his Ph.D. in African history from Northwestern University. Dr. Harris accepted the invitation of the University of Nairobi to be visiting professor of history in 1972. He is currently professor of history at Howard University. He is also the author of several academic books on African history.

AFRICANS AND THEIR HISTORY

Second Revised Edition

Joseph E. Harris

A MERIDIAN BOOK

MERIDIAN
Published by the Penguin Group
Penguin Group (USA) Inc., 375 Hudson Street, New York, New York 10014, U.S.A.
Penguin Group (Canada), 90 Eglinton Avenue East, Suite 700, Toronto,
Ontario, Canada M4P 2Y3 (a division of Pearson Penguin Canada Inc.)
Penguin Books Ltd., 80 Strand, London WC2R 0RL, England
Penguin Ireland, 25 St. Stephen's Green, Dublin 2, Ireland
(a division of Penguin Books Ltd.)
Penguin Group (Australia), 250 Camberwell Road, Camberwell, Victoria 3124, Australia
(a division of Pearson Australia Group Pty. Ltd.)
Penguin Books India Pvt. Ltd., 11 Community Centre, Panchsheel Park,
New Delhi – 110 017, India
Penguin Group (NZ), 67 Apollo Drive, Rosedale, North Shore 0632, New Zealand
(a division of Pearson New Zealand Ltd.)
Penguin Books (South Africa) (Pty.) Ltd., 24 Sturdee Avenue, Rosebank,
Johannesburg 2196, South Africa

Penguin Books Ltd., Registered Offices: 80 Strand, London WC2R 0RL, England

Published by Meridian, an imprint of Dutton Signet, a division of Penguin Books USA
Inc. The first and revised editions were published under the Mentor imprint.

First Printing, August 1972
First Meridian Printing (Second Revised Edition), August, 1998

20 19 18 17 16 15

Ⓜ REGISTERED TRADEMARK—MARCA REGISTRADA

LIBRARY OF CONGRESS CATALOGING-IN-PUBLICATION DATA:

Harris, Joseph E.
    Africans and their history / Joseph E. Harris.—2nd rev. ed.
        p. cm.
    ISBN 978-0-452-01181-6
    1. Africa—Politics and government. I. Title.
DT31.H28   1998
960—dc21   98-14409
                                                                        CIP

Printed in the United States of America
Set in Times New Roman

Dedicated to two distinguished African-American historians whose teaching and scholarship in African and African-American history have contributed immeasurably to those fields and to the inspiration of scores of students, black and white:

Rayford W. Logan, Professor Emeritus, Howard University; and John Hope Franklin, Professor Emeritus, Duke University (formerly at Howard University)

Contents

Preface to the Second Revised Edition

The original volume, like any other African history text, needed revisions before it went to press; so it was with the last edition of this volume. Such is the scope and dynamic rapidity of change in the research and contemporary times of Africa.

Given the great diversity, complexity, and dynamism of African history, I have organized this volume around selected themes, which should be supplemented with more specialized studies. I have identified some relevant studies for this purpose in the bibliography. For general readers who may wish only or primarily an overview to identify trends in African history for an understanding of contemporary times, this volume should suffice. However, in our highly literate society, additional reading can hardly be avoided.

Since the publication of the second edition of this book, UNESCO has published the complete eight-volume *General History of Africa*, which contains the work of experts around the world and appears in the major languages of the world. Its board of editors includes Africa's most renowned scholars. This series therefore is recommended to all readers interested in Africa's history.

A number of very significant developments have occurred since the last edition appeared, requiring revisions of the text. Ethnic conflicts have continued to threaten national borders in Africa, and in at least one case, a new and independent country has appeared, Eritrea. While a text this size cannot detail that story, it should be noted that the implications for other secessionist movements are clear, in spite of the Charter commitment members of the Organization of African Unity made to respect the national borders won at independence.

Two other events of great magnitude are independence of Namibia, and the transition from minority to majority rule in South Africa. Both of these events had implications far beyond their own experience, in part because both shared a history directly related to international organizations, the League of Nations and the United Nations, that over many decades took action that affected those states, thereby directly involving the nations of the world. In addition, both countries were subjected to apartheid, a racial ideology that most countries found repulsive and many took actions to change.

As was observed in the last edition, the African diaspora continues to require an understanding of the African background and context in historical and contemporary times. This trend has gained momentum, with the result that many Africanists as well as diasporists now recognize the vital relationship between African and African diaspora history.

The central thrust of this volume remains continental Africa and the evolution of its societies within the context of the world. The approach is topical and draws on relevant examples to demonstrate particular points of view. There are many other examples of people, countries, organizations, and events that one may wish to select; I have not attempted to exhaust all the cases or topics.

The last chapter in particular is designed to examine broad issues of continental significance. Not all the issues apply equally to all the countries, but I believe they are matters of great concern to most of the states. In addition, this approach should stimulate debate and analyses of the great issues confronting contemporary Africa.

I thank my colleagues, students, and Africanist friends whose discussions and candid evaluations helped to make this revised volume possible. I again thank my family—Rosemarie, Joanne, and Earl—for their critiques, inspiration, and forbearance.

—Joseph E. Harris
Department of History
Howard University

Preface to the First Edition

Although much more is known about Africa's history in 1972 than was the case even a decade ago, there is still the crucial task of reconstructing and reinterpreting it with both a consciousness of the need to compensate for the centuries of distortions and omissions, and the ultimate goal of approximating truth, insofar as that is possible. To compensate, in this instance, means to identify and rectify imbalances in earlier historical presentations; to approximate truth means to apply as best one can the techniques, data, and perspectives available in one's own time.

It hardly need be stated that the increased world interest in Africa accompanied the appearance, since the 1950s, of scores of independent African countries. That development underscored the ignorance non-Africans had about Africans, and among the results of this realization has been the emergence of numerous courses and programs of African studies on various educational levels throughout the world, with an increasing demand for materials to train specialists and to inform the general public. The special implications of these occurrences for black people are obvious: the affirmation of an identity, a source of pride and fulfillment, and the substance and perspectives necessary for a liberating movement. This book attempts to contribute to these several needs.

The vastness and diversity of Africa, and the many unexplored sources, make it virtually impossible to write a complete history text. Consequently, I have been selective in presenting chapter themes and data to support them. I have made no attempt to be all-inclusive; rather, I have preferred to present a theme and to illustrate it with examples from various geographical and cultural regions of the continent. While all regions of the continent, and indeed the diaspora, receive appropriate treatment, the primary stress has been put on the black societies because of their greater numbers and larger roles in Africa's past, and because racial denigration placed them in a uniquely disadvantaged position, which, for many centuries, significantly affected the course and interpretation of African history and from which their continued struggle for political, economic, cultural, and psychological freedom is already causing major transformations in our own times and will, no doubt, in its own way help to free millions of nonblacks in and outside Africa.

I alone am responsible for the presentation and interpretations in this book; but I have benefited more than I can explain from the direct and indirect influences of many former professors, students, Africans in many walks of life, and innumerable authors, some of whose works appear in the bibliography.

I am very grateful to the Clark University Cartographic Laboratory and its designer Norman T. Carpenter and draftsman David Spinney for producing the maps for this book. I also extend thanks for the kind assistance of the Stetson Library staff at Williams College and Howard University.

Of course, my immediate family—Rosemarie, Joanne, and Joseph Earl—and the extended family provided both the initial inspiration and the continuing support necessary for the completion of this task.

—Joseph E. Harris
Williams College
Williamstown, Massachusetts

1

A Tradition of Myths and Stereotypes

The history of Africa is relevant to the history of black people throughout the world. This is partly because persons of African ancestry are dispersed throughout the world, and partly because of the general derogatory image Africans and black people everywhere have inherited from Western history. A recognition of the magnitude of this problem is the acknowledgment of the heavy burden on the shoulders of the historian who seeks honestly to reconstruct the black historical experience, but who at the same time realizes that even before that task can be fulfilled, a solid historical foundation must be established by confronting and destroying the multitude of myths fashioned by Europeans of yesteryear and transmitted to the contemporary world.

Race in general, and myths and stereotypes surrounding physical features and skin color in particular, have been so pervasive and basic in black-white relations and in accounts of those interactions that in spite of a stream of scientific evidence to the contrary, the concept of black inferiority continues to thrive in many minds. Since the origin and perpetuation of that concept have been supported by the denial of a meaningful and intellectual cultural and historical African experience, it is appropriate that this concise history of Africans should present an analysis of the effects of historical myths and stereotypes about Africans.

Perhaps the best approach to an understanding of this problem should begin with an examination of some of the early characterizations of Africans in history in order to see how the roots of racial prejudice became interwoven in Western culture, which internationalized the concept of black inferiority and colonized Africa's history. The denigration of Africans can be traced back beyond the Christian era into antiquity; and in later times, anyone who wished to employ degrading stereotypes about black people could easily establish reference points in classical times when outstanding scholars and writers described Africans as strange and primitive creatures. Many of those descriptions have remained with us and have contributed immeasurably to the perpetuation of denigratory myths about Africans, and black people generally.

That the Greeks and Romans knew a great deal about and were sensitive commentators on the physical features of blacks in Africa is confirmed by the copious evidence provided by classical writers and artists. Although Professor Frank Snowden, in his book *Blacks in Antiquity: Ethiopians in the Greco-Roman Experience,* is not convinced that racism was cultivated in the Greco-Roman experience, he has nonetheless confirmed that skin color was "uppermost in the minds of the Greeks and Romans" when describing Ethiopians, and that artistic representations are sufficient in quantity from the sixth century B.C. to permit the conclusion that "tightly curled or woolly hair; broad, flattened noses; lips thick, often puffy and everted; prognathism" were African characteristics familiar to the Hellenistic world.

Admittedly, the psychological interpretation of history is extremely difficult to document, especially for the classical era, and thus highly vulnerable to criticism; but all critics must know that the psychological factor is crucial to an eventual understanding of the roots and growth of an attitude that is so fundamental a determinant of history. The preeminent preoccupation with the blackness and physical type of Ethiopians must have made a deep imprint on Greek and Roman minds, particularly on the less sophisticated ones. That Ethiopians were "blameless," as Homer described them, need not have signified equality, but could indeed have been intended to describe their remoteness from civilization—"the farthermost men"—and imply that they were thus ignorant of and not responsible for the complex problems of the "civilized" (Greek) world. How profound and extensively employed was the following proverbial expression of the times, which is cited by several authors, including Snowden: "To wash an Ethiopian white"? On the one hand this expression could and no doubt did signify the futility of trying to alter that which nature had made. But note the contrasts: *blackness* represented *dirt,* which one could not wash *clean* (white). In short, not only might libertarian interpretations be drawn from these classical descriptions of Ethiopians, who were also described as pious and just by classical writers, but there is also evidence for the view that seeds of color prejudice were sown, consciously or unconsciously. It is interesting to note that of the two streams of information, the one that has survived and has had the greater impact is that of the mysterious and savage.

With a few selected quotations from some of the classical writers, the African could be shown to be a strange, barbarous, and subhuman creature. Although this was not the primary focus of those writers, it is nonetheless important, especially for the Renaissance and Age of Reason, when Europeans took a greater interest in the outside world, from the point of view of trade, politics, and exploration. Maps were made, and the areas unknown to Europeans were gradually filled in and described. Thus, Europeans interested in Africa turned to the writings of the ancients, so many of whom had had a firsthand glimpse of parts of the continent. Based on these early accounts, maps and books were produced and became valuable to European readers: merchants, missionaries, explorers, students, and others.

Although the "father of history," Herodotus, made significant contributions to the evolution of history as a field of study, in attempting to explain African culture, which was so different from his own, he sowed seeds of racial prejudice that shaped black-white images for centuries to come. He frequently referred to Africans as "barbarians," and characterized the people of Libya by saying "their speech resembles the shrieking of a Bat rather than the language of Men." "Barbarian" and "savage" were terms that embodied no racial significance as such, for they were used to describe many other groups of people; but they did connote inferiority. The point to be emphasized is that once European "savages" refined their lifestyle, there remained no visible label of inferiority, whereas the blackness of Africans became identified with and lingered in the minds of Europeans as a badge of primitiveness. A part of this must be explained by the way in which Africans were described as animals and monsters. The bat was the reference point for Herodotus, but Pliny the Elder discussed Africans who "by report have no heads but mouth and eies [eyes] both in their breast," and others "who crawled instead of walking."

The third-century geographer Solinus wrote a book entitled *Collection of Wonderful Things,* which was available to men during the Middle Ages. In it Solinus described "Aethyop, of the filthy fashion of the people of that countrey, of their monstrous shape, of the Dragons and other wyle beasts of wonderful nature there." Solinus did not need to refer to the people as inferior or subhuman; that was rather clearly established by describing their "monstrous shape" and juxtaposing them next to "Dragons and other wyle beasts." These were indeed "strange" people whom European readers could easily consider subhuman, or at most would regard as less worthy than themselves. Descriptions such as these are scattered in much of the European literature up to the present time. Even if that tradition were unconsciously developed, and much of it probably was, the Christian era ushered in another dimension.

A most decisive derogatory racial tradition stems from the biblical interpretation of Noah's curse of Ham. The Bible did not apply any racial label, but the idea of race later became attached to the descendants of Ham. A collection of Jewish oral traditions in the *Babylonian Talmud* from the second to the sixth centuries A.D. holds that the descendants of Ham were cursed by being black,[1] and this belief received even greater elaboration during the Middle Ages when, according to one source, Noah's curse was explained.

> "It must be Canaan, your firstborn, whom they enslave . . .
> Canaan's children shall be born *ugly* and *black!* . . . Your grand-
> children's hair shall be twisted into kinks . . . [their lips] shall
> swell." Men of this race are called Negroes; their forefather
> Canaan commanded them to love theft and fornication, to be
> banded together in hatred of their masters and never to tell the
> truth.[2]

Indeed, that passage includes not only a pretty clear description of the color and physical type of the "cursed" people, it also presents the principal stereotypes associated with blacks—thieves, fornicators, and liars.

The translation of a Hebrew manuscript of Benjamin ben Jonah, a twelfth-century merchant and traveler from Spanish Navarre, not only supports the same theme but also suggests that it was fairly widespread:

> There is a people . . . who, like animals, eat of the herbs that
> grow on the banks of the Nile, and in the fields. They go about

[1]Thomas F. Gossett, *Race: The History of an Idea in America* (Dallas, 1963), p. 5.
[2]Robert Graves and Raphael Patai, *Hebrew Myths* (New York, 1964), p. 121.

naked and have not the intelligence of ordinary men. They
cohabit with their sisters and anyone they find. . . . These sons
of Ham are black slaves.[3]

Not only was Benjamin Jonah sure about the characteristics of
those blacks, he was also certain they were the sons of Ham. To
the extent that this latter point was generally accepted by Europeans, to that same extent could the inferior position of blacks be
explained by Noah's curse and thus rationalized biblically.

The image of Africans as inferiors was reinforced further by
arguments of several Christian missionaries, ministers, and others
who explained that an African was better off a slave in a Christian society than free in "African Savagery." One is reminded that
most missionaries or other Europeans did not visit Africa until
the latter part of the nineteenth and early twentieth centuries, but
all the same, Africa was presumed to be savage. It was also
argued that the Bible spoke of slavery without condemning it. No
doubt these arguments were convincing rationalizations to many
Europeans, especially during the era of the slave trade. The European settlers in America became increasingly apprehensive about
the apparent contradiction of maintaining in slavery a converted
African. That apprehension was soon overcome, however, when
several of the American colonies passed statutes that held that
conversion did not necessitate manumission. These acts encouraged the importation of Africans as slaves and removed the fear
masters had that baptism might place them in violation of Christian teachings. In fact, from the latter part of the seventeenth century, conversion of the slave was argued both as a rescue
operation from barbarism and also as an effective instrument of
social control. The extension of black slavery abroad and its ratio-
nalization by Christians were historic occurrences in the internationalization of the idea of black inferiority.

[3]Robert Hess, "The Itinerary of Benjamin of Tudela: A Twelfth Century Description of
North-East Africa," *Journal of African History,* Vol. VI, No. 1 (1965), p. 17.

Several writers on the slave trade illustrate the trend. William Bosman, a Dutch slaver, dismissed black culture out of hand in his book *A New and Accurate Description of the Coast of Guinea* (1705). His book was widely read and for many years was regarded as authoritative. In 1725 James Houston wrote *Some New and Accurate Observations of the Coast of Guinea* in which he described Africans thus: "They [Africans] exactly resemble their Fellow Creatures and Natives, the Monkeys." Thomas Phillips's slave journal noted that Africans were "generally extremely sensual, . . . so intemperate, that they drank brandy as if it were water; deceitful in their dealings with Europeans." It is strange that Phillips condemned Africans for deceiving European slavers!

Another prominent slaver and writer during this period was John Barbot who published *A Description of the Coasts of North and South Guinea* (1732). He explained that the slave's conditions in his own country were so appalling that it was kindness to ship him to the West Indies and more considerate masters, not to mention "the inestimable advantage they may reap of becoming Christians, and saving their souls." It is curious, however, that Barbot continued: "tho it must be owned, they are very hard to be brought to a true notion of the Christian religion . . . being naturally very stupid and sensual, and so apt to continue till their end." On the one hand he saw Christianity as a rescue effort that would save the African's soul; on the other hand, he doubted that Africans would ever become Christians. One is reminded of the note of irony expressed by the French philosopher Montesquieu in 1748: "It is impossible for us to suppose these creatures to be men, because, allowing them to be men, a suspicion would follow that we ourselves are not Christians." At least this philosopher seems to have detected the dehumanization of Africans by European Christians.

Geographers also made a contribution to the European image of Africa. Robin Hallett, in *The Penetration of Africa*, quotes from an African map published in Paris in 1761:

It is true that the centre of the continent is filled with burning sands, savage beasts and almost uninhabited deserts. The scarcity of water forces the different animals to come together to the same place to drink. It happens that finding themselves together at a time when they are in heat, they have intercourse one with another, without paying regard to the difference between species. Thus are produced those monsters which are to be found there in greater numbers than in any other part of the world.

Hugh Murray, a popular geographer of the early nineteenth century, described the continent as an area of mystery with wild and strange aspects of man and nature. Africa was a strange place, inhabited by strange people, where monsters dwelt and strange things happened. These were all part of the evolving image of Africa, a place where "creatures" less than human survived in an order less than civilized.

African or black inferiority as a concept reached its high point when it became intellectualized by philosophers of the Enlightenment. In a footnote to his essay entitled "Of National Character," which appeared in his *Essay and Treatises* (1768), the influential Scot philosopher David Hume wrote:

I am apt to suspect the negroes . . . to be naturally inferior to the white. There never was a civilized nation of any other complexion than white, nor even any individual eminent either in action or speculation. No ingenious manufacturers amongst them, no arts, no sciences.

Hume probably did not realize how monumental his ignorance was, but it is doubtful that such a philosopher did not realize his great contribution to the stereotypic image of black people.

Another ignominious pronouncement came from the German philosopher Georg Hegel in his *Philosophy of History*. After a cursory discussion of Africa, he noted:

It is manifest that want of self-control distinguishes the character of the Negroes. This condition is capable of no development
or culture, and as we have seen them at this day, such have they
always been. . . . At this point we leave Africa, not to mention
it again. For it is no historical part of the world; it has no movement or development to exhibit.

Having given Africa about eight of a hundred pages, Hegel dismissed it from the remaining 358 pages.

Most of these myths were formulated long before anything like
serious relationships were established between Africans and
Europeans. One can only surmise about the impact of those
myths on European attitudes toward blacks, and one can imagine
what early European sailors and explorers thought when they
landed in Africa and saw the objects of those centuries-old stereotypes. For indeed it is clear that Prince Henry the Navigator and
others had access to the early writings and oral accounts about
blacks in Africa.

Even before the peak of the Atlantic slave trade, there were
already signs of racial prejudice among Europeans. There is the
example of an unusual African visitor to Scotland in the Middle
Ages, a lady about whom a poem was later written. She achieved
a kind of fame with knights and nobles, but in spite of her sexual
charm, she was described as having a mouth like an ape, a catlike
nose, and looking "just like a toad." Similar examples may be
found in Shakespeare's works. For all its liberal aspects, *Othello*
shows some of these stereotypes. Brabantio, for example,
expresses disgust that his daughter might incur disrespect by
seeking the "sooty bosom of such a thing as thou," referring to
Othello. The black slave in *Titus Andronicus* is referred to as
"thick-lipped," while Tamora is reviled for loving "a barbarous
Moor," another degrading description of the times. These are all
light touches of black devaluation, but they had a message that
demeaned black people. It is certainly possible that by the six-

teenth century, for many Europeans such stereotypes had become so common as to go seemingly unnoticed. It is noteworthy, however, that in 1601 Queen Elizabeth reacted to the growing number of blacks in England by ordering their deportation.

Clearly, degrading racial descriptions developed in parts of Europe prior to the high point of the Atlantic slave trade. This is particularly significant, since a sizable number of Africans were taken to Portugal and other places in Europe as slaves long before the Americas were visited by Columbus. It should be stressed, therefore, that these denigratory judgments about blacks were being strengthened in Europe at the same time that Europeans were establishing serious contacts with Africans, a relationship that culminated in the slave trade to America. Thus, some Europeans were aware of and had owned black slaves, who were identified as inferiors, long before the extensive trade in Africans was extended to Brazil and elsewhere in the Americas.

It is essential to stress that a combination of European attitudes about blacks, the fact of black visibility, and the demand for cheap labor all combined to entrench the institution of slavery and the deeply embedded myths that were used not only to justify slavery but black inferiority as well. Consequently, the racial conditions that followed in the Americas, especially in the United States, were logical sequences to those earlier attitudes about Africans; and Western institutions—the governments, courts, and churches, for example—supported those beliefs. Given that position, it was natural for Europeans to conclude that Africans had no history and no written language, two other great myths. But a society that justified its expansion overseas, and into Africa in particular, in terms of the "civilizing mission to uplift the heathens and savages of Africa," could not regard the history or language of the latter group as being worthy of serious study. That would have amounted to retrogression rather than the progression by now so deeply ingrained in the Western tradition. It must be emphasized, therefore, that one of the greatest contributions

Europeans made to the New World was the expansion and entrenchment of the concept of black inferiority.

Of the many Americans who helped stigmatize blacks during the era of slavery in the United States, John C. Calhoun, one of the most influential political leaders of his time, stands out. In many ways Calhoun spoke for whites, especially planters, when he explained that the black man as an inferior should occupy the doorsill so that the more superior whites could develop civilization. Calhoun is reported to have stated that if he could find a black man who could understand Greek syntax, he would consider the black race human. The Kenyan political scientist Ali Mazrui, in a pamphlet entitled *Ancient Greece in African Political Thought,* refers to a speech in which Kwame Nkrumah cited the case of a Columbia University Zulu student who, in a speech of 1906, responded to Calhoun:

> What might have been the sensation kindled by the Greek syntax in the mind of the famous Southerner, I have so far been unable to discover, but . . . I could show him among black men of pure African blood those who could repeat the Koran from memory, skilled in Latin, Greek, and Hebrew, Arabic and Chaldaic.

It is doubtful that Calhoun's beliefs would have been altered by that oration, especially from a black student, but he might have wondered about his general ignorance of black people and their history.

A great landmark in this historical drama occurred during the latter part of the nineteenth century when modern industrial nationalism in Europe and imperialism abroad contributed to the development of ideologies that sanctioned as necessary and natural white donors and black recipients of civilization. It was the great contribution of Darwin's theory of evolution and the subsequent emergence of the concept of Social Darwinism that synthesized the old ideas and provided fresh support for old beliefs. Given the racial situation in the United States immediately following the Reconstruction era, it was only natural that white Americans would contribute to the expansion of Social Darwinism and the theory of black inferiority. Among the most influential proponents of Social Darwinism were William Graham Summer, professor of political science at Yale University; Josiah Strong, a popular late-nineteenth-century historian, lecturer, and Congregational clergyman; John Burgess, William Dunning, U. B. Phillips, and several other prominent professors at Columbia University.

This is a very small but important sample of the great array of United States scholars, politicians, and writers who spread the stigma of black inferiority. In 1885 Strong envisioned that the Anglo-Saxons "will move down upon Mexico . . . over upon Africa and beyond. And can anyone doubt that the result of this competition of the races will be the 'survival of the fittest'?" In his *Our Country: Its Possible Future and Its Present Crisis*, Strong answered his own question:

> It seems to me that God, with infinite wisdom and skill, is training the Anglo-Saxons for an hour sure to come in the world's future . . . the final competition of races, for which the Anglo-Saxon is being schooled. . . . Whether the extinction of inferior races . . . seems to the reader sad or otherwise, it certainly appears probable.

In 1896 William Summer emphasized that "if you asked Thomas Jefferson . . . whether in 'all men' he meant to include negroes, he would have said that he was not talking about negroes." In fact, in his notes on the State of Virginia (Paris, 1784), Jefferson observed that ". . . never yet could I find that a black man had uttered a thought above the level of plain narration; never saw even an elementary trait of painting or sculpture."

In his book *American Historians,* Harvey Wish provides perhaps the best concise statement on the influence of the Burgess–Dunning–U. B. Phillips school of thought: "They convinced textbook writers that Radical Reconstruction was a basic error" because the Thaddeus Stevens–Charles Sumner group "assumed that Negroes were capable of self-government"—the inference clearly being that blacks were not capable of political responsibility.

Some critics have observed that Joseph de Gobineau's *Essai sur l'inégalité* (Essay on Inequality) was the most directly influential publication on racism in the nineteenth century. Gobineau, a Frenchman, extolled the racial purity of the Nordics and explained that as the Franks (Nordics) mixed with Gallic stocks, the former became weaker and more decadent, which eventually led to their overthrow by commoner elements, the leaders of the French Revolution. In his book *The Foundations of the Nineteenth Century,* Houston S. Chamberlain, an Englishman who later became a German citizen, expanded on Gobineau's ideas. Chamberlain attempted to show that almost everything worthwhile in history had been accomplished by Nordics. He combined the ideas on the evolutionary struggle with the will for power and presented a doctrine of the master race, later adopted by Hitler.

Another influential person in this context was Francis Galton, an Englishman who developed the mental tests and statistical methods for understanding individual differences. Galton wrote *Hereditary Genius* (1869), in which he argued that the intellectual standard of the "Negro race" was low and would remain so. Although these and other protagonists of white superiority did not elaborate on Africa or the African, their frame of reference provided an inferior place for blacks, both scientifically and socially.

Indeed, simultaneous with the appearance of Social Darwinism and Gobineau's *Essai* was the accelerated expansion of Europeans into various parts of Africa. Concurrent with both of these occurrences was the academic division of Africa into two areas, the Hamitic in the North and the "Negro" in the south. The significance of this division related directly to the subject of stereotypes of the African past. Egypt's place in history is indisputable, and there remain various kinds of documents to confirm a rich, ancient civilization that had a great impact on Asia and Europe. Moreover, Egypt is geographically a part of the African continent, and the blood of indigenous Africans has always been there. Yet some scholars and other observers even today exclude Egypt from African history and include it as part of the Middle Eastern world. The questions that logically emerge from this are: Who were the Egyptians and what was the relationship between them and other Africans?

One of the foremost proponents of the division of Africa into Hamitic-Negro areas was C. G. Seligman, an English anthropologist who later became a German citizen. In simplified terms, Seligman applied the concept of Social Darwinism to African ethnography, which amounted to the attribution of absolute values of white and black physical types, with the latter at the lower rung of advancement. According to Seligman, "the Hamites— who are 'Europeans,' i.e., belong to the same great branch of mankind as the Whites," civilized Africa. "The civilizations of Africa are the civilizations of the Hamites, its history the record of these people and of their interaction with the two other African stocks, the Negro and the Bushman." Seligman described the ancient and modern Egyptians as Eastern Hamites. With a few strokes of the pen Seligman thus denied that Africans had developed a civilization, and attributed the meaningful aspect of their history to outsiders! The clear inference of this hypothesis was that inferior blacks were civilized by superior Hamites (whites), and that the degree of political and cultural evolution of Africans depended on the amount of white blood the blacks had.

Sir Harry Johnston, a popular observer of Africa in general and the Bantu in particular, graphically portrayed his views in *A Comparative Study of the Bantu and Semi-Bantu Languages:*

> The Negro, in short, owes what little culture he possesses,
> before the advent of the Moslem Arab and the Christian white
> man, to the civilizing influence of ancient Egypt; but this influ-
> ence travelled to him, not directly up the White Nile, but indi-
> rectly through Abyssinia and Somaliland, and Hamites, such as
> the stock from which the Galla and Somali sprang, were the
> middlemen whose early traffic between the Land of Punt and
> the countries round the Victoria Nyanza was the main, almost
> the sole, agency by which the Negro learnt the industries and
> received the domestic animals of Egypt.

Three Americans who greatly influenced anthropology in the
United States—Samuel G. Morton, a physician and professor of
anatomy, who wrote works on the human crania, Josiah C. Nott,
a scientist, and his collaborator George Gliddon, an American
consul in Egypt—collected and studied crania from Egypt and
concluded they were Caucasian crania. Nott, Gliddon, and others
thus explained the accomplishments of the Egyptians as products
of the Caucasian race and not of blacks.

Thus it was Egypt, which was not regarded as African, that
served as the civilizing force; the Hamites (whites) who were the
carriers; and the blacks who were the waiting recipients. The
stamp of racism thus not only made its indelible imprint generally
on Africa, Africans, and all black people, it also prejudiced schol-
arly studies of black people up into the present. One is reminded
of how the French history textbooks castrated African history by
teaching Africans, up to a few decades ago: "Our ancestors the
Gauls." The French were not sharing their biological or racial origin, but indeed were entrenching the idea that meaningful African
history and culture came with the French.

The most impressive challenge to the Hamitic concept has

come from the Senegalese writer Cheikh Anta Diop who, drawing on evidence from eyewitness accounts of Herodotus and others, concluded that the Egyptians were indeed black and their
contributions to the world—agriculture, science, religion, the cal-
endar, writing, etc.—were all contributions of black people.
According to Diop:

> It remains . . . true that the Egyptian experiment was essen-
> tially Negro, and that all Africans can draw the same moral
> advantage from it that Westerners draw from Graeco-Latin
> civilization.[4]

If Plato, Eudoxe, and Pythagoras remained in Egypt for thirteen
to twenty years, "it was not only to learn recipes." Diop concluded:

> Many of the guiding lights of Western civilization—scholars,
> scientists, and public officials—continued to believe in the
> classification of the races, with blacks occupying the lower
> rung, and much of the terminology applied to Africa is still
> stereotypic. From what has already been said, it should be clear
> that the term "Hamitic" is unacceptable as a racial label,
> because it has a long historical association with the concept of
> black inferiority. For an objective approach to the understand-
> ing of any group of people the language should be as precise
> and free of prejudice as possible.

Two other terms that denigrate Africans are "native" and
"tribe." Regarding native, even the English historian Arnold
Toynbee, who maintained that Africans were civilized by Europeans, wrote that when Europeans call people "natives," a cultural distillation takes place and the former do not understand the

---

[4]Cheikh Anta Diop, "The Cultural Contributions and Prospects of Africa," *Proceedings of
the International Conference of Negro Writers and Artists, Presence Africaine,* Special
Issue, June–November 1956.

latter. The term "native" usually connotes a person of a lower order. One rarely if ever refers to the "natives" of the United States unless depicting the Indians. Yet the term is still applied to Africans without regard to their national or ethnic origin. Toynbee's observation, in this instance, is a telling one, for as long as Africans are regarded as "natives," the approach to them will no doubt remain paternalistic. European colonial officials and apologists so distorted the term in reference to "native courts," "native administrations," and "the natives" that it is not an authentic description of Africans.

The classification of African political units as "tribes" also made a major distinction between Europeans and Africans. Historically, the term was used to denote subordinate units, such as the divisions of the ancient Romans into Sabines, Latins, and Etruscans. The tribe was regarded as a more primitive unit, which in time evolved into a civilized one. The tribe was too small and lacked the complex organization and functions of the nation. Social Darwinism of the nineteenth century justified this as the order of things for Africa. The Caucasian type was represented as possessing superior linguistic, political, and cultural capacities. Since, in the European view, African politics had not reached the level of complex, centralized systems of government, without which the higher attainments of civilization could not be achieved, the term "tribe" was employed. One hardly needs to state that the term "Negro" also is pejorative, stereotypic, and meaningless as a description for Africans. In short, as with the terms "Hamitic" and "native," "tribe" and "Negro" as general labels for Africans suggest denigratory characterizations and therefore prejudge the African or black experience.

From the dawn of the twentieth century the concept of black inferiority was full-blown and internationalized. It was even poetized in Kipling's "The White Man's Burden." With it, imperialists and racists justified the power of whites over blacks. The coming of radio, movies, and television further entrenched blatant and subtle forms of the concept. Thus, since prejudice, as learned behavior, is a result of observation and participation in social patterns and institutions, and, as the foregoing pages have shown, the derogation of blacks became deeply rooted in Western traditions, the conclusion is that Westerners in general from childhood became exposed to socializing patterns of behavior that in its stratification and separation of blacks and whites nourished an explicit and implicit ideology of racism. Westerners also carried this idea to the global communities they colonized.

Some critics argue that myths and stereotypes are only peripheral concerns in African history. But others believe that stereotypic Africa is deeply embedded in intellectual history and thus continues, consciously or unconsciously, to influence relationships with and accounts of Africans. When critics generalize about "tribal wars" in Africa, the "inability of Africans to govern themselves," the "excessive corruption" in African societies, whether correct or not, the implications often are that Africans are unique in those regards. One therefore senses the need to emphasize Africa's enormous size and diversity and the fact that there is multiple causation, much of which stems from an oppressed past rooted in gross derogation that shaped perceptions of Africans and non-Africans alike.

The efforts to redress these issues have been continuous. Of particular note were movements such as the Harlem Renaissance in the United States, Negritude in France, and Negrismo in Cuba, which sought an intellectual redemption of Africa and African peoples by revealing the diversity, scope, achievements, longevity, and complexity of African cultures and their influence in Europe, Asia, the Americas, and elsewhere. More recently, building on pan-Africanism and black studies/consciousness movements, the Afrocentric perspective, often grossly exaggerated by critics, has gained widespread appeal among Africans and their descendants especially. That perspective focuses on the study of blacks as subjects instead of objects of history and culture and on initiatives as well as reactions to outside forces. This approach not only centers the study of the black experience on the indigenous peoples of Africa; it also seeks to reveal the values, goals, aspirations, and the vision of African peoples in the course of history.

The most blatant forms of stereotypes have been muted, thanks in part to scholars, writers, and others, including Africans in particular. African critics have increased in number as has the volume of their candid assessments of the African condition. One is thus able to assess the comparability of Africa's first generation of independence and that of other powers—in Europe, Asia, and the Americas. Africa's struggle to affirm its identity is paramount. The accommodation of Africanity, Islamic, and Western influences—the triple heritage, as Kenyan political scientist Ali Mazrui has characterized it—is a complex phenomenon rooted in ideas about the worth and achievements of peoples and their values.

The major challenge for African peoples, their descendants abroad and non-Africans alike is how to transcend deeply ingrained Eurocentric biases, establish more relevant guidelines with language expressive of the mutually understood meanings, and thus reveal the historical and contemporary reality of Africa, Africans, and their descendants abroad.

2

The Evolution of Early African Societies

Geography has been a major factor in Africa's history. Virtually contiguous to Asia via the Near East, Africa thus shares linguistic and cultural ties with that area. It is separated from Europe by the Mediterranean Sea, only about ten miles wide at its closest point, the northwest corner, and thus has age-old contact with that region. The continent is about five thousand miles wide from the Atlantic to the Indian Oceans and is about the same distance in length.

Africa is over twice the size of the United States and several times the size of Western Europe. The continent is also very diverse: mostly tropical with great mountain ranges, rough and abrupt rivers, great climate diversity and vegetational varieties, perhaps 25 percent desert, and one of the richest continents in minerals. The interaction of human beings and this tremendous environmental diversity is the essence of this continent's frequently controversial history as the world's oldest human habitat.

For many years it was generally believed that man, in the generic sense, originated in Central Asia, but as early as the nineteenth century, Charles Darwin in *Descent of Man* (1871) projected the idea that future evidence would prove that man and higher primates originated in Africa. He wrote: "It is somewhat more probable that our early progenitors lived on the African continent than elsewhere." About ninety years later, Louis and Mary Leakey and their team produced fossil evidence to support Darwin's prophecy.

Human beings belong to the primates and the family is the Hominidae, but a definition of when a hominid became man has caused some difficulty. An early definition held that man appeared when he began to make tools in a regularly set pattern, but subsequent research showed that chimpanzees meet that requirement. Consequently, a more recent definition is that humans emerged at that stage of evolution when their carriage or posture became erect as they walked on two legs and possessed the ability to make cutting tools for future use. Inherent in this definition is conceptualization as revealed in making tools for a preconceived rather than an immediate purpose.

Although work began in the Olduvai Gorge in northern Tanganyika in East Africa in the early years of the twentieth century, the major achievements occurred in 1959 when the first big discovery was made. The Leakeys and their team located a skull in the gorge, and when it was finally pieced together, it was a hominid type, subsequently named Zinjanthropus or Man of Zinj, the latter being the term of the East African coast in early history. Zinjanthropus, also called "The Nutcracker Man" because of its large molars, was found in proximity to primitive stone tools, which, under the earlier definition, suggested that this was man. In 1960, however, a second discovery was made, and it was named Homo habilis (man with skill). Zinjanthropus and Homo habilis seem to have been contemporaries, but the latter had a greater brain capacity. In addition, while Zinjanthropus had teeth adapted for a coarse vegetable diet, Homo habilis had teeth more adapted to a meat diet, which would have required greater reliance on the making and use of tools. The latter also had hands with opposable thumb and forefinger (an adaptation that facilitated tool-making), a much more necessary technique for the survival of Homo habilis as a meat eater than for Zinjanthropus, although the nature of the latter's hands is not known. The evidence thus far available, therefore, points to Homo habilis as the maker of the tools associated with Olduvan culture, the earliest fully established Stone Age culture. Those earliest of tools were made of pebbles (pebble tools) and evidence of them has been found scattered throughout the African continent. Homo habilis then seems to be the direct ancestor of humans, dating back about two million years.

Archaeologists and paleoanthropologists continue to recover data to affirm Africa as the original habitat of human beings, and those efforts will no doubt continue. Without chronicling each development, it is noteworthy to call attention to another significant find in recent years. In 1974 Donald C. Johanson discovered in Ethiopia parts of a skull and skeleton of an ancient female hominid (erect-walking ancestor of humans). That discovery, dubbed "Lucy," is dated at 3.5 million years old and is the oldest, most complete hominid found to date.

Homo erectus, the main human type, emerged over a million years ago, and had migrated to Asia, Europe, and possibly elsewhere. It may be assumed that early humans evolved as scavengers of carcasses, using their hands to make tools necessary to cut the flesh. This would have led them increasingly to become hunters, though remaining scavengers and also gatherers of wild fruits and vegetables. Over a long period of time, therefore, humans developed more refined tools for hunting, cleaning, and butchering game. But as long as they remained scavengers and hunters, they were almost completely dependent on the environment for life and security. As animals moved from place to place in search of water and food, early humans had to follow. This ever-present, direct concern with the very basic search for food forced them to remain nomadic, which in turn meant that sedentary communities where complex social institutions could develop rarely if ever could emerge.

Somewhere between fifty thousand and one hundred thousand years ago, it seems that humans in Africa became regular users of fire. The benefits derived from this discovery were great: It increased the potential for collecting, producing, and cooking food; making and repairing tools; and adjusting to colder and wetter climatic conditions by living in caves and shelters heated by fire. Humans could make tree gums into glue; and they could process poisons of fruits and vegetables for use on arrows and spears during the hunt. These factors were all the more important in view of the fact that humans in an upright posture reproduced their young in a more premature state, which required longer and more attentive postnatal care. This longer withdrawal of the mother from other duties, such as helping to collect food, made humans more dependent on a settled abode, at least temporarily. The use of fire, therefore, contributed greatly to their better nourishment, comfort, and security; it also encouraged and facilitated greater group activity.

Food Production

The almost complete dependence on the environment and the continued nomadic existence of humans led to another major breakthrough in their evolution—the discovery and development of food production with a reasonable guarantee of its constant availability. The development of better means of acquiring food, which occurred sometime during the Neolithic Age, resulted essentially from the domestication of animals and plant cultivation.

These two developments evolved in Africa during ancient times, and, contrary to earlier views, were indigenous. No one knows how and when humans began plant cultivation, but it is not unreasonable to assume that as they collected and ate various kinds of berries and vegetables, seeds fell on the ground and eventually reproduced themselves, a process humans gradually understood and developed for their own benefit. This would have led them to experiment with water control, tilling the soil, weeding planted areas, and sowing seeds. These developments must have stimulated greater experimentation, greater animal domestication, and crossbreeding of plants and animals.

The domestication of animals for work, various kinds of clothing (skins, wool), and food (milk, meat, eggs) greatly improved humans' life, while at the same time animals thus domesticated were assured better protection, survival of the species, and controlled crossbreeding. Pastoralism thus provided one means of food production, and at the same time became a stimulus for migration, conquest, settlement, and political development. It appears that from about the seventh millennium B.C. the pastoral way of life spread across most of the northern third of the continent.

The transition from reliance on wild food collection to food production may have occurred as early as the ninth century B.C. The earliest known food-producing communities in Africa, however, were in the Nile delta, located at Merimdeh, Fayum, and Luxor—all in Egypt. The most significant was Fayum Lake. The inhabitants there had an environment conducive to agriculture, and kept domesticated cattle, goats, and pigs. They cultivated emmer and flax, and some of their tools were polished stone axes, gouges, bone harpoons, and pots. The Fayum economy is said to date from about 6200 B.C. A comparable development probably occurred at Merimdeh in Lower Egypt, where graves were found with the dead buried in a contracted position and facing eastward, suggesting a belief in a spiritual life.

In Upper Egypt evidence has revealed an economy that grew barley, emmer, and flax and domesticated sheep, goats, and cattle. Flint sickles, grain storage pits, and pottery have also been recovered there. The latter shows decorations of painted animals and boats. Near Khartoum (Sudan) another site was excavated that was probably a settled community subsisting on agriculture. The Upper Egypt and the Khartoum sites date back to about 4000 B.C.

Although the nature of the soil seems to have made the hoe the dominant technology, there is evidence that the plough was also part of that development, with Ethiopia and the Horn of Africa as the early examples. From Ethiopia southward along stretches of the Rift Valley, terraced agriculture evolved, probably because of the greater rainfall in the mountains, and natural resources to support crop varieties, and to establish and protect self-contained settlements. These communities had to control water for irrigation and drainage, skills which they passed on to future generations.

In southern Algeria a Neolithic culture has been traced to about 3500 B.C. Agriculture, fishing, and domesticated cattle were part of that culture, which stretched into the savannah. Neolithic cultivators were also in West Africa. In northern Nigeria, for example, where Nok culture developed, cultivators existed as early as 2000–1000 B.C.; and around the Niger River in the present country of Mali there were also cultivators during the late Stone Age. The existence of arrow and spear points, bone harpoons, and fish hooks confirms that West Africans had begun to specialize in food production. Polished stone axes and hoes over a wide area in West Africa, especially in Ghana, attest to an agricultural economy. The Nachikufu caves in northern Zambia have revealed tools associated with vegetable foods and are dated as early as 4300 B.C.

The question of water and irrigation has permeated much of this discussion. It is therefore important to note that between seven thousand and ten thousand years ago, Africa as a whole was far wetter than in subsequent years. Waterways stretched from the Nile basin to the Atlantic Ocean, most of which today is desert. It is not clear that the people of that era were agriculturalists, but the waterways certainly provided food and no doubt stimulated techniques to control lakes and rivers, and could indeed have been an incentive for plant cultivation.

By about 5000 B.C. desertification had set in. A wet phase recurred around 3000 B.C., but was not as widespread as before. Then from about 2500 B.C. an arid phase was reestablished, thereby further minimizing the economic and political regional influence of the Nile Valley.

As the Sahara began to receive less rain and became dryer, from about 2500 B.C., grazing lands became scarcer and less capable of supporting large numbers of people, cattle, and wildlife. Consequently, a significant population emigration to more favorable agricultural and pastoral areas in other parts of the continent stimulated a more intensive effort to acquire food. In this process not only were large numbers of different people merged or assimilated over time, but also the intensified search for food made farming a more important aspect of human survival.

The desertification of much of northern Africa has also been a basis for explaining the relative lack of blacks north of the Sahara in more recent times. Several specialists, for example, have concluded that those aquatic people were "Negroid." Thus the arid phase of life forced the widespread migration of those "Negroids" (blacks) to areas farther south. This point is plausible and deserves further investigation.

Further investigation is necessary for all of those developments. Only a small portion of the archaeological and botanical evidence has been uncovered. Consequently, it is entirely possible that much of the present position on the emergence of economies based on cultivation may have to be revised, and areas like western, eastern, and southern Africa will share a larger place among Neolithic societies.

As of now it seems that the following crops are indigenous to Africa: rice and Guinea corn in Guinea, sorghum in Sudan, teff and eluesine in Ethiopia, and yams and ensete in several parts of the continent. Research is increasingly placing less emphasis on the diffusion of agricultural crops and techniques from outside Africa and more concentration on both the evolution of food plants in Africa and their paralleling and combining with imports both outside and from different regions of the continent.

Iron Culture

It was the appearance of iron culture that greatly accelerated developments in farming and led to decisive changes in the lives of Africans. With iron, Africans made more durable and effective agricultural tools, which helped them to bring under control more rugged land, much of which was outside their bounds because the tsetse fly prevented the use of draft animals. Heavier and sharper axes were manufactured to provide lumber for construction and fire. Iron also led to an improvement in armaments: The iron-tipped spear and arrow provided a more reliable means of capturing bigger game; allowed hunters to venture deeper into the forest to explore and settle; and gave people a superior means of defending their settlements. The acquisition of iron culture was therefore one of the great human achievements, and in Africa as elsewhere the future was changed radically by that discovery.

The acquisition of iron-smelting techniques spread throughout Africa at different times, depending on the availability of natural resources (ore and wood for charcoal), the extent of contact with people in possession of the technique and resources, and the recognized need for such innovation. Human-made iron objects have been reported in Egypt from about 2000 B.C., though they do not seem to have become common until about 1200 B.C., and only from about 700 B.C. does it seem likely that iron was locally smelted there. The principal sites were at Defenneh (Dophnae) and Naucratis, the latter having been regarded as an international emporium, primarily because it supplied much of the Greek demand.

From about 500 B.C. or possibly earlier iron was in fairly general use among the northern African Berbers, the Kushites of the Nile Valley, and the Axumites of Ethiopia. Iron was used on some of the Napatan pyramids early in the fourth century, and around 200 B.C. an iron-smelting industry of great importance operated at Meroë, which had replaced Napata as capital of the kingdom of Kush. Indeed, the potential of the iron industry was very likely one reason for the choice of Meroë as capital. To the east of Kush iron appeared in Ethiopia around the third century B.C., though it is not clear that it was smelted there. By the first century B.C. iron trade had developed along the coast of the Red Sea.

Between 500 and 200 B.C., iron-making appeared along the plateau area of the Niger-Benue rivers in central Nigeria. That industry is identified with Nok culture, which was well established over a wide area and named after a village where terra-cotta and other artifacts were recovered in the 1930s. Nok culture, in addition to revealing an iron-making transition from the Stone Age to the metal era, also shows wonderful artistic qualities of the artists of that culture, discussed in chapter 3.

The knowledge of iron smelting appeared in the area of the Zambesi by the first century A.D., about the same time as its appearance in East Africa, and probably also in more southern areas. It is extremely difficult, hardly possible, to establish definite dates and direction of possible diffusion. Indeed, the whole question of diffusion raises the fundamental issue of the original area from which iron culture spread. Some commentators hold that the Assyrians spread knowledge of iron smelting to Egypt, which disseminated it south to Meroë, from which it was diffused south along the east coast and into the western Sudan. Others hold that Carthage disseminated the knowledge across the trans-Saharan caravan trade routes from about 500 B.C., and that the western Sudan learned the industry through that influence. Still others believe that iron culture reached East Africa through contact with Asia. However, there is no conclusive or decisive evidence for any of these points of view, and it is entirely possible that Africans in the Sudan, East Africa, and elsewhere where resources were available, developed their own skills with iron. It has been claimed, for example, that Nubians were smelting iron as early as 700 B.C. and taught their skills to the Egyptians. But as with the question of the origin and direction of early agrarian skills, what concerns us most is the effectiveness of the uses to which that knowledge was put and the resultant effect on historical developments among Africans.

Early Artistic Expression

Although early humans in Africa to a great extent were preoccupied with the bare necessities of physical survival, they also found time for aesthetic expression. Their artistic talent in prehistoric Africa is revealed in a number of rock paintings and engravings over most of the continent from the Mediterranean coast to South Africa. In North Africa, chipped figures of animals have survived on rock walls in the Atlas Mountains in Algeria. Rock paintings are found in the Sahara regions of Tasili, Ahaggar, Tibesti, and around several oases of the Nubian desert of Libya and Egypt. Stylized cattle have been found in Nigeria and Mauritania, while a number of rock paintings, especially of humpless cattle, are found in the Horn of Africa (Ethiopia and Somalia). Rock paintings in Tanganyika are numerous and vary from cruder patterns to highly finished drawings of animals and people. Engravings are rare in Tanganyika, though there are some of animals. Other rock paintings appear in Zimbabwe, Zambia, and South Africa. All of these paintings and engravings not only attest to prehistoric Africans' artistic knowledge and style as well as their developments with durable paints, but in addition, valuable data are provided about their life, history, and their environment during and after the Neolithic Age.

Conclusion

Even before early humans in Africa reached the era of metals, there was a clear need to develop basic forms of social organization beyond the immediate family. Inasmuch as culture is learned behavior, the knowledge and rationale for tool-making, the cultivation of plants and domestication of animals, and the use of fire, all of which no doubt resulted from centuries of imagination and experimentation, were transmitted to future generations who improved on techniques and developed newer tools. As hunting groups became larger, weapons more deadly and with a longer range of fire, competition for game more intense, specialization more advantageous, and longer conditions for settlement more necessary, the pressures increased for the organization of food production, collection, storage, and distribution; the regulation of relationships of individuals in the group; control over labor and surplus; the provision for the young, sick, and deserted; the definition and identification of areas of habitation; and protection from hostile intruders. These and other social demands doubtless led early humans to the evolution of social organization and state formation.

3

Early Kingdoms and City-States

The Nile Valley

Egypt

The beginning of Egyptian history is estimated at 3200 B.C.; there has been positive identification of several dynasties from that period to the conquest of the kingdom by Alexander of Macedonia in 332 B.C., which marks the beginning of the Hellenistic era. Egypt, as noted in the previous chapter, is generally acknowledged as pioneering African agricultural development. Confirmation of this results from the discovery of ancient tools and the location of terraced hills for farming in several places along the Nile Valley, most significantly at Fayum and Merimdeh.

During the early dynasties Egypt frequently raided Nubia for supplies and slaves, and in the process extended its political, economic, and cultural influence. Pharaoh Snefou of the Fourth Dynasty (2680–2258 B.C.), for example, is reported as having said that he returned with seven thousand prisoners and two hundred thousand cattle from a military expedition in Lower Nubia.

If those figures are even half correct, the capture of so many Nubians with a large number of cattle suggests both that Nubia had a prosperous economy and that Egypt relied on it.

By the Sixth Dynasty Nubia seems to have been a very active area for Egyptian expeditions. Nubia was a crossroads area with routes connecting Elephantine, El Fasher in Darfur, Red Sea ports, points around Lake Chad, and regions farther south. Although little is known about the extent to which Nubians and other interior Africans traveled to Egypt and the Red Sea coast, it is clear that inhabitants of an area as active politically and economically as Nubia, which attracted such diverse people as traders, soldiers, and adventurers, must indeed have been very much involved in wide areas extended in all directions. Inner Africa must have dispatched its merchants and emissaries outward; their presence as slaves in the north is established.

Egypt and Nubia shared in the benefits from their relationship: Egypt for the labor, resources, and passageway to the south and west; Nubia for the commerce, skills, and Egypt's links to the Mediterranean Sea. Both areas emerged as viable economic, political, and cultural centers in northeastern Africa with links to other regions of the continent.

Some scholars believe that commercial relations between Egyptians and Greeks were established as early as 3200 B.C., but certainly by the eighteenth century B.C. both commercial and diplomatic relations existed between the two peoples. That this early contact exposed the Greeks to the Africans of a darker hue is revealed by the terms "Aethiopia" and "Aethiopes," which applied to the whole area and its inhabitants south of Egypt. Aethiope was a general term meaning burnt (dark or black) face, and is comparable with the Arabic *Bilad-es-Sudan,* meaning land of the blacks. An Ethiopian was thus a person whose skin color was considerably darker than inhabitants in the Greco-Roman world. It would seem, therefore, that at least since the dawn of history Egypt has served as a great magnet attracting people from Asia and Europe

Ancient Egypt, Ethiopia, and Nubia

to join blacks in the drama of African history. At the same time, Egyptians were themselves active in affairs abroad.

As Egypt expanded its spheres of influence, the political authority of its rulers became more vulnerable. Increasingly, more administrative control was assumed by nobles, and a greater degree of local autonomy was achieved in Upper Nubia. However, Egyptian influence there was great; its achievements in agriculture, technology, writing, engineering, religious ideas and ceremonies, and political organization spread in all directions and affected future developments in Asia and Europe as well as various other parts of Africa.

Kush

The ancient kingdom of Kush is one of the least known of early world powers, in spite of the fact that it was powerful and influential during its time. Of the several classical writers who referred to Kush, Herodotus seems to be the first to mention it by name; others simply called it Ethiopia. Herodotus visited Egypt and traveled as far as Elephantine (modern Aswan), which he regarded as the frontier separating Egypt from Ethiopia. In his description of the world he devoted a chapter to the Nile Valley, discussing mostly geography and myths. About four hundred years later Diodorus Siculus wrote of Ethiopia as the source of the Nile. Strabo's geography included a discussion of agriculture and the Meroë army. Pliny the Elder in his *Natural History* wrote about Meroë, military campaigns, and geography, but he also listed several towns, many of which no longer exist. There are many other references that indicate that Kush and some of its towns were fairly well known in ancient times. However, none of these sources nor all combined are sufficient to reconstruct Kush's history. By the late third century B.C. Kush developed its own language, which is still undeciphered; thus the most important sources about Kush's past remain untapped.

While the origins of the kingdom are not known, it is clear that there was a long period of interaction between the eastern Sudan and Egypt. The area as far upstream as the Fourth Cataract was occupied under the New Kingdom of Egypt (1580–1100 B.C.). During this period Egyptian influence was strong; there were Egyptian administrators and priests, craftsmen and artists introducing Egyptian techniques and art forms. During the eighth century on the periphery of Egyptianized territory there emerged the state around the capital, Napata, which was the ancestor of Meroë. The origins of Napata are unknown, but there is no reason to think the state did not emerge around local rulers (some have argued that they were Libyans). It is known that it was under Piankhy that the conquest of Egypt was completed by Napata, and he with his successors controlled the country until 654 B.C. when the Assyrians broke Sudanese power, and the Kushites retreated south under King Tanwelanani. It is generally believed that after this defeat the capital of the kingdom was moved to Meroë. No exact date is agreed on other than somewhere in the sixth century B.C. This seems reasonable, especially in view of the fact that in 591 B.C. the Egyptian pharaoh carried out a military campaign that reached Napata, suggesting the need to move the capital for security reasons.

One must also recognize, however, that in spite of the pressure of military events, there was the greater attraction of Meroë in its own right. It was situated in a region of better annual rainfall and could thus produce a greater abundance of food and provide better pastures for cattle. The town was also better located for trade, being on a navigable stretch of the Nile at the end of a caravan route from the Red Sea. The Egyptians and the Romans after them depended on several imports from the Sudan, including gold and ivory. Kushites had already developed the trade route along the Red Sea, bypassing much of the desert and the rough cataracts of the Nile. Moreover, it seems that routes eastward from the Nile had been of importance since early times. There

long was considerable interaction between the Horn of Africa and
Arabia. Indeed, some of the people of Ethiopia still claim descent
from Arabian peoples, and some authorities see an Eastern influence in some of the art and monuments of Meroë and other areas
of northeastern Africa. While the earliest document about this
commercial contact is the Greek guide for sailors, *The Periplus,*
which was written about eighteen hundred years ago, there is no
reason to think that the relationship does not stretch back much
farther in time. So indeed, Meroë was more strategically conducive to international trade than was Napata. Its location was
also favorable because of the abundance of iron ore and timber
for its smelting; thus when the knowledge of iron working was
learned, the town became a major producer of iron tools. This
obviously made Meroë especially important in the northeast.

There are many large mounds of iron slag (cinders) thought to
be the remains of iron smelting. They have been the cause of
much speculation about the importance of iron in Meroë's economy. There are six large mounds within the town. It is generally
believed that the ore was smelted in furnaces fired by charcoal,
the material that was in abundance in the groves of acacia trees
along the Nile. Meroë was therefore fortunate in having the two
basic requirements for iron production—the ore and the fuel—
and this was probably what made the kingdom powerful for a
long time. By the early Christian era iron was fairly common in
northeastern Africa, though stone, bronze, and copper continued
to be used in many areas.

Since the language of Meroë has not been deciphered, and
since there is no great abundance of information otherwise about
the kingdom, the description of the people and their life must
remain skeletal, being reconstructed mainly from archaeological
materials. Admittedly the discovery of palaces, temples, cemeter-
ies, and other such things, while important, especially as far as
artistic achievements and some history are concerned, tells us little about the life and social organization. But it seems that the

main activity of most people of Meroë was some form of agriculture and cattle raising. Some of this activity is shown in artistic reliefs. The tending and milking of cows are shown, for
example. Horses were used both for riding and for pulling chariots, and on occasion they were buried with their owners. Strabo
reported that millet was one crop, and the discovery of fragments
of cloth made from cotton suggests that this plant was grown.
This view is strengthened by the presence of spindle whorls (fly-
wheels) and loom weights. Some cloth fragments made from flax
show that it too was probably a crop of the area. Elephants and
lions, animals rarely seen in Egyptian art, were in evidence. The
lion is frequently shown on reliefs as well as in sculpture. The ele-
phant is shown many times and is thought to have been used for
war and ceremony. The elephants used in Ptolemaic and Roman
times are believed to have been trained by Meroites.

What about the significance of Meroë in African history? It
has been argued that with the fall of the kingdom in the fourth
century A.D., many Kushites migrated westward and southward, taking with them their specialized skills and concepts
such as state organization, but this remains only speculative
with no conclusive evidence to support it. There are objects in
some parts of Africa that resemble Egyptian ones and are therefore viewed as of that origin (headrests, musical instruments,
ostrich fans), but even if such objects resulted from diffusion,
there remains the question of direction. P. L. Shinnie has
pointed out that, in the main, the objects of Egyptian appearance are not such as were known to be common in Meroë, and
no object of certain Meroë origin has been found away from the
Nile to the west.

There is the argument that Kushites carried with them ideas
about metal-working techniques. The existence of a long and
skilled tradition of bronze working (by the cireperdue method)
among the Yoruba and the Bini of Nigeria has raised the question
of relationship to Egypt. While this is possible, again there is no

evidence to support it. Moreover, there seems to be a gap of about a thousand years in the established chronology.

On the question of knowledge of iron smelting, there is the same kind of argument: Who was responsible for the dissemination of that knowledge? Meroë is a possible source from which such knowledge could have spread. It was long in contact with areas to the south and west. But so too were areas in North Africa. Carthage was long in contact with areas in the Sudan, and it had begun to work with iron as early as about 500 B.C. and is a possible source. But one should not overlook or minimize the possibility that the people who had the material resources could have developed those techniques themselves.

The kingdom of Kush, however, was indeed an important kingdom in history in its own right. It was urban, materially advanced, literate, and existed in the interior of the continent for about a thousand years, with dynamic relations not only with its immediate neighbors but, through trade, with an international community. In the first century A.D., after the Roman conquest of Egypt, Kush sent ambassadors to Rome, and Emperor Nero sent Roman emissaries to Kush.

This was the high point of Kush. From about A.D. 200 the vital trade routes converging in the kingdom were increasingly invaded by desert nomads and neighboring merchants from Axum.

Axum

The ancient kingdom of Ethiopia evolved around and became known by the name of its capital, Axum. Much of Axum's early history is shrouded in legend. The best known is that of the Queen of Sheba who went from Ethiopia to King Solomon's Jerusalem, where they fell in love and had a son, Menelik. That son thus became the founder of the ruling dynasty—the Lion of Judah—from which the late ruler, Emperor Haile Selassie, claimed descent. In addition, Ethiopia's tradition includes a written lan-

guage, which has provided nearly two thousand years of historical documentation. Although the identity of the original inhabitants of the area in which the kingdom emerged is not clear, it
seems likely that sometime during the first millennium B.C., the
Sabaean people of South Arabia, already in commercial contact
with the African coast on the Red Sea, settled in the area and
intermarried with the indigenous inhabitants. The Sabaeans
spoke a Semitic language, Sabaean, and brought their own customs. Out of this culture-sharing emerged the kingdom of Axum,
with the port of Adulis becoming a major entrepôt where
Africans from the interior brought iron, tortoise shells, animals,
hides, rhinoceros horn, gold, and slaves to exchange for iron
tools, weapons, copper implements, trinkets, cloth, and wine.

Axum thrived on this international trade, which involved merchants from regions of the Mediterranean and Red Seas and the
Indian Ocean. As a wealthy cosmopolis, Axum included residents
from Egypt, the eastern Roman Empire, Persia, and India. Greek
was commonly spoken there, and King Zoscales, who reigned
about two thousand years ago, was described as being well versed
in Greek literature. But the Axumites also developed their own
distinct civilization. They evolved their own language, Ge'ez,
with a special script. Unlike Sabaean, it included vowel signs in
each letter and was written from left to right. Several stone
inscriptions appear in Sabaean, Ge'ez, and Greek. The Axumites
became reputable architects and builders in stone, as the famous
monolithic stele still seen in Axum reveal. The kingdom also produced bronze, silver, and gold coins.

Axum became a powerful kingdom that extended its control
over Africans and Arabians. From the second century A.D. military conquests were made along the Red Sea and the Blue Nile,
and during the third century Axum established its authority over
peoples on the Arabian coast as far as Aden. It controlled the
important trade routes to Meroë, Egypt, and Red Sea ports, and
had a major influence over the Red Sea trade in general. The

kingdom reached its apogee during the fourth century when King Ezana unified Axum, integrated Yemen into the empire, invaded and ultimately destroyed Kush around A.D. 330. Ezana's armies swept as far as the confluence of the Atbara and Nile Rivers. This was indeed an epic victory that gave Axum even greater control over caravan routes in northeastern Africa and established the kingdom as an important international power. Indeed, Axum became an ally of Byzantium. Byzantine emperor Justin I sent an emissary to the Axumite king Ella-Atsbeha (Caleb) in 524 and secured the latter's promise to invade Yemen, where Christians were being persecuted. After successfully completing the expedition, the king sent a report to Justin. This close diplomatic cooperation was still in evidence in 531 when Justin's successor, Justinian, sought Axum's support against Persia, but it seems that in this instance Ella-Atsbeha did not have the power to match Persia, which, as one of the great powers in Arabia in the latter part of the sixth century, overran Arabia and gained control over much of the Red Sea trade, including ports that served Axum. Axum was unable to maintain its hegemony in Yemen and was challenged along the Nile by the kingdoms of Nabatia, Makuria (Makurra), and Alodia (Alwa). Finally, Islam's expansion into Egypt in 639, the Muslim destruction of Adulis in 710, and the establishment of Umayyad control over the Dahlak Islands in 715 signaled a new era for northeastern Africa. From Egypt and the coastal towns on the Red Sea Islam spread along the trade routes to the Ethiopian interior where Ifat, Adal, and other Muslim states appeared at about the same time that Axum was expanding across Shoa and other areas. While the Muslims and Axum maintained a fairly peaceful relationship, the latter was increasingly isolated from the major international centers along the Mediterranean and Red Seas, centers with which she had established long-standing and influential relations.

Axum's decline on the international scene did not signal stagnation at home. The kingdom continued a trend toward unifica-

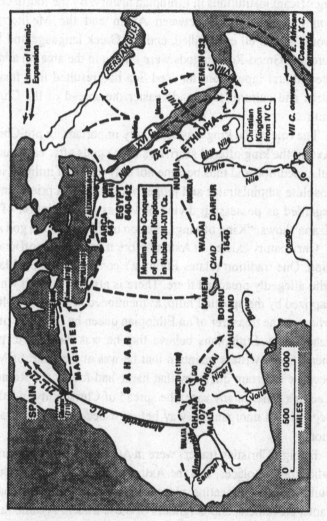

Expansion of Islam

tion and the development of its own culture, which was manifested largely in the Ethiopian Church, one of the oldest and most significant institutions in Ethiopian history. By the fourth century commercial relations between Axum and the Mediterranean world were well established, and the Greek language and literature and Greco-Roman gods were known in the area. In addition, the cultural input from the Red Sea had resulted in a fusion of ideas and cultures that made easier the spread of the Christian faith.

The role of the king was especially important. In pre-Christian Axum, the king offered sacrifices to the gods after each successful expedition and thus became not only the chief military leader, absolute administrator and judge, but the highest priest, and was regarded as possessing divine power, as an inscription of King Ezana shows: "King of kings, the son of the invincible god Ares."

Christianity existed in Axum before it became the official religion. One tradition relates Ethiopia's conversion by St. Matthew who allegedly preached there. There is also the eunuch who was baptized by the apostle Philip, as mentioned in Acts 8:26–40, and who was the treasurer of an Ethiopian queen by the name of Candace. Many Ethiopians believe that he was the first to preach there. Some writers maintain that he was at the court of Meroë, because a certain queen by that name had fought the Romans in Caesar's time. In any case, the spread of Christianity in Ethiopia began in an unorganized way before it became the official religion.

Foreign Christian traders were in Adulis, the city of Axum, and other trading places, and the Axumite kingdom allowed them to build their own meeting places. It is entirely possible that servants, customers, and neighbors of those traders became familiar with the faith and thus prepared the way for organized proselytizing. Christianity became the official religion in the fourth century A.D., officially established by Frumentius, a Syrian student of philosophy. He found his way to Axum after encountering an accident at sea. Shortly after his arrival at the capital, the king died and left the kingdom to the queen, who requested Frumentius to help in its administration. This gave him the opportunity to exercise influence over the education of the princes and the construction of prayer houses. It was he who later became the first bishop of Ethiopia and converted King Ezana, who reigned sometime between 320 and 360 and recorded inscriptions of his achievements on slabs of stone. In the first four he showed adherence to pre-Christian beliefs, but the last one showed a change in his beliefs. He no longer attributed his success to Ares, but according to an inscription: "By the power of the Lord of heaven, who in heaven and upon earth is mightier than everything that exists."

With regard to theology, the Ethiopians accepted the position of the Council of Nicea (325) that Christ is fully God and Man, that Christ is of the same nature as God (consubstantial), and that there never was a time when Christ did not exist (a counteraction to Arianism). When the Council of Chalcedon in 451 supported the view that Christ is of two natures, divine and human, Egypt and Ethiopia severed their relationships with the Church of Constantinople and Rome, and became leaders of a new group, the monophysites, the Coptic Church of Egypt and the Ethiopian Orthodox Church respectively.

The growth of the church was assisted toward the end of the fifth and early sixth centuries by missionaries, and the support of kings. When the Monophysites were condemned at the Council of Chalcedon and persecuted by the Byzantine emperors, they received refuge under the Ethiopian Church and helped evangelize in the country. Among these immigrants were the Nine Saints who went to Axum about 502 and taught in different places. They turned some of the pre-Christian temples into churches, relating themselves thereby to a local institution and thus appealing to the local inhabitants, because they made no major effort to destroy existing houses of worship. Pilgrimages to these places were made by people from different parts of the country.

These religious communities depended on the surrounding villages for supplies and gradually received substantial assistance from various kings. In the sixth century King Gabre Maskal presented the monastery of Debra Damo with lands that included many villages. He also gave grants to other communities, setting an example that other kings followed, thereby making these monasteries great land-owning institutions through gifts that were not to be taken away either by the giver or any other ruler. Thus, while this practice limited the resources of the state, it strengthened the church and became a source of conflict to the present day.

The monasteries also became centers of learning. During the sixth century the Nine Saints began translating the New Testament and other relevant books into Ge'ez, which became the basis for Ethiopian literature and ecclesiastical expression. Some of the Saints also served as advisers to the kings. The great Ethiopian scholar Yared received his education in one of these church schools. He compiled the Digua, a hymn book that called for the use of such instruments as sistrum and drums to accompany the human voice. In addition to contributing church music, Yared also made important contributions to the development of Ge'ez poetry.

A most impressive cultural achievement occurred during the thirteenth century when the famous rock-hewn monolithic churches were constructed during the reign of King Lalibela. The churches were carved out of solid rock mountains by chipping away at the top to a depth of some forty feet. The churches were thus approached by descending a stairway leading to a hewn-out courtyard surrounding the church. The interiors of the churches were decorated with colorful religious figures. These churches have been called one of the wonders of the world and bear some resemblance in style to the earlier constructed stele at Axum, suggesting a possible continuity in architectural style.

Without a doubt the Ethiopian monarchy and Christian Church reinforced each other and became symbols and bonds of unity and identity for Ethiopians in ancient times, and this whole process was buttressed by the international image of the country provided by the legends of the Queen of Sheba and Prester John and the involvement of the country in world affairs.

By the dawn of the modern era, with the persistent expansion of Europeans into Africa, several kingdoms in the northeast had been participants in and contributors to a remarkable history. Attempts to establish a foundation for unity among a great diversity of people in the region, which were unsuccessfully undertaken by Kush, were much more successfully carried out by Axum. Indeed, nation building was in the making.

Nubia

Between the Axumites' conquest of Kush around A.D. 330 and the Arab conquest of Egypt in A.D. 639, there emerged at least three small Nubian kingdoms along the Nile—Nobatia, Makuria, and Alodia. Exactly when they were formed is unknown, but there are references by classical writers to the Nobatae (of Nobatia) invading Egypt and fighting the Roman armies there. Early in the sixth century the Nobatae expanded southward up to the Third Cataract probably in the consolidation of their kingdom. Their Merotic heritage met the influence of Byzantine Egypt and could have been Christianized by that contact. By 566 a bishop was appointed in Nobatae, and shortly thereafter Christian churches were built; and Greek was adopted as the language of the church, diplomacy, and official documents.

During the latter part of the sixth century two other kingdoms emerged in Nubia, Makuria with its capital at Dongola, and Alodia with its capital at Soba. Alodia is believed to have sprung from migrations of people south of Meroë. Both Makuria and Alodia converted to Christianity during the sixth century and were influenced by the Byzantine Empire. In 573 Makuria dispatched an emissary to Constantinople where a friendship convention was negotiated with Justin II. Alodia was converted by Egyptian Monophysites. Thus, by 580 many Nubians were Christians and resisted the advance of Islam for about eight hundred years.

These Nubian kingdoms developed their own culture, only part of which has been reconstructed—thanks to the results of archaeology. Church ruins have been recovered, and the pottery and paintings that adorned them seem to indicate an artistic peak between A.D. 800 and 1000. Inscriptions in Greek, Coptic, and Nubian have been found. Remnants of houses built of sun-dried brick reveal something of their architecture.

Islam made its thrust into Nubia when it besieged Dongola in A.D. 651. This led to a treaty of friendship and trade that lasted for many centuries. An inscription of 1317, however, reveals that Dongola may have been an independent Muslim state; but as late as about 1340 Al Omari wrote that the people of northern Makuria were Christians with a Muslim king. Conversion of the masses to Islam thus seems to have been a slow process in which Nubians retained their own language and customs. Some of them did, however, migrate and settle in southeastern Sudan where they helped to spread the faith. Over the years Nubians developed great military strength. They maintained friendly relations with Egypt, the principal outlet for their trade, which included slaves. This friendship with Egypt later led the Nubians to assist the Fatimid dynasty in its struggle for power.

Thus, in spite of the sparse documentation, enough is known to conclude that Nubia, in the early tradition of Kush, remained a dynamic factor in the history of northeastern Africa. It kept open the north-south channel of reciprocal communication and cultural diffusion. It helped first to Christianize, later and more effectively to Islamize, much of the Sudan; it also retained much of its own character and carried north inner Africa's presence and influence.

Western Africa

Carthage, Ghana, Mali, and Songhai

Political evolution in northeastern Africa was shaped to a great extent by the geographical, economic, and social impact of the Nile River, which linked Egypt and the several interior societies. The Nile had no such counterpart in the west, which was distinguished by the harsh Sahara desert. In spite of the many difficulties that this situation posed, however, the people of the great western bulge of Africa developed viable societies of their own, maintained contact among themselves, and established direct and indirect relations with the non-African world. In short, the inhabitants of this part of Africa did not allow the tremendous obstacles of the Sahara to stifle their cultural growth.

Carthage, like Egypt, benefited from its strategic northern location, which allowed it to become the major African entrepôt in the western Mediterranean Sea. It controlled much, if not most, of the western trans-Saharan trade in ancient times; it also sought to tap the sea trade on the Atlantic side of Africa. Sometime in the sixth or early fifth century B.C. the Carthaginians dispatched an expedition under the command of Hanno, who reportedly sailed past Gibraltar and continued south. The expedition, which consisted of sixty vessels and an estimated crew of thirty thousand, was to explore the western coast of Africa and set up trading stations along the way. How far Hanno sailed is in dispute. Some writers believe he reached the area of Mt. Cameroon, while others believe his voyage extended only to Sierra Leone. Whatever the extent of the voyage, however, the motive seems to have been to establish a more direct access to trade, gold in particular, and Hanno's expedition does appear to have established some contact with "the Ethiopians."

Commerce formed the basis of the Carthage economy. Herodotus explained how the Carthaginians practiced silent barter with interior Africans during ancient times. The main commodities of the Carthaginian markets were textiles, glassware, pottery, ivory, and precious stones. However, the Carthaginian influence was cut short by the Roman conquest in 146 B.C. Under Roman rule Carthage became more integrated into that empire, which it supplied with grains, olives, and vineyards. This in turn further stimulated the growth of urban life in Carthage, which continued to attract merchants from the Sudan and Sahara and encouraged northerners to journey in the south. Indeed this two-way commercial and cultural interaction continued through the religious schisms and nomadic raids of the Roman Empire and the subsequent conquests of the Vandals, Byzantines, and Arabs, all of whom contributed to the cultural mosaic of northern Africa in general and Carthage in particular. Throughout all of this, the indigenous people, the Berbers, retained their ethnic identity, language, and culture, and maintained their contacts along the trans-Saharan trade routes and in the western Sudan.

In the interior of the western Sudan—from the Lake Chad region to the Atlantic, which includes the buckle of the Niger, where some scholars believe independent agricultural developments were contemporaneous with those along the Nile—several different African groups devised cultures and political systems that had a tremendous impact not only in the immediate area, but in northern Africa and beyond. The western Sudan contained several forms of material wealth—gold, ivory, gums, and kola nuts—which were early exploited by the local inhabitants who engaged in a vigorous commerce with peoples throughout much of the continent. This trade expanded considerably with the acquisition of iron-making skills, which led to the modernization of their military weapons, their agricultural implements, and other working tools.

In addition to their iron-making skills, the several great kingdoms that emerged in the region had the advantage of strategic location along commercial highways that were part of an interna-

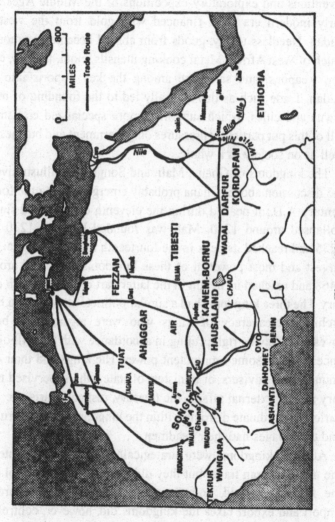

Western African States

tional mercantile network. Goods purchased in the western Sudan by Berbers were sold to northern African merchants who in turn sold them to Europeans or Asians. Indeed, many of the European inventions and exploratory expeditions of the Middle Ages and early modern era were financed with gold from the western Sudan. Needless to say, goods from abroad became common in much of West Africa. Metal cooking utensils, cloth, jewelry, copper, weapons, and salt were among the key imports into the Sudan. Trade such as this naturally led to the founding of more towns and cities, which supported more specialized craftsmen. All of this put particular pressures on government and business as well as on society as a whole.

The kingdoms of Ghana, Mali, and Songhai are illustrative of the discussion above. Ghana probably emerged during the fourth century A.D.; it peaked during the eleventh century, and finally collapsed around 1240. Mali was founded between 1230 and 1235 and reached its peak in the fourteenth century. Songhai, the largest and most powerful of these kingdoms, appeared around 1468 and reached its height in the latter part of the sixteenth century. The three kingdoms had a similar political structure—a hierarchical bureaucracy of kings who were regarded as being invested by divine right, ruling in accordance with the will of the ancestors and some omnipotent power. The kings had their own councils and advisers, or ministers of state, who supervised military affairs, external affairs, the treasury, justice, courts, etc. The various subordinate districts within the kingdoms had their rulers, and the villages had their headmen.

All three kingdoms were strategically located along routes of the trans-Saharan trade, but they did not have basic control over the sources of gold, known as the Wangara mines. Through import and export taxes the kingdoms did, however, control the trade routes, which crossed their territory. Of the several routes, four deserve special mention. The westernmost route linked Ghana with the principal trading town of Audaghost, and continued across the western edge of the Sahara, and along the Atlas Mountains in southern Morocco to Sijilmasa, a crossroads commercial community that tied in to feeder routes north to Marrakesh, Fez, and beyond. Ghana also connected with Timbuktu on a route north through the salt-mining regions of Taodeni and Taghaza to Sijilmasa. The third route became especially prominent during the time of the Mali Empire. It stretched from Gao on the eastern buckle of the Niger River and across the Sahara to Tunis. There were several oases along the route where merchants stopped for water and rest. Around those oases, Agadès and Ghat, for example, commercial activities stimulated the growth of towns. The fourth route to be mentioned here was the mainstay of the Songhai Empire, and connected the Bornu region, in what today is northern Nigeria, with Bilma, and continued into the Libyan hinterland of Fezzan where it branched off at Murzuk to Tripoli and Benghazi, two principal entrepôts for trade in the eastern Mediterranean. These north-south routes were connected with east-west routes, primarily one which linked Timbuktu and Gao to the Bornu region, which was tied in with the Nile Valley trade. In addition, the southern Sudanic entrepôts had feeder connections with areas in the forest zone. So in fact none of the kingdoms, large or small, was without some contact with the vigorous trans-Saharan trade.

Those were the main routes during the Middle Ages. The first two were controlled in the Sudan by Ghana, though Berbers and later Arabs were the principal traveling merchants. On both routes gold was the principal export and salt the main import along with cloth, jewels, trinkets, etc., from the north. The third route carried a more mixed trade—gold, salt, shells, skins, ivory, cloth, kola nuts, etc.—and was traveled to a great extent by Mandingo merchants, reflecting the impact of the Mali Empire as its people and their language, Mandingo, became more widespread after Mali peaked as a kingdom in the fourteenth century. The fourth route was essentially a slave route supplying the Arabs through Tripoli and Benghazi. This route peaked under Songhai at a time when Islam helped cement closer relations with the Muslim Arab east.

For a description of what the Sudanic kingdoms were really like, the best accounts have come from contemporaries. Although Ghana seems to have been mentioned by Arab writers as early as the ninth century A.D., and the Sudanic historian in Timbuktu, Mahmud Kati, in his book *Tarikh-al-Fattash,* discussed Kanissa'ai, a seventh-century Ghana king who had a thousand horses, the best source of information about the kingdom at its peak is *Description of North Africa* published in 1067 by al-Bakri, an Arab geographer who spent much of his life at Cordova, Spain, collecting data from merchants who had eyewitness reports of Ghana. Bakri described Ghana as two towns, one with the king and traditional society, and the other one Muslim. The houses were built of stone and wood. At the king's court there were interpreters, a comptroller, and advisers. All the gold nuggets belonged to the king, and the gold dust to the people. Tenkaminen, the king, around 1065, had an elaborate court and could put in the field two hundred thousand soldiers, more than forty thousand of them armed with bows and arrows. With this kind of power, backed up by skilled iron workers producing iron weapons, one can understand how Ghana was able to extend its control over the lesser states of Tekrur, Audaghost, and others.

Kumbi, which is located about two hundred miles north of Bamako in present-day Mali, is considered the site of the Muslim town. Excavations there have revealed stone houses, a mosque, tombs, and Koranic inscriptions. It has been estimated that Kumbi had as many as fifteen thousand inhabitants. When Islam continued its spread across northern Africa from the seventh century, and as the several coastal entrepôts came under Muslim control, Muslim Arabs settled in larger numbers throughout much of the Sahara and Sudan, primarily as merchants. The king of Ghana apparently recognized the political and economic significance of those developments because he not only tolerated them and allowed the construction of a Muslim town in his realm, he also employed several Muslims as trusted advisers. This was of great consequence for West Africa. First, it facilitated a more peaceful penetration of Islamic influence at an early stage of Muslim expansion into the region. In time, the presence and activities of the Muslims prepared the way for great cultural change. Second, this cooperation between the king of Ghana and Muslims paid dividends to the kingdom through increased trade and better relations with the Muslim north.

The eleventh century, however, witnessed an important shift of events when along the Senegal River there emerged a militant Muslim reform group known as the Almoravids. They launched a two-pronged attack, one north and another south, with dual objectives—military conquest and Islamic proselytization and reform. The movement fanned out of the Senegal Valley northward into the Iberian peninsula, thereby bringing a part of Europe under the authority of a black kingdom. There had been other large Muslim kingdoms established in the Maghreb, but they had been set up by alien conquerors; the Almoravids, however, were Africans—Berbers and inhabitants of the Senegal Valley. The empire, through the control of trade from the Sudan on up into Iberia, became very prosperous and lasted for about a century before it was overcome in the north by the Moroccan-based Almohads who ruled for another century. The latter not only gained control over northwestern Africa, including Tripolitania, they also replaced the Almoravids in Muslim Iberia.

The major impact farther south, however, was the destruction of Ghana in 1076. The fact that Ghana had accepted and indirectly encouraged Muslim settlers in the kingdom meant that the expansion of Islam by the Almoravids met with some internal support and popular adherence. Two noteworthy points on the defeat of Ghana are the destruction of the ancestral citadels and the subsequent rule over the state by Muslims. Over the next few years, therefore, Sudanic Africans in increasing numbers converted to the faith. Whether this resulted from a basic religious conviction or from the imperative of protecting one's interest in the Muslim-controlled state is less significant than that such conversions strengthened the links between the Muslim world and blacks in Africa.

The destruction of Ghana encouraged greater unrest in the region as various small kingdoms sought liberation from the rule of Ghana and competed for the wealth accruing from the trade routes. The most successful in its struggle for hegemony was Mali, which finally emerged between 1230 and 1235 under Sundiata. Although Mali encompassed much of the old kingdom of Ghana, the principal trade entrepôts shifted toward the east, reflecting greater cultural and commercial relations with the Muslim world. The main caravan route became Gao-Ghat-Tunis, which carried a great diversity of goods—gold, salt, metals, cloth, jewelry, kola nuts, etc. In addition to its control over much of the trade, Mali also encompassed the fertile lands along much of the Niger River, which provided a more balanced economy and secured a network of communication via water transport.

The growing relationship between Islam and the Sudan became more apparent, as, increasingly, the rulers of Mali and the next great kingdom, Songhai, were Muslims. Indeed, the most influential, colorful, and well-known sovereign of Mali, Mansa Musa, was a Muslim who established himself as a great leader. His position was dramatized mainly as a result of his historic pilgrimage to Mecca in 1324. This seems to have been the first time a great Sudanic ruler had made a voyage from western Africa through Egypt to Mecca, and in such splendor.

Within fifty years of that pilgrimage there appeared in a European atlas the following inscription accompanying a picture of Mansa Musa:

This Negro Lord is called Mansa Musa, Lord of the Negros [sic] of Guinea. So abundant is the gold which is found in his country that he is the richest and most noble king in all the land.

This description resulted from Mansa Musa's liberal distribution of his wealth as he passed through the Sudan, Egypt, and into Mecca. He took with him an estimated entourage of eighty thousand people carrying gold bars and sacks of gold dust. Some twelve years later an Egyptian historian wrote that Egypt's economy had not then recovered from the effects of Mansa Musa's gold.

While on his pilgrimage the king persuaded a number of Muslim scholars, jurists, architects, and others to return with him to Mali. The result of this was to be a great flowering of African civilization, with a momentous impact far and wide. One of the architects, es-Saheli, designed several buildings, notably mosques, which became testaments to Islam's influence as it built on the indigenous mud architectural tradition. But what is much more important is that some of the Muslim teachers began establishing Koranic schools that taught reading, writing, and comprehension from the Koran. The great university at Timbuktu, Sankoré, built by es-Saheli, attracted students and professors not only from the immediate area but also from northern Africa and the Middle East. Timbuktu thus emerged as a significant intellectual center of Muslim learning.

Mansa Musa appointed judges as advisers to him and some of the provinces. While Muslim law did not then become dominant in the kingdom, it must be reckoned that Mansa Musa laid the foundation on which Muslim tradition would later be established. These were only beginnings, but they represented the work of the sovereign and therefore gave a meaning and established religious goals that must have helped win many converts to the faith.

It is entirely possible that Mali extended its activities across the

Atlantic Ocean. Mansa Musa is reported to have said that his brother Abubakar equipped several hundred ships and instructed his captains not to return from a trip across the Atlantic until they had discovered land. One vessel seems to have returned, and it reported that the others had been lost at sea. Thus Abubakar himself led a second expedition, leaving Mansa Musa in power. This is the last we know of this venture. But whatever one may think of its authenticity, it is remarkable that the rulers of Mali, at least during the early fourteenth century, thought of and possibly launched a trans-Atlantic voyage.

This was a golden age in West Africa, and Mansa Musa was part of it, but with his passing, rivalry for rule, competition for wealth, and religious reform movements began to bring Mali to decline. Its strength waned first in the eastern provinces, where religious reform and missionary activities were greatest, sometimes reflecting the waves of Muslim unrest from the Middle East. The king's rule in the western region continued with greater force. Indeed, in 1494 when the Portuguese were penetrating various parts of the continent, they established diplomatic relations and exchanged ambassadors with Mali. Mali engaged in trade with the Portuguese and remained an important kingdom until the sixteenth century.

The greatest challenge to Mali came from the area around Gao, home of the Songhai, which played key roles in the trade around the eastern buckle of the Niger. From 1468, under Sonni Ali, the Songhai eventually formed the largest and greatest of these Sudanic kingdoms. It included all the major north-south trade routes in the area. comprised the fertile lands of the Niger River, and influenced several of the Hausa states, which were well known for their crafts. This kind of economic balance underlay the greatness of Songhai.

During this time the eastern trade route thrived on the sale of slaves to northern Africa, the Middle East, and Turkey. Slaves were marched from the region of Bornu, through Bilma, and eventually sold in Tripoli and Benghazi whence they were carried to Egypt and Turkey primarily, while others were taken to other parts of the East. While this trade did not even begin to approach the volume of the Atlantic slave trade, it was nonetheless a brutal enterprise, with skeletons of Africans strewn across the Sahara. The heat, cutting winds, attacks by animals, raids by renegade slavers, thirst, and hunger all took their toll on African lives; and yet, rulers and traders thrived on this kind of business, which helped to make Songhai a great kingdom.

Askia the Great (Muhammad Touré) became the most prominent king of Songhai, and in many ways he went beyond the efforts of his great predecessor, Mansa Musa. He too made a pilgrimage to Mecca (in 1495) with a large entourage, carrying gold, which he distributed along the way. He also returned to the kingdom with several scholars and other professionals. He appointed Muslim advisers and attempted to enforce Islamic law. Indeed, Askia was determined to rebuild the greatness of the area, which had not regained the point of its earlier prominence. Thus, there occurred at Timbuktu a cultural revival which was shared by other centers, especially Jeanné, where educational endeavors were also encouraged. Timbuktu at this time surpassed its earlier reputation. It was in this period that indigenous African writers published books: Ahmad Baba composed many works on Islamic law, a dictionary of Muslim scholars, and thirteen of his works are still in use in parts of West Africa; Mahmud Kati wrote *Tarikh al-Fattach* (Chronicle of the Seeker after Knowledge) in Arabic; Abdal-Rahman as-Sadi wrote *Tarikh as-Sudan* (Chronicle of the Sudan). These have become crucial documents for the reconstruction of West African history during the Middle Ages.

The greatness and prosperity of Songhai continued to attract Arabs and Berbers as visitors and settlers for many years, and kingdoms to the north continued their proverbial talk about capturing the rich kingdoms to the south. Finally, in 1591, El Mansur of Morocco dispatched a large army to attack Songhai and establish control over the rich gold mines. After defeating Songhai and routing its armies, the Moroccans discovered that the kingdom did not control the gold mines, which were located in the northern forest areas. When the Moroccan forces pushed their attack to the forest, they faced a different kind of warfare, guerrilla warfare in which the bow and arrow were effective against the cavalry of the northerners, who were unaccustomed to the dense forest. Although they were unsuccessful in gaining control over the gold mines, the Moroccans remained in the region and over the years intermarried with the local inhabitants. Some of the Moroccans ruled as independent pashas over small districts up to about 1660 when the non-Muslim Bambara states of Segu and Karta became powerful, and Islam in the Sudan entered a period of eclipse.

Thus the greatest kingdom of the western Sudan was destroyed, and with it the glory of the African achievement in the region was temporarily shattered. No large unit would emerge in this region until the nineteenth century, by which time a new force was gaining momentum. That was the European presence.

Kanem-Bornu

In the central Sudan, around Lake Chad, another great and powerful kingdom emerged as a contemporary of Ghana. Like the other early kingdoms, Kanem-Bornu's origins are obscure, but it probably appeared early in the ninth century. Its position paralleled that of the western Sudan by being favorably located along trade routes to Tunis, Tripoli, and Benghazi in the north, the Nile Valley and Egypt to the east, the Niger River area to the west, and the southern forests of the Guinea coast. To the north, mainly at Bilma, there were salt deposits and some copper; oils, gums, nuts, and some cotton goods came from the south; kola nuts, ivory, and some gold arrived from the western Sudan; from the east, horses and metalware were imported. A trade in slaves also developed with the north. There were relay and rest stations scattered along all the routes, north-south and east-west. The early inhabitants of Kanem were thus in direct contact with diverse areas, peoples, and events.

The Sefawa family produced the early kings (mais) of Kanem, and during the eleventh century one of them, Hume, accepted Islam and thereby set an example that led eventually to the Islamization of the kingdom. As elsewhere, Islamization facilitated better trading relations with surrounding Muslim-controlled areas. In addition, the arts of writing and scholarship in Arabic were introduced by Islam.

The core of Kanem were the Kanuri people, who produced the early kings and councils. Each ruler over districts of the kingdom was a member of the council whose advice the king had to consider. With Islamization a greater degree of centralization occurred as each subordinate became linked to the king by religion as well as birth. Muslim law led to greater standardization over the Kanuri and other groups in the kingdom.

This was old Kanem, to the east of Lake Chad, but it collapsed in a fifteenth-century revolt by the Bulala people, and west of the lake a new center of the kingdom arose, Bornu. However, Kanem had laid the commercial, political, and religious basis for the new kingdom, whose greatest king was Idris Alooma, who reigned from 1580 to 1617 and became one of the strongest and most successful kings of Kanem-Bornu. He united most of the savannah lands from Darfur to Hausaland, established firm diplomatic relations with Tripoli and Cairo, and exchanged gifts with the sultan of Ottoman Turkey.

The Hausa City-States

Spread across northern Nigeria were the Hausa states, fertile in land, skilled in crafts, and experienced in trade. These states were not united until the nineteenth century, but were instead a series of merchant states. Each town developed its government, and nearby farmers often took refuge there in time of war. For this protection the farmers paid taxes to the rulers of the city-states who maintained the armies. Each city-state was also a market-place, the economic mainstay of the polity. The principal cities were an integral part of the great international trade already described in the western and eastern Sudan. In addition, com-mercial connections developed with the forest zones in the south.

The principal Hausa states were Daura, Gobir, Katsina, Kano, and Zaria. Although they did not form an empire or a kingdom, they did occasionally band together for their mutual interests and thus achieved a great commercial influence throughout the immediate region. During the early modern period, about 1500, Katsina and Kano emerged as the strongest Hausa states. Indeed, Kano eventually surpassed the great commercial cities of Tim-buktu and Gao. What was especially unique about the Hausa states was their handicraft. They made cotton and leather goods, which sold throughout much of the western and central Sudan.

The Guinea Forest States

Much less is known about the Guinea forest states prior to European contact. The Arabs and Berbers, to whom we are so indebted for historical accounts of the Sudan, do not seem to have penetrated the forest zones until much later, and then on a small scale. We do know, however, that the hot and humid climate, dense undergrowth, and tsetse fly greatly limited both trade and agriculture. The Guinea coast comprised many mangrove swamps and rough beachlines that restricted communications via the sea. Moreover, torrential rains and humidity along with ter-mites made the preservation of documents most difficult, while the acid soils seem to have limited the preservation of fossils. However, one should not conclude that the inhabitants of the for-est zone were completely isolated and unindustrious in cultural and political developments. Some of the greatest African kingdoms emerged there, and their roots must reach far into the past. As already pointed out, several species of yam, the kola tree, and oil palm are said to be indigenous to West Africa. The cultivation of these crops developed even before the use of iron became common in the region, sometime between A.D. 300 and 500.

Trade was a great factor in the evolution of these states. The kola nut was in great demand in the Sudan; the gold of the trans-Saharan trade brought fame to Guinea; ivory was also in great demand, and slaves later became a major commodity. The trade routes were rugged, passing through dense forests and along rivers and lagoons. Human porterage was the chief means of transport, except for small boats in the rivers. But through their ingenuity, the forest people retained contact with the great commercial highways and entrepôts of Hausaland and the Sudan, and were therefore a part of the progress, though perhaps not always so rapid, that occurred in other parts of the continent.

Some Guinea states developed political institutions and concepts similar to other states. They were ruled by a divine king who had his council of advisers and subrulers. In the case of the Yoruba the rich oral traditions reveal a deep concern for cosmogony. At the very heart of Yoruba life is Ile Ife, which is regarded as the cradle of humans. Several myths and legends describe the creation. One version holds that Olorun, the sky god, sent Oduduwa, father of all original Yoruba kings, to establish land in the ocean. He distributed soil and placed a cock and a palm nut on the ocean and when the cock scratched the soil it became earth, and the nut grew into a tree. All Yoruba versions seem to agree on the descent of Oduduwa to establish earth, but other details vary. For example, one account holds that Obatala, a follower of Oduduwa, fashioned man out of clay. Although the Yoruba concept of creation is much more complex than this, the point here is that the Yoruba developed an elaborate metaphysical philosophy that explains the relationship of man to the universe.

It also explains the source from which the major Yoruba rulers derived their divine sanction, which became the center of Yoruba religious beliefs.

What is much more widely known about Yoruba history is the world-famous bronze and terra-cotta sculptures that were discovered in Ife in the nineteenth century. The figures, mostly human, are naturalistic in style and are believed to be idealized portraits. Some are life-size. A number of stone monuments have also been found at Ife. Those include carvings of humans and animals and decorated stools. Very little is known about the identity of the artists, when the art flourished, the purpose of the art, or the relationship between that art and the art of the Yorubas' neighbors. However, a Benin tradition holds that the art of bronze casting came from Ife, although Benin's art is less naturalistic and is said to have evolved in wood, terra-cotta, and ivory in addition to bronze. Further, Nok art and culture, which are referred to in chapter 1 and which date between 900 B.C. and A.D. 200, were found throughout much of northeastern Nigeria, which has led to the belief that Nok was the ancestor of both Ife and Benin art. Clearly Nok, Ife, and Benin art and culture were products of a highly creative genius, which even in the absence of fuller descriptions of the societies themselves, does allow deductions that the kind of stability and patronage required for such works could only have come from highly organized and secure states.

The East African Coast

Written accounts of the East African coast date back nearly two thousand years to the *Periplus of the Erythraean Sea,* a sailor's guide written by an Egyptian Greek merchant. It was probably written during the latter part of the first century A.D., and along with Ptolemy's *Geography,* which for East Africa probably dates from the end of the fourth century A.D., constitutes the most informative source up to the tenth century when al-Masudi, an Arab, wrote his very valuable accounts, and the fourteenth century when Ibn Battuta's travel accounts became invaluable sources. There are also chronicles of particular towns written in Arabic or Swahili with Arabic script. The *Kilwa Chronicle*, written about 1530, is the oldest and probably the most reliable. Most of the other town chronicles were written from the latter part of the eighteenth century. These written sources supplemented by oral traditions, archaeology, linguistics, and anthropology provide the main substance of the history of the East African coast up to modern times.

The precise ethnic identity of the original inhabitants of the eastern coast is unknown, but it is generally agreed that they were probably hunters and gatherers of food. They were probably part of the Khoisan ("click") language family, as are the Sandawé, who live close to the main rock-painting area in central Tanganyika, and the Hadza (Tindiga) around Lake Eyasi. Early stone implements have been found at various coastal locations. Subsequent to these early inhabitants, however, the principal components of the present population settled along the coast: The Oromo (Gallo), with linguistic relations with Arabs and long contacts across the Red Sea, established settlements in the northern part of the Horn of Africa (Eritrea and Somalia), and later penetrated into northern Kenya. They remain essentially a nomadic, pastoral people. The Somali also had prolonged contact with the Arabs and settled along the southern shore of the Gulf of Aden. They more readily adopted Islam, probably as early as the tenth century A.D., and intermarried with Arabs to a great extent. Their influence has been greatest along the coast, but they also migrated into the interior where communities now reside in Kenya and Ethiopia. The Bantu probably began settling on the coast in small numbers very early, increasing in number by about A.D. 500–600, so that by the end of the first millennium A.D. most of the area had become Bantu-speaking. However, recent research challenges the earlier view that the great wave of Bantu migrations to East Africa probably originated in present-day Cameroon and moved through Congo and along the Zambezi River to Mozambique and into Tanganyika and Kenya. Today the Bantu represent the largest group of Africans in East Africa.

Some historians have stated that Egyptians, Phoenicians, Persians, Arabs, and others may have settled on the coast long before the Christian era. In fact, Herodotus relates an account of the circumnavigation of Africa by Phoenicians, but few historians seem to accept this as fact. It is important to note, however, that East Africa, particularly the area south of the Horn, has been in continuous contact with the whole Indian Ocean complex since the *Periplus* was written, and probably centuries before that. These contacts were facilitated by the monsoon winds that from November through March blow from the northeast and carried dhows from Asia to the East African coast. From May through September the winds reverse themselves, blow from the southwest and so carried the dhows and their crews back to the Arabian peninsula, India, and elsewhere in Asia. This meant that, with the winds blowing from east to west for five months, Arabs, Hindus, and other Asians could visit several points on the East African coast, and spend several weeks or months at various places selling their wares and solidifying contacts with local inhabitants. Some of those Asians took up residence, intermarried with the Africans, and thereby provided the genesis of present-day Asian communities in East Africa and the emergence of persons of Arab-African descent, the Swahili.

To the early writers this area was known as Azania and to the Arabs as the land of the Zenj. The most important pre-Islamic commercial town on the coast seems to have been Rhapta, about which little is known except that it was the center for the export of ivory that Arab merchants controlled. Rhapta was probably located on the northern coast of Tanganyika. The East African products exported were ivory, gums, shells, copper, leopard skins, gold, rhinoceros horn, coconut oil, and slaves. From Asia came such items as glass, cloth, spears, hatchets, daggers, awls, lances, beads, and porcelain. The inclusion of the several metal (iron) tools as imports supports the view that iron smelting either was not developed or was underdeveloped. Moreover, near the coast iron ores are very poor.

There is a disputed tradition that following their defeat in Oman by an Umayyad army in the seventh century, two brothers, Suliaman and Said, emigrated from Oman to the land of Zenj. There are also stories of heretic Muslims settling along the coast, and there may indeed be truth in these. Certainly the Arabs could easily have started communities. At Merca a colony of Muslim Arabs dates from the tenth century and another emerged at Manda near Lamu, and in Zanzibar. Arabs from the area of Bahrein reportedly founded Mogadishu and Brava, probably in the eleventh century.

By the tenth century Muslim settlements had appeared on the islands of Zanzibar and Pemba. Settlements had also emerged in Kilwa, which became the prominent town near the end of the twelfth century. The power of Kilwa is traced to the Shirazi—a derivative of Shiraz, capital of the Persian province of Fars—who very possibly were part of the group of Persian settlement in Mogadishu, Shungwaya, and other points along the Somali coast. They intermarried with Africans wherever they settled, became Africanized, and established a ruling dynasty at Kilwa and Kisimani Mafia, both of which eventually became very important coastal entrepôts. The Shirazi were essentially merchant-rulers who capitalized on the lucrative gold and ivory trade from Sofala, a town south of the Zambezi River on the coast of Mozambique. Kilwa is reported to have gained hegemony over the Sofala trade around the late thirteenth century and probably levied taxes on other merchants trading there. That Kilwa's wealth and influence increased during this period is revealed by the architectural achievements that resulted in the commercial emporium of

Husuni Kubwa, Ndogo, and major extensions to the Great Mosque. Stone houses became more common, and valuable Chinese porcelain appeared in larger quantities.

The key items from the coast were gold and ivory, which arrived from the interior to Kilwa and Zanzibar, both of which were favorably located near the coast and in the path of the monsoon winds. The source of the gold and ivory was probably Zimbabwe, about which our knowledge is limited. However, archaeology has uncovered some very important evidence that includes impressive ruins of stone structures (probably royal buildings) built between the eleventh and fifteenth centuries. Some of the walls of the buildings are thirty-two feet high, seventeen feet in thickness at the base, and between eleven and fourteen feet at the top. One wall extends about eight hundred feet in length. The walls were constructed of dry stone mortar, and there is no evidence of the use of scaffolding. Contrary to earlier hypotheses, it is generally agreed that Phoenicians, Arabs, and Europeans had not penetrated so deep into the interior so early and could not have constructed those edifices. The general consensus is not only that Africans were the builders of those structures, but that to have done so required a highly developed social and political system to organize and supervise the huge labor force, to secure and transport the materials, and to design and construct the buildings—all of which required many years to complete. Moreover, gold and ivory were abundant in the area and no doubt played a significant part in supporting the state through trade with the coast.

During the fifteenth century, in addition to undergoing serious internal dynastic strife, Kilwa was challenged commercially and politically by several other coastal entrepôts. Zanzibar exerted its independence and minted its own coins, as did Kilwa. Trade increased at Gedi, where many stone houses were constructed. Pate extended its trading activities, while the rising power of Mombasa became particularly ominous for neighboring towns. It was at this juncture that the Portuguese entered the scene, thereby adding another contending influence, which will be considered later. Suffice it here to note that the supremacy of Kilwa was already being undercut prior to the arrival of the Portuguese.

Trends in the interior were affecting coastal developments. This was especially the case among the Yao of northern Mozambique and southern Tanganyika. They were active merchants in large areas of the interior and as such responded to coastal developments. As the interior demand for goods from the Orient increased, the Yao pushed farther toward the coast, where they established commercial links at least by the sixteenth century and probably earlier. Conceivably other people, like the Kamba and Nyamwezi, also had commercial links with the coast. As the merchant states or cities on the coast increased in number, the competition to attract or influence the interior trade increased. Thus, the Portuguese arrived as East Africa was undergoing a commercial expansion stimulated in large measure by Indian Ocean influences, which also helped determine East African political trends.

The several city-states along the East African coast were governed by sultans and sheiks with their councils. They periodically established cooperative alliances with a neighbor, but never became unified in an empire or a federation. They were, instead, essentially city-states whose strength rested on their land trade with the interior and their maritime trade overseas. The coast, therefore, was an integral part of a continental and an international mercantile system.

Arabs engaged in trade with East Africans long before the development of Islam, but once the faith appeared, its identity with the Arabic language and culture and its acceptance by ruling and commercial interests in Arabia and North Africa caused Arabs and Swahili on the coast to become centers for the propagation of the faith. This was done partly by war but mainly through daily contact and intermarriage with Africans. This led to an identification of East Africans with Islam and Muslim trade, somewhat similar to the West African experience, with this important exception: In West Africa Arabs at the outset came to stay, either permanently or for an indeterminate time. While this may have been true of some Arabs in East Africa, the attraction and accessibility of Arabia where Arabs in East Africa maintained close, direct contacts with relatives, friends, and businesses, and the absence of a strong, centralized force of government to assert an African imperative allowed the continuation of a stronger identity of East African Arabs with the wider Arab world, and thereby limited their fuller identification with the broader African community.

But much of that was not then as evident as the fact of the cosmopolitan character of the East African coast. The Bantu, other Africans, the Arabs, Indians, Persians, and possibly some Greeks traded and intermingled in this part of Africa. Such contacts and intermarriages over the centuries led to what is commonly called but more difficult to define as Swahili culture or civilization. It is characterized by Islam, coastal settlement, and the Swahili language, which is basically Bantu with the incorporation of foreign words, mainly Arabic. This was the civilization the Portuguese found when they sailed around the southern tip of Africa near the end of the fifteenth century. To find such a civilization surprised the Portuguese, as their reports reveal in the description of the tall, many-storied buildings, well-laid-out streets, gardens, and parks, and harbors full of ships from the Orient. There was much evidence of luxury and wealth.

The Muslim Factor

The strategic geographical and economic position of North Africa accounted for much of that region's influence on other parts of Africa—the Sudan especially. Trade across the northern coast carried with it the culture of foreigners, thereby spreading influences in both obvious and imperceptible ways. Nubians and

Berbers were the critical agents of change in this regard; the Sudanese were to follow.

From about the eighth century B.C., when the Phoenicians founded colonies in northern Africa, until the Arab expansion there in the seventh century A.D., Africans along the northern coast were directly involved in the vigorous and decisive commercial and cultural life of the Mediterranean Sea. The Phoenicians had migrated from around Syria and established trading stations along the route; Carthage became the most successful station in the western sector, which controlled a series of neighboring towns. But the indigenous inhabitants, the Berbers, continued to develop their cultural institutions and script, Tifanagh. The immigrant Phoenicians, however, with their wide commercial relations, which necessitated the establishment of a more complex administrative system, had a decisive impact on many Berbers who became Punicized, and adopted the Phoenician language, Punic, as a lingua franca for trade.

The Phoenicians were later challenged by the Greeks, who successfully planted colonies in Egypt and Cyrenaica, but were repulsed by the Carthaginians. From 332 B.C. at least, when Alexander the Great conquered Egypt, the latter became the key connection between Africa and Europe, serving as a two-lane highway of cultural and commercial exchange. During the second century B.C. Carthage fell to the Romans; the next century witnessed Cyrenaica and Egypt fall under Roman control. These events more nearly integrated northern Africa as a unit into the Mediterranean cultural and commercial complex. On the cultural side, Christianity was a great factor. The faith spread in various parts of northern Africa and eventually involved Africa and Africans in the fourth-century Nicene Creed, which resulted from doctrinal differences. In 451, after the Council of Chalcedon, the indigenous Egyptians debated and accepted the Monophysite interpretation of the nature of Christ and rallied behind their Coptic Church, which was also adopted by the Nubian kingdoms and Ethiopia.

Commercially, the Roman era brought prosperity to parts of the area, such as Leptis Magna, which was no doubt a major outlet for the trans-Saharan trade passing through the Fezzan. The reports of Herodotus about chariots in the Fezzan and the discovery of rock drawings of horse-drawn carts add support to the hypotheses about this early caravan trade and contacts between Sudanic and northern Africa. The introduction of the camel in northern Africa during the Roman era further increased the ability of the Zenata and other northern Africans to travel long distances and raid the desert and its fringes. This greater African mobility contributed to the breakdown of law and stability and hastened the decline of Roman power. Then came the Vandal invasions from Europe in the fifth century, later followed by the Byzantines. These later invaders had much less of an impact but in a sense paved the way for the expansion of another, more decisive wave of colonizers—the Muslim Arabs.

Two points deserve emphasis if one is to understand the appeal of Islam among Africans. First, it is obvious that Islam spread across the northern littoral in the wake of long and often predatory conflict and insecurity for most of the people. Second, Islam, unlike the ideologies of the earlier immigrants, proved itself capable of providing a kind of unity and a greater political stability and economic security for diverse peoples. Not that the faith achieved the ideal, but it did offer an attractive promise of equality in a Muslim community that required little basic change from traditional African life. Indeed, it is noteworthy that except for the northern coast, Islam spread rather peacefully until the eighteenth century, with one significant interruption—the Almoravid conquests. This more peaceful expansion may be explained further by the fact that early African rulers tolerated the Muslim presence in order to enhance their economic and diplomatic relations with Muslim-controlled areas. Two points should be stressed in this connection. First, Islam traveled the trade routes and won its early, most numerous, and most effective converts in the towns

and cities. It was thus urban-based. Second, it was in the centralized states, which encouraged and protected trade and in which
the elite embraced the faith, for a variety of reasons, that Islam
thrived. This was achieved by the practice of employing Muslim
advisers and judges, establishing Koranic schools, and in general
fostering Muslim immigration, all practices that in very subtle
ways eventually embraced the Muslim and non-Muslim inhabitants. These were policies that could be successfully pursued only
by centralized bureaucracies.

Much of the appeal of Islam, however, was inherent in the faith
itself. In addition to the promise of equality, Islam's heritage, like
traditional Africa, included the extended family and polygamy.
Magic and divination were tolerated. Further, Islam was presented as a way of life without particular emphasis on abstract,
complicated theology. Belief in Allah and the teachings of the
prophet Mohammed were more important than comprehension.
Indeed, performance of the rituals and recitation of the creed
were sufficient to distinguish the believer from the nonbeliever.
Finally, the Muslim God and the great creator-power in African
cosmogonies were sufficiently comparable to facilitate the acceptance of Islam as an additive cultural factor. In fact, in some
African societies Allah is embodied in terms for traditional
deities: *waq* among the Oromo and Somali, *winam* among the
Mossi, *mungu* in Swahili, and *soko* in Nupe. All of these factors,
and the intermarriages in which offspring became Muslims, contributed to the steady increase in Muslim African converts. One
is reminded, however, that this was a gradual process that, except
for northern Africa, did not really embrace the masses until the
nineteenth century, by which time the faith itself had acquired
many local characteristics.

The schisms of the wider Muslim community also affected
Africa. Thus, the rise of the Fatimid dynasty, founded in the
Maghreb in the tenth century, was initially embraced by many
Berbers, whose loyalty was later lost as the Fatimids shifted their

capital and focus to Egypt and the Middle East. A result of this was the emergence of small Berber kingdoms under the Sanhaja confederation. Seeking to abort this development, the Fatimids encouraged Bodouin nomads with the Bani Hilal to invade wide stretches of Berber country. What was perhaps more important in the Bani Hilal invasions than their "locust" effect on the area was the inauguration of a process of Arabization and Islamization of Berbers not before so seriously undertaken south of the coast. Later, the Almoravids benefited from some of those effects by solidifying contacts with Muslim Berbers who helped to continue the thrust of the movement into the western Sudan and Muslim Iberia.

The Islamized Berbers' influence in the Sudan, however, resulted less from war and more from their role as merchant and settler in commercial towns like Audaghost, Kumbi, and various oases in the Sahara, a development that predated Islam and perhaps preceded Phoenician contacts. The spread of Islam through commercial relations was a slow process, reaching the western Sudan probably by the tenth century, though the earliest conversions of great consequence seem to have been the king of Gao in 1010 and the king of Kanem-Bornu in 1086. These and similar early conversions were probably motivated primarily by economic and political reasons. Even in the fourteenth century when Mansa Musa made his historic pilgrimage, and the rulers of the Hausa city-states (Kano and Katsina) became Muslims, and during the middle of the fifteenth century when Muslim Fula teachers went from Mali to various parts of Hausaland, the overall effect was essentially the extension of the faith to the ruling dynasties and their advisers, who were concentrated mainly in the capital cities and the large commercial centers.

The influence of traditional beliefs and practices was a powerful force even during the reign of the great and respected ruler of Songhai, Askia the Great. He came to power in 1493 and performed the pilgrimage in 1495, on which occasion the sharif of Mecca appointed him khalifa (deputy) over the western Sudan. On his return and during his early years of rule Askia wisely employed Islam as a political instrument, but sought a balance between Islam and traditional religious beliefs and practices. This was necessary because in spite of the several advantages of Islam, in reality, most of the Africans were not Muslims. Thus, in the tradition of the founder of Songhai, Sonni Ali, Askia had to pursue a cautious policy of identification on both sides. Askia stayed in touch with the ulama (a learned body of Muslims serving as custodians of Muslim law and theology) and sought their sanction for his acts. He respectfully rose to greet the ulama, returning pilgrims, and other Muslim leaders, and only they were allowed to eat with him. Later, however, when his power became more secure, Askia discontinued these privileges. Moreover, he made little effort to reform his administration along Islamic lines, preferring to keep titles and offices inherited from Sonni Ali. Askia retained certain symbols of indigenous culture, e.g., a seal and sword, drum, sacred fire, and the appointment of a high priest for ancestral ceremonies. The same may be said of his son and successor, Musa, and even Askia Dawud, who assisted the development of Islamic education; non-Muslim ceremonies remained features of the court along with Islamic influences. Indeed, the strength and persistence of traditional beliefs and practices largely account for the eclipse and slow resurgence of Islam in the western Sudan after the defeat of Songhai by the Moroccans. Over the years, however, the tension and cross-purposes, cultural and economic, between the Muslim-oriented towns and the agricultural countryside led to intrigues and war. Political rulers found themselves seeking a balance between the towns and countryside, both of which were crucial for political tenure and economic prosperity. This also was part of the assimilative process that led to the evolution of an Africanized Islam and an Islamized Africa.

In East Africa the early Arab merchant communities that emerged on the coast were the vanguard of the spread of Islam in that area. As cohabitation and intermarriages occurred, the resulting members of the settlement constituted the Swahili community and culture. Along the Horn of Africa from the island of Dahlak, and the towns of Zeyla, Berbera, Mogadishu, Brava, and Marka, Arab traders advanced the faith to surrounding regions of Ethiopia and Somalia. The expansion of Islam, however, was cut short by the Christian community, which had been established in Ethiopia much earlier. The eastern and southern fringes did remain Muslim.

Conclusion

This survey has aimed at describing and assessing some of the diversity of African societies from early times to about 1600. Although many African societies have not been discussed here, enough has been presented to reveal the dynamism and continuity of the African past from ancient times. Not only did Africans develop their own languages and fashion their own political structures, they also displayed a genius in agriculture, technology, architecture, trade, and metaphysics. Ideas including Christian and Islamic theology diffused among Africans and between them and non-Africans; and societies in all categories discriminatingly selected and adapted cultural forms to their own needs and goals.

The geographical position of Carthage and Egypt determined the role they played as part of Africa: their political, economic, and cultural tentacles influenced and were influenced by other parts of Africa and the outside world. In this endeavor, Egypt was unmatched. Its greatest historical role was that of bridging world cultural difference through the dissemination of ideas and skills to and from Asia, Europe, and Africa, and in the process it became an international mainspring rightly to be claimed as a key component of world civilization. In that way, Africa became a touchstone of ancient world civilization that continued to be fed for centuries by a continuous and abounding input from Africans and Africa.

4

Africa and the World, 1400–1850

Early European Contacts

One of the most difficult chapters of African history to understand and place in perspective is the one that involves the developing relations between Africa and Europe after 1400. From that general period onward, Africa, previously encompassing great societies whose influence was felt abroad and whose innovative characteristics greatly enriched African culture, was eclipsed at the very time when certain European states not only achieved national unity but made great technological advances that led to an overseas expansion that further increased Europe's economic and technological capacities. Much of this extension into the continent resulted from years of trade with Africans for gold, which helped to finance European technological advance and overseas expansion. That commercial expansion was fired by the imperial ideology of Christianity, which, like Islam, expanded and converted others abroad. Indeed, that commitment to universal conversion to their faith reflected the belief in their superiority which later manifested itself in policies and practices during the colonial occupation.

The years from the fifteenth century on were a period of transition for Africa because, for reasons to be discussed, several important kingdoms were disrupted by political and religious conflicts. Islam, for example, was both stabilizing and unsettling. It established among the elite (rulers and nobility) common interests that led to diplomatic relations with other sovereigns and thus maintained for years a kind of law and order that fostered trade and brought economic prosperity to many Africans. Furthermore, as we have seen, Islam provided for greater administrative bureaucracy and centralization. But in addition to these and other stabilizing forces, Islam, as already noted, fostered a slave trade and created tensions between urban and rural areas and between Muslim and traditional cultures. Among the Muslims arose religious schisms, political rivalries, and economic competition for commercial towns and control over trade routes. These several factors were manifested in varying degrees over much of the continent: Kilwa's hegemony was being seriously challenged during the fifteenth century by Zanzibar, Mombasa, and other coastal cities in East Africa; during the same period Mali began to disintegrate in the central Sudan because of Muslim reform pressure and economic competition, and by 1600 the kingdom had been eclipsed; Songhai was crushed by the Moroccans during the 1590s; Ethiopia remained essentially contained by Muslim states. While some states remained relatively powerful, like Kanem-Bornu and the Hausa states, the several great kingdoms and city-states that earlier had manifested such dynamic and innovative energies were in transition. There is little doubt but that new forces were fermenting and very likely would have matured into meaningful institutions had the powerful external impact of Europe not intervened and altered the course of events.

From the early 1400s Portugal and other European countries became unified and pursued a policy designed to break the Muslim monopoly of the southern Mediterranean Sea, the Red Sea, and the Indian Ocean. Spain and Portugal, which had had some contact with Africans through Muslim control, began to push the Muslims across the Straits, and began to apply their knowledge to exploration and greater overseas trade. Prince Henry the Navigator (1394–1460) formulated a plan to outflank the Muslims by circumnavigating Africa. The motives for this policy were several: to tap the Asian trade and thus avoid paying the high prices demanded by the Venetians who dominated the European trade in the Mediterranean; to secure direct trade in the gold south of Muslim-controlled northern Africa; and to establish political and economic links with African Christendom, about which Europeans knew very little.

By 1445 the Portuguese had reached the Cape Verde Islands and the mouth of the Senegal River, and by 1471 they had found a rich gold trade at what became the Gold Coast. In the 1480s they began establishing a series of coastal forts to tap these commercial opportunities. In 1488 Bartholomew Diaz rounded the southern tip of the continent, and a decade later Vasco da Gama sailed up the East African coast and on to India. These Portuguese ventures not only outflanked the Muslims, they signaled several changes in Africa itself. The Sudanic merchants now had to compete with increasing European commercial power on the coasts, and the slow, more limited capacity of the camel caravans was no match for the sea merchants. Thus, the trans-Saharan trade routes would not regain their importance, and the great kingdoms of the Middle Ages would not be matched in the modern era. Instead, powerful new states emerged along the Gulf of Guinea.

Similarly, the East African city-states now had to contend with the European presence. The Portuguese in 1502 forced Kilwa to recognize their authority and pay an annual tribute; the next year Zanzibar was confronted. Subsequently Mombasa was looted and burned, Lamu and Brava were defeated, Sofala was occupied and became a headquarters for Portugal; the town of Mozambique was colonized. Within about eight years of their arrival, the Portuguese could claim influence over much of the East African coast. Although the Portuguese could not in fact control the coast and, indeed, failed in many respects, they seriously disrupted the commercial patterns of the Arabs and Africans. Much the same was true in the Congo and elsewhere. But it should be emphasized that although European influence remained along the coast, African and Arab sovereigns retained political control of most areas until the latter part of the nineteenth century. However, the appearance of the Portuguese, followed by other Europeans, was a portentous event. It led to the European slave trade from Africa and the tremendous dispersion of Africans throughout the world.

The Atlantic Ocean Slave Trade

It would be an exaggeration to imply that Portugal at the outset intended to inaugurate the Atlantic slave trade. Indeed, during the early years of exploration, Europe's primary demands were for such legitimate goods as silks, spices, perfumes, and sugar, which came from Asia. With the exception of gold at the Gold Coast, most of the African stations did not fulfill Europe's economic desires in the early years. However, the European acquisition of gold and silver mines in America and the evolution of the plantation system led to the establishment of unfree labor, first with Indians, and finally and more successfully with Africans.

The question of traditional servitude in Africa is often raised in connection with the development of the overseas slave trade. It should be noted at the outset that much of Africa resembled a feudal society with rulers, vassals, and subjects. Although vassals were free men, they owed services and tribute to their ruler who provided general protection and helped to resolve various kinds of disputes. Vassals in turn provided protection for their subjects in exchange for labor and goods. Societies were essentially communal and stratified, with no one working for money, but virtually everyone provided duties individually or collectively to someone else. Even so, there was domestic slavery as well as other classes of people with virtually no freedom: community outcasts, adulterers, debtors, prisoners of war, and persons convicted of witchcraft. These persons had few rights that rulers or societies were obliged to observe. But, with these few exceptions, servants were regarded as human beings and not chattel. They could marry, own property, maintain their family unity, freely worship their god, and sometimes they became military commanders and even rulers. This kind of servitude, therefore, should not be confused with American slavery in which the slave was regarded as chattel, and in some cases defined as property and real estate.

It is important at this juncture to stress a point made in chapter 1: namely, that it was a combination of European attitudes about blacks and the demand for cheap labor that sired the Atlantic slave trade and New World black slavery. When the Portuguese arrived in Africa they began seizing Africans to take to Europe as "curiosity pieces," which confirmed that a "new" land had been reached. The early African victims were honored in Portugal, taught Portuguese, and used as informants and guides for future Portuguese voyages to Africa. However, as the number of Africans increased in Lisbon they gradually were relegated to menial tasks, and by the middle of the fifteenth century, a lively trade in African labor (slaves) developed. Thus, even before the Americas were settled by Europeans, Europe witnessed the development of black slavery, especially in Portugal, Spain, Italy, and Sicily. It has been estimated, for example, that between 1458 and 1460, from 700 to 800 slaves were exported annually from Africa to Europe, with an estimate of 35,000 from 1450 to 1500. Some authorities have calculated that from 50,000 to 100,000 Africans were taken to Europe during the whole course of the trade. Whatever the numbers, the point to emphasize here is that a half century prior to their settlement in the Americas, many

Europeans (especially the inhabitants of Spain and Portugal, the two countries that spearheaded American settlement) had become accustomed to the enslavement of Africans.

The tropical plantation system was introduced in Africa during the fifteenth century. The Spanish introduced it in the Canary Islands, and the Portuguese started it in the Cape Verde Islands, and São Thomé. The latter two became especially profitable as slave-based plantation economies and as re-export areas for slaves to Brazil. For the most part, the plantation system in Africa did not become an important factor this early. What should be underscored at this point, however, is that in these few African offshore islands and in several European countries, Europeans had already linked black visibility with bonded servitude by the time the Americas were settled.

This was a gradual process, but in time the European population in the African offshore islands increased, and in some cases intermarriages or cohabitation with local women occurred. This latter occurrence gave birth to a class of mulattoes who were part of two cultures, African and European, but the material attractions of the plantation, in which they had a direct interest through their European fathers, caused many mulattoes to use their knowledge of African language and custom to assist European planters in capturing and enslaving other Africans. Indeed, the African offshore islands not only used enslaved Africans, they also served as re-export areas to Europe and America. As the overall demand increased, especially before the Europeans established themselves more firmly along the coasts, settlers and mulattoes of the offshore islands supplied many slaves by launching raids on the mainland.

The expansion of the slave trade had a direct effect on early Portuguese–African relations. The kidnapping of Africans made the Portuguese vulnerable to attacks and could not, in any event, fill the increasing demand for slaves in the Americas. Moreover, the Portuguese also wanted other commodities—gold, ivory, pepper—that could best be purchased under more stable, peaceful conditions. Primarily for these reasons, the Portuguese and other Europeans preferred not to kidnap Africans, but instead successfully encouraged African merchants, kings, and others to provide supplies of slaves.

In order to understand why Africans participated in the slave trade it is necessary first to realize that many Africans had long been accustomed to European goods, first coming across the Sahara desert and later on European vessels. There was thus a demand for those items that African merchants had already engaged in supplying (cloth, metalware, trinkets, and most significantly, firearms and gunpowder) in exchange for ivory, gold, and kola nuts. Another crucial factor is that European merchants dealing in gold, ivory, or other legitimate goods were established on the coast from the early fifteenth century. Consequently, they had various kinds of contacts and were quite knowledgeable about local African politics in several regions. As the demand for slaves grew, they used their knowledge of African factionalism to play one leader against another or one group against another: Kings were sometimes given firearms and other goods to raid neighboring areas in exchange for war prisoners; one faction of a dynasty was armed against another; and young men were hired to raid for slaves in another region.

It must also be remembered that African labor built many of the European homes, business establishments, mission stations, and so on; it is very conceivable, therefore, that some of those laborers supplied by African kings and merchants could have been shipped abroad as slaves without an awareness on the part of the wider African community. In any case, when Europeans demanded laborers or slaves, the African merchant had to comply or lose his business.

The acquisition of firearms by one group encouraged another to acquire the same, and the main source was the European. This caused keen competition between European merchants, sometimes resulting in one European group supporting a particular African ally and another group supporting other Africans. In either case Africans were captured and enslaved. Once arms were acquired, a supply of parts and powder had to be maintained. Thus a given king had to maintain the flow of slaves, first by supplying prisoners, debtors, social outcasts, and the destitute, but later by conducting frequent raids, sometimes in outlying areas of his own kingdom. The slave trade, therefore, caused and perpetuated many wars of devastation and depopulation over four hundred years.

Other examples could be cited to show how this trade originated and persisted over the centuries, but the conclusion would be the same. A minority of African rulers and merchants, like their counterparts elsewhere in the world, succumbed to the attraction of wealth and power to the point that they sold fellow human beings into slavery. It was also a minority of Europeans supported by powerful political and mercantile interests who organized and financed the Atlantic slave trade; obviously the Europeans were much more powerful and possessed much greater knowledge of the overall picture and consequences than the Africans. One must not forget that the Atlantic slave trade involved three continents—Europe, America, and Africa. Europeans controlled the first two regions and had great influence in the third. Moreover, they demonstrated through kidnappings and slave hunts that they were determined to secure slaves even without African allies.

Portugal's dominance in the trade was challenged by the Dutch, who between 1642 and 1648 captured the Portuguese forts in the Gold Coast and Angola. By the eighteenth century Britain and France were the principal competitors, though traders from virtually all of western Europe were involved at some point. The latter half of the eighteenth century saw British ships take over half of the trade. By the nineteenth century European settlers in America—mainly the United States—dominated the trade. In fact, from the time of its independence, the United States began to play a major role.

The African side of the trade was essentially the same throughout the period. African rulers remained in control. Their consent was necessary for the construction of a trading station or fort, and they levied taxes on trade and land where European buildings stood. Their slaves were usually sold first and they had the pick of European goods.

Slave trading in Angola was an exception. Portuguese colonial rule was established there during the sixteenth century, so the governor-general gave the trading licenses and levied the taxes. In order to encourage settlement, the Portuguese government made huge land grants to retired soldiers and missionaries. These grantees participated in the slave trade and paid taxes in slaves.

The Indian Ocean Slave Trade

The Indian Ocean slave trade differed in certain respects from that in the Atlantic. First of all, it predated the Atlantic traffic by several centuries, having been in existence at least since the *Periplus,* which reported on slave trading along the Somali coast. This activity increased and very likely expanded southward as Muslim Arabs settled along the coast from the early eighth century. The overall volume of this trade probably was small, because gold and ivory remained principal commodities even during the height of the slave traffic in the nineteenth century. The principal demand for East African slaves, prior to the nineteenth century, came from the Arabian peninsula, Persia, India, and very likely China. On the Arabian peninsula, in Persia and India, African slaves were used primarily as mercenary soldiers, domestic servants, concubines, crewmen on dhows, and dock workers. A number were also used as pearl divers in Bahrain, while the date plantations and coconut groves of Basra, the Batinah coast, Bandar Abbas, Minab, and a few other areas along the Persian Gulf employed slaves as gang labor.

Arabs were the principal slave dealers in the Indian Ocean areas. Prior to the nineteenth century, they seldom ventured into the hinterland, but instead profited from their legitimate business contacts on the coast and thus purchased slaves from coastal allies, many of whom were persons of mixed Arab-African descent—Swahilis. This peaceful trade, however, developed alongside kidnappings and raids. An advantage Arabs had in East Africa that Europeans did not have in West Africa was a long history of trade and settlement among Africans. Indeed, from the late eighteenth century, and especially the nineteenth, Arab political rule on the coast virtually assured a lucrative slave traffic to Asia. When Said ibn Sultan established authority over Zanzibar in 1806, several of his Omani compatriots migrated to the island in search of economic gain. Cloves were introduced in 1818, and as large plantations developed, the demand increased for cheap labor to clear the land, keep it worked, and to harvest the crops twice a year. Coconut palms for copra, which produced four times a year, also created a big demand for labor. The inevitable consequence of these developments was to accelerate the expansion of the slave trade. More traders arrived on the island and mainland, new routes extended farther inland, slavers penetrated the interior, and reports of slave caravans increased.

European and American slavers also tapped the East African supply, purchasing slaves from Arab and Indian merchants. In addition, European and American merchants also sought gums, vegetable oils, and ivory. (The latter, because of its relative softness for carving, long remained in heavy demand in India.) Thus, East African slaves were increasingly seen carrying ivory from the interior, and on their arrival at the coast they and the ivory were sold. This was indeed a profitable business and was one reason why the Omani sultan moved his capital from Muscat to Zanzibar in 1840.

Other factors affecting the expansion of the slave trade in East Africa included the gradual effectiveness of the abolition of the traffic in West Africa from 1807, when Britain and the United States legally abolished the trade. The harassment and punishment of slavers in West African waters caused many slavers to seek supplies in East Africa. Further, as European political and economic influence in North Africa increased from the 1790s, the northern slave entrepôts of the trans-Saharan and Nile Valley were gradually drawn into the European orbit of legitimate trade. In order to meet their Asian demand, Arab slavers shifted their activities to the Red Sea and East African coast. Finally, from about the middle of the eighteenth century, French settlers in the Indian Ocean colonies of Mauritius and Réunion developed sugar and coffee plantations, which relied on labor from East Africa. In short, East Africa during the nineteenth century became a major source of slaves for Asian and European settlers in the Orient. And most of this was regulated and taxed by the Arab sultan of Zanzibar.

The major source of West African slaves remained Angola, which by British and Portuguese agreements was not patrolled by the West African Slave Squadron. Angola became the main supply base for slaves to Brazil, and eventually suffered perhaps the greatest depopulation from the traffic. The other Portuguese territory, Mozambique, was in East Africa and supplied fewer overseas slaves because of the development of *prazos*, or private slave-worked plantations, in the colony itself. But the governor of Mozambique received a percentage of the profit on those slaves who were shipped abroad.

Farther inland a number of merchants and rulers extended the slaving enterprise. A prominent example in this regard was the Swahili Tippu Tibb who in the 1870s formed alliances with Swahili traders and interior African merchants and chiefs. He built an empire with roads, plantations, and a trade network based on slaves and ivory in eastern Congo. He maintained good relations with the sultan of Zanzibar, even after he accepted an administrative appointment from the Belgian-controlled Congo Free State, which gradually limited his power and prevented him from acquiring arms. Finally, in 1890 he retired to the coast a dejected but wealthy man. Tippu Tibb's legacy includes both the promotion of the slave trade, collaboration with Europeans, and the extension of Islam and Swahili, which established the base for a new cultural force in eastern Congo.

The mechanics of the trade in East and West Africa are generally known: the raids and the purchases in the interior; the long, harsh marches to the coast; the minute inspections of slaves by Arabs and Europeans; ultimate sales on the coast; prayers by Christian missionaries as slaves were boarded on ships; cramped, filthy, and diseased conditions on Arab, European, and American vessels; heavy losses at sea; and slave revolts on board the vessels and sales abroad—these are all familiar parts of the tragic trade in Africans.

African Resistance to the Slave Trade

While the slave trade developed with the assistance of certain elements of the African population, it was resisted by others. In fact, one of the main reasons most Europeans and Arabs refrained from kidnappings was the fear of African retaliation and attack. Resistance marked the whole endeavor from the initial raid to sale abroad. When it became clear that the Portuguese were more interested in slaving than in legitimate relations, the king of Kongo angrily protested to the Portuguese king. Nzenga Meremba, christened Alfonso, explained that the slave trade hurt his country and that all he wanted from Portugal was "priests and people to teach in our schools, and no other goods but wine and flour for the holy sacrament." He told the Portuguese sovereign that "it is our will that in these kingdoms of Kongo there should not be any trade in slaves nor any markets for slaves." Kongo kings also sent appeals to the Holy See through missionaries, but neither the Church nor the Portuguese kings asserted the power necessary to end the trade.

Queen Nzinga of the Angolan region led armed resistance against Portuguese slavers to end the slave trade, and negotiated treaties to entrench her rule. King Agaja in Dahomey sent armies to capture Andrah (Allada) and other slave-dealing centers on the coast in 1724. He also sent a message to the British explaining that he wanted the export of his people to stop. But Agaja, like Alfonso, and other kings in Futa Toro, Benin, and elsewhere, all lacked the local and international power to change the situation. In the long run, much of Africa became captive of the trade in people, and the impact was incalculable.

Impact of the Slave Trade

That the slave trade had a great negative impact on Africa hardly needs to be stated, but the following points should be included in the assessment. The most obvious effect was depopulation. The Atlantic slave trade could have caused the uprooting of up to fifty million people, some earlier critics suggested. More recent research, however, places the estimate of those who landed in the Americas closer to twenty million. In addition, several million were taken across the Sahara desert to Europe, the Middle East, and Asia. Firmer figures are not available. Both estimates should be regarded as "educated guesses," for there is no way to calculate losses due to raids, marches to the coast, deaths in coastal quarters, and high mortality rates during the sea voyage. These losses were spread over several centuries and the rate of depopulation was uneven: Certain areas were hard hit rather continuously (Angola, for example), and other areas suffered intensely during shorter periods—the eighteenth century being the most active for the Atlantic trade. Also noteworthy is that a greater proportion of Africa's youth was exported, thus adversely affecting future social relations, reproduction, labor, and cultural and political leadership. The fear attendant upon the slave raids and the trade generally created a climate unconducive to cultural growth. The uncertainty of the future discouraged long-range planning for crops, trade, and artistic developments, and it disrupted normal political growth and development. With the principal commercial emphasis on human merchandise, the traditional craftsmen, if they escaped the slave traffic, found less of a market on the one hand; and on the other hand, their products had to compete with European and Asian goods exchanged for slaves. These and many other factors may be subsumed under the effects of the transplantation of human labor from Africa. For nonreproductive merchandise, Africa lost its greatest source of productive wealth—manpower, which provided the brawn for economic development abroad and whose value generated the accumulation of the capital needed by shippers, bankers, textile manufacturers, and others to launch the era of the Industrial Revolution. The economic impact is less clear in the Asian area, but certainly the pearl industry, date plantations, salt flats, and shipping businesses, all of which used African slaves, contributed to the accumulation of capital and economic development of the Arab and Asian worlds. In short, the forced dispersion of millions of Africans throughout the world—Asia, Europe, and the Americas—extended a decisive presence of Africans in world civilization and contributed to an enormous accumulation of capital, however inhuman the means.

Finally, the era of the slave trade further entrenched and indeed extended the concept of black inferiority. This was much less the case among Muslims than Christians. Missionaries and other Christian spokesmen participated in the trade and cited the Bible to justify enslavement of Africans. The future of Christianity in Africa and the evaluation of whites in general were greatly affected by this negative legacy, whereas Africans were made more welcome by Islam, which related more closely to African society and manifested greater brotherhood and equality (see pp. 72–73).

The slave trade eventually led some African political and religious authorities to abuse traditional practices in order to secure slaves. There is the case of a small element among the Ibo, called the Aro, who perverted the spiritual oracle, Chukwu. Those accused of offending Chukwu were called on to provide sacrifices of people, who were later sold as slaves.

That the slave trade was brutal and inhuman and devastated large areas in Africa was known by many Europeans and Americans, but it was not until toward the end of the eighteenth century that those few individuals who early protested the trade succeeded in marshaling support for complete abolition. Since most of this story belongs to European and American history, only a few of the main thrusts will be mentioned here. In response to the increasing number of African slaves brought to England by West Indian planters, a group of Englishmen organized to persuade public opinion and the government to abolish the slave traffic. Their first success came in 1772 when the court ruled against slavery in England. This success encouraged other persons, largely evangelical Christians, to launch a relentless campaign against British participation in the trade. This culminated in an 1807 law that made the slave trade illegal for all British subjects. Once having prohibited British participation, the campaign proceeded to suppress the trade internationally. Denmark had abolished it in 1804; the United States in 1807; the Netherlands in 1814. France abolished the trade during the French Revolution, but Napoleon reestablished it when he came to power; it was finally abolished in 1818. Other nations abolished it, but this was only legal abolition. Enforcement provisions were always weak, and persistent slavers continued to engage in the trade as long as there was a demand. Thus, an illegal traffic continued as the United States, Brazil, and Cuba expanded their sugar and cotton plantations during the second half of the nineteenth century and continued to demand African slaves. We have already observed that as abolition was attempted in West Africa, several European slavers shifted their business to East Africa. However, proponents of abolition succeeded in including in their campaign all dimensions of the exportation of African slaves. The result was that Britain negotiated agreements with African and Asian sovereigns to limit and eventually prohibit the eastern traffic in 1873.

The story of abolition is frequently portrayed as humanitarianism. While the curtailment of the traffic in itself was humane, it is clear that economic imperatives in large measure accounted for the success of abolitionism. The huge profits accrued from the slave trade made possible greater industrial development, which created a demand for legitimate products such as oil for lubricants and soap. In order to exploit these and other products that were known to exist in Africa, peace and stability, which could not occur alongside the slave trade, had to be established. Moreover, once participation by British slaveowners and traders was prohibited, they sought to end the whole trade. Britain had lost the American colonies in 1776 and then sought to undercut United States commercial competition. It should be acknowledged, however, that some of the abolitionists were very likely motivated solely by the desire to eliminate the inhumanity that the slave trade engendered. It should also be noted that the antislavery movement so fired the enthusiasm of certain religious groups that they expanded their efforts to proselytize seriously among Africans, a development to be discussed later.

It is noteworthy that some Africans who had been freed or had escaped learned European languages and devoted themselves to the cause of African dignity and freedom. While they came under strong European influence, they spoke on behalf of Africans and some voluntarily returned to the homeland. Anton Amo, who was never a slave, studied in a Dutch mission and returned to help his fellow Africans in the Gold Coast; Philip Quaque and Jacobis Capitein of the Gold Coast studied abroad and returned to work at home.

Ottobah Cugoano was captured as a child and enslaved, but was freed by the English court decision of 1772. He later wrote "Thoughts and Sentiments of the Evil and Wicked Traffic of the Slavery and Commerce of the Human Species." Olaudah Equiano (Gustavus Vassa) was a slave who purchased his freedom. Although his *Narrative* presented theological and humanitarian arguments against slavery, he focused primarily on the cruelty of the slave system.

These Africans are examples of the black protest and resistance against slavery, which reached greater heights among Africans in the United States, where organized efforts for asserting pride, maintaining an African consciousness and identity, and involvement in Africa reached considerable proportions during the nineteenth century.

Early Chinese Contacts

Although much less is known about China's historical contacts and relations with Africa, some significant data are becoming available. A Chinese scholar, Professor Ge Ji, has written a historical survey in which she discusses intercourse between the two areas during the following Chinese dynasties: Han, 206 B.C.–A.D. 220; Tang, A.D. 618–907; Song, 960–1279; Yuan, 1260–1368; Ming, 1368–1644. Indeed, between 1405 and 1433 official Chinese and East African envoys exchanged visits on several occasions.

In 1954 a figurine with "typical African feature[s]" was

unearthed in a Tang tomb near Xi-an where it had been buried in A.D. 854 as a funerary object. In addition, novels written by Chinese during that period often depicted black Africans as heroes. Those blacks were usually slaves of Chinese nobles.[1]

---

[1]This fascinating information about China is based on a translation of Professor Ge Ji's research for the author. This significant area of study deserves much greater attention by scholars, as does the study of other regions where Africans visited and settled voluntarily or involuntarily.

5

The Expansion of Africa

One may wish to trace the dispersion of Africans abroad to pre-historic times. Whether by trade, adventure, or warfare, Africans established their presence along the southern coasts of the Mediterranean Sea and the Middle East in ancient times. Ethiopia's victory over Yemen in the sixth century A.D. provided another source of African settlement abroad. In the ninth century African slaves revolted in Mesopotamia, where they were used, among other things, to construct dams. Even earlier, in the eighth century, African slaves were observed in China and in the twelfth century several were reported in Canton.

Not only did the Muslim-conducted slave trade continue to take Africans abroad, the expansion of Islam itself also took African converts to Iberia after 711, and during the ensuing Muslim–Christian warfare Africans fought as soldiers and were enslaved by both sides. And in the thirteenth century Moorish merchants were selling sub-Saharan Africans at fairs in Guimares, in northern Portugal.

The fifteenth-century exploration of Africa by the Portuguese ushered in a sustained European penetration of Africa with the consequences of the forced migration of Africans in the Atlantic slave trade. Europe generally and Portugal in particular became adopted homes for African slaves and ex-slaves. As noted in chapter 4 thousands of African slaves were in Portugal by the seventeenth century.

The papal bulls of Nicholas V (1454) and Calixtus III (1456) had provided the justification for the slave trade by proclaiming Portugal's expansion into Africa as a Christian crusade. The enslavement of Africans therefore was regarded as advantageous to the "savages."

Slaves in Portugal and neighboring Spain worked in mines, on farms, in construction, as guards, soldiers, domestics, couriers, stevedores, concubines, and factory workers. The principal slave communities were in Lisbon, and in Spain the Spanish cities of Barcelona, Cadiz, Seville, and Valencia.

After William Hawkins sailed to West Africa in 1530, more and more Africans were seen in England. By 1556 Elizabeth I observed that there were too many "blackmoores" in the country and that they should be returned to Africa. From the eighteenth century in particular, West Indian planters brought slaves with them on home leave, and so did military officers. By the nineteenth century this African presence had increased considerably and led to the abolitionist movement and the repatriation of Africans in the West African colony of Sierra Leone.

From the fifteenth century Africans were observed in France, and although a royal court proclaimed that France did not permit slavery, the institution did emerge there. Both enslaved and free Africans lived in the cities of Anjou, Lyon, Orleans, Nantes, and Paris. They worked as servants, menial laborers, pages, and entertainers. From the seventeenth century Africans arrived in France in greater numbers, and during the eighteenth century royal policy allowed French slave owners in the Americas to bring their slaves to the metropole.

Other parts of Europe became residences for African slaves and free persons. A number of Ethiopian envoys and pilgrims, for example, visited Europe in the late Middle Ages, and several Ethiopian monks, and free and enslaved Africans resided in Venice, the Vatican, and neighboring cities from the fifteenth century.

The situation in Eastern Europe is less clear. For centuries southern Italy, Greece, and Turkey were entrepôts for African slaves. While some of these, especially from Turkey, were re-exported to the Middle East, little is known about re-exports to other areas. The case of Pushkin's ancestor is just one example of an African slave taken from Turkey to Russia. Other blacks there as well as blacks in Yugoslavia very likely derived from that trade in humans.

In addition to the Arabian peninsula, where Africans resided since ancient times, Muslims in the Persian Gulf, especially around Bandar Abbas and Shiraz, also had African settlers as slaves and free persons. Africans were seen as merchants, dock workers, clerks, and agricultural laborers on salt marches and sugar and date plantations.

The Dutch took African slaves to Indonesia; the Portuguese took them to India; the British and French took them to India and the Mascarene Islands in the Indian Ocean. Observers reported African slaves reaching Malaysia with Muslim merchants and pilgrims from Mecca.

Far too little research has been published to allow a satisfactory identification of the global scope of the African diaspora in Asia. However, Arabs continued to conduct a trade in Africans across the Sahara desert, the Mediterranean Sea, Red Sea, and the Indian Ocean and took them to Turkey, Arabia, the Persian Gulf region, India, and the Far East. These enslaved Africans worked in the salt mines, coconut groves, and date plantations of the Persian Gulf region; as pearl divers in Bahrain; as palace guards, domestics, farmers, dock workers, craftspeople, etc. in Arabia and India. They served as eunuchs and concubines throughout much of the Muslim world.

Today, there are mixed and discrete communities of African descent in Iran (Bandar Abbas, Jiruft, Shiraz, and Tehran); Iraq (Baghdad and Basra); in India (Hyderabad, Surat, Cutch, and Gujarat); and Pakistan (Karachi, Lahore, and Baluchistan). Although there is evidence that Africans were taken to Macao and Hwangchou in China and Nagasaki in Japan, there is little evidence of a contemporary presence in these places today. However, it seems that most diaspora Africans resided in South Asia, India in particular. That may have resulted from the long trade with and settlement of Indians in East Africa and their return to India with Africans.

Known as Habshis and Siddis, Africans settled in several parts of India. In the Bengal region several of them became rulers following slave revolts in the fifteenth century; in Gujarat large numbers served in Muslim armies from the thirteenth century at least; on Janjira Island several of them seized control in the fifteenth century; and in Diu and Goa the Portuguese used them as sailors and domestics; many others lived and worked along the Malabar coast.

In the seventeenth century an Ethiopian, Malik Ambar, organized African slave soldiers and seized control of Ahmadnagar in the Deccan (central India). He ruled the area from 1601 to 1626, during which time he founded towns, constructed canals and roads, and fostered trade, scholarship, and the arts. He was proud to be an African, and employed Africans, Arabs, Indians, and Persians at his court.

Siddi Sayeed, an ex-slave, became wealthy and built a noted mosque in Ahmadabad in 1573. Several experts have praised this structure as comparable to architecture in medieval Greece. Siddi Bashire was also lauded for his construction of a renowned mosque in Ahmadabad.

That Africans had a dynamic presence in parts of Asia is clear. They affirmed their identity, struggled for freedom, and contributed to the development of their adopted countries. They would later be inspired by other Africans, and some would return to the homeland.

The greatest dispersion of African slaves was to the Americas, where the largest diaspora now resides. However, during that trade in humans, Africans also participated in the exploration of the Americas. Thirty accompanied Balboa during the exploration of New Mexico and one reportedly planted and harvested the first wheat crop there; two hundred accompanied Alvarado to Quito (Ecuador) and some joined Pizarro's expedition in Peru. Estevanico explored New Mexico and Arizona. Africans also participated in a number of expeditions in Canada.

Only a few Africans remained free in the North American English colonies after the 1660s, when slavery was officially established. Meanwhile, the sugar plantations led to furious competition between England and Spain in the Caribbean and ended when Barbados (1627) and Jamaica (1655) became British territories. Large numbers of slaves were subsequently imported into those territories from the Gold Coast, Angola, Congo, Nigeria, and Madagascar.

The struggle for freedom by African slaves began at the point of capture and continued on the slave ships and in the diaspora. They relied on their languages and cultures to survive. Although they often were randomly caught, sold, and packed on ships, they spoke related languages, frequently came from the same area, and in a number of cases were members of the same ethnic group. For all these reasons they could communicate and did, as several examples of slave mutinies on board ships confirm. Investigation of some of these mutinies revealed that African slaves conspired for days to revolt, some of which were successful. The Amistad mutiny of 1839, for example, resulted in freedom of enslaved Africans and their return to the continent.

As debilitating as the slave ship experiences were, Africans cultivated friendships that lasted into the system of slavery in the Americas. Confirmation of this friendship or group identity is evidenced by the following terms that referred to those relationships: "shipmate" in Jamaica, "sippi" in Suriname, "mulongo" in

Brazil, and "batiment" in Haiti. These terms in the diaspora signified "brother" and "sister." The extent to which these examples may point to a synthesis of African culture abroad during slavery is a question that deserves serious research.

The hope for freedom was reinforced by these relationships and culminated in many slave revolts, a few of which were: the Maroon War in Jamaica in 1725 and the signing of a treaty in 1739 between Britain and Captain Cudjoe from the Gold Coast; the resistance in Guyana under the Caromante leader Adoe in the 1740s and Cuffy in the 1760s. Similar revolts led by Africans under their African names occurred in Mexico, Cuba, Panama, Colombia, Venezuela, Peru, and the Leeward and Windward Islands, in the sixteenth and seventeeth centuries especially.

The most impressive armed struggle for freedom prior to 1800 occurred in Brazil, where Palmares was established in 1605 under its leader Zumbi. This was an autonomous settlement of an estimated 20,000 Africans largely of Bantu origin. Zumbi attempted to duplicate the development of an African community. He and his followers resisted the Portuguese military in several battles until 1695 when they were finally defeated.

Similar struggles were mounted in North America. Africans fought for freedom in Virginia, Maryland, and Louisiana, for example, in the seventeenth and eighteenth centuries. But not only were there armed struggles in the South where slavery was harshest; in 1712 a Gold Coast African organized a group to burn New York City, and in 1739 another African, Cudjoe, led a revolt in South Carolina. Another movement to burn a town occurred in Boston in 1723. These and numerous other efforts, aborted and realized, were led by slaves recently imported and still fighting to be free.

Disillusioned and frustrated in the slave societies but confident in their ability to develop their communities, diaspora Africans also formed institutions to express their collective identity and aspirations. In many North American colonies they referred to themselves as "Africans" and "Ethiopians." And although legal codes forbade them to speak African languages and to practice their religions and culture, many of them did, often in secret. They in time also learned the European languages and established parallel institutions labeled African churches, African schools, lodges, etc. Indeed, the lodges, like the masons, reflected not only Western influence but the African tradition of secret societies, especially the *pora* and *sande* along the West African coasts from which so many African slaves came.

These organizations represented group identification as Africans; they also were vehicles for socialization among the Africans. Moreover, these organizations, especially the churches and schools in the United States, would seek to utilize their Western values, skills, and ideas to liberate and educate Africans throughout the world, including the homeland itself. The most dramatic examples of this occurred in the long history of Sierra Leone, Liberia, and Freretown in Kenya (see chapter 6).

The most successful freedom struggle by diaspora Africans prior to the post–World War II era occurred in Haiti and reflected the combination of African and Western ingredients. In 1791 Boukman, born in Africa, who bound his followers with voodun rituals and African-style secret oaths, led the island's black masses against the slave masters. He was joined by the diaspora-born Christian son of an African father, Toussaint Louverture, who organized guerrilla warfare, which defeated Napoleon's army in 1804. Haiti thus became the second republic in the Americas (the first black one) and a symbol of black or African freedom throughout the diaspora. Descendant Africans in the United States in particular were inspired by Haiti's example, but white Americans followed with more stringent legislation and tightened security.

These several freedom struggles revealed a nascent African nationalism in the diaspora. The aims were more than vengeance and escape, but meant primarily to establish control over replicate

African societies that would promote traditional African religions such as Voodun in Haiti, with influence from Benin (Dahomey); Candomble in Brazil, with influence from Orisha or Nigerian Yoruba; Pocomania in Jamaica, with influence from the Ghana Akan; or the Efik-derived Abakwa secret society in Cuba. There was and is also in Brazil the influence of Islam brought to Bahir by the Hausa and Yoruba slaves.

The dawn of the nineteenth century thus witnessed the maturation of an African identity in the diaspora. That identity was expressed in culture and political struggles throughout wide stretches of the diaspora. Although descendant Africans abroad were pariahs, they contributed significantly to their adopted diaspora homes and became sources of mutual inspiration abroad and in Africa.

6

Repatriation and the Development of a Pan-Africanist Tradition

The return of Africans from the diaspora and their repatriation into continental African societies laid the foundation for greater cross-ethnic and cross-regional collaboration. Although there were several cases of return movements, including the return of Africans from Cuba and Brazil to West Africa in the nineteenth century, the focus of this chapter is on the larger movements primarily to Liberia and Sierra Leone, which had great and sustained impact on Africa and the diaspora.

Sierra Leone

When Lord Mansfield held in 1772 that a master could not forcibly remove his slave from England, abolitionist propagandists portrayed the decision as the abolition of slavery, as it indeed came to be regarded. That decision and the influx of Africans who had been liberated because they fought with England during the American War for Independence resulted in a sizable free black community in London. While some of them found employment in domestic service and on ships, the majority did not secure jobs and did not readily assimilate. Thus, in the wake of the 1772 decision, for which they claimed credit, abolitionists pursued the idea of resettling liberated Africans in Africa, where it was hoped that a society founded on free labor could spread Christianity, develop a Western-style economy, and contribute to the restriction of slavery on the African continent. Resettlement therefore won the support of humanitarians, evangelical Christians, and businessmen, all of whom joined the increasingly popular move "to civilize and Christianize the Africans." Finally, in 1787 a group of 411 settlers left Britain to found a new society on land purchased from a Temné ruler in Sierra Leone. This was the first practical application of repatriation of liberated Africans. Hard times, and the failure of Africans in Nova Scotia to receive land promised them for fighting on the British side during the 1776 war, caused Thomas Peters, a former United States slave, to lead approximately twelve hundred free blacks from Nova Scotia to Sierra Leone where they founded Freetown. Eight years later about five hundred Maroons from Jamaica also settled in Sierra Leone.

The colony was governed by the Sierra Leone Company, which received its charter in 1791. The company forbade slave trading and attempted to suppress it through the introduction of Christianity and the development of trade based on legitimate goods. But the colony had a very inauspicious start. Many of the settlers died of fever and a variety of diseases; funds were limited and supplies were scarce; slaving continued; indigenous Africans periodically attacked the colony, and in 1794 a French naval force attacked it. Supporters of the colonial experiment became disillusioned as their will was severely tested. However, in 1807 the British government outlawed the slave trade and in 1808 assumed direct control over the colony. Freetown thus became the base for the British West African Slave Squadron, which patrolled the West African coast to enforce abolition treaties signed by the several powers. Africans liberated by the squadron were settled in Sierra Leone, which by mid-century had some seventy thousand African repatriates.

The growing number of black repatriates severely taxed the ability of the crown government to administer the colony. Protests, rebellions, and indifference demonstrated that British officials were unable to rule effectively. Consequently, the repatriates increasingly asserted their autonomy in local matters. New arrivals frequently established themselves in isolated corners of the colony and provided for themselves with a minimum of involvement by the British government, which showed little desire to invest the funds necessary for effective administration. Although the liberated Africans did receive government food rations by 1819, the repatriated Africans continued to evolve a new society incorporating African and European culture.

The new arrivals usually spent a few months in Freetown where they were freed and processed. While there they made new acquaintances and sometimes organized voluntary associations for mutual aid. When they were free to establish a permanent residence they frequently sought communities of their own ethnic background, which facilitated the perpetuation of their culture in song and dance, religious beliefs, and crafts. As they acquired capital, they bought land, developed farms, and opened shops. They maintained control over local politics through the selection of a headman who supervised the settlement of disputes and the general maintenance of law and order.

Because the first settlers had come from England and America, they knew the value of education within the context of their Westernized society. They enrolled their children in the several mission schools, and some of them sent their sons and daughters to English universities. This African desire for education, and the missionaries' belief in education to "civilize" Africans, led naturally to the founding of Fourah Bay College by the Church Missionary Society (CMS) in 1827; in 1841 Edward Jones, the first

African college graduate in the United States, became president of Fourah Bay, which became a center for training teachers and catechists. In 1876 a connection was established with Durham University, thereby bringing university education to Sierra Leone where it became available to students across West Africa. In a very real sense, therefore, Western education in general and Fourah Bay College in particular distinguished Sierra Leone.

Shortly after the founding of Sierra Leone, some of the liberated Africans began to migrate to other parts of West Africa. In general, Europeans saw Africa as a single mass and were little concerned about the fact that most African slaves had not come from Sierra Leone, and therefore had not really been returned "home" by the establishment of the colony. Consequently, hundreds of settlers began to migrate in search of their original homes and families. Others migrated to expand their commercial activities, and still others felt called on to spread the Christian faith. As early as 1838 a group signed a petition stating their intention to go to Badagry in Nigeria. In 1841 an official report recorded that several vessels owned by liberated Africans were transporting hundreds of persons along the Guinea coast. One boat, owned by William Johnson, made several trips between Freetown and Badagry during the 1840s. Among the several emigrants to Nigeria were Thomas Babington Macauley and Samuel Crowther. Macauley studied at Fourah Bay College and later took charge of a mission station in Abeokuta. He also founded a grammar school in Lagos. Crowther was the first student of Fourah Bay College, and became a missionary in Badagry and Abeokuta, and was consecrated bishop in 1864. He wrote several books in the Nupe and Ibo languages and compiled a Yoruba vocabulary. He was also part of the Niger Expedition in 1854, when quinine was successfully used against malaria. These are only a few examples to illustrate the contributions of immigrants from Sierra Leone to West African history of the nineteenth century.

Sierra Leone was an omen of future relations between Africans and their descendants in Africa. The pioneer settlers, partly because their earlier life in the Western world identified them with European culture and partly because of their belief that they brought benefits to African culture, did not regard the recaptured indigenous Africans as equal to themselves. But as the number of recaptives greatly surpassed that of the early settlers, and as the former accepted Christianity and Western education, the gulf between the two groups narrowed, intermarriage occurred, earlier distinctions disappeared, and by midcentury a new group and culture emerged as a combination of interaction between the settlers and recaptives. That was Krio society, a blend of Christianity and African beliefs, Western and African cuisine, with Africanized English as the language. The Krio thus constituted the elite of African society in Sierra Leone and naturally achieved the greatest mobility in trade and the Western-style professions. As pioneers in Western education they were appointed by the British to civil service posts and seats on the executive and legislative councils in Sierra Leone and other British colonies in West Africa. They produced scholars like Samuel Crowther, linguist and bishop; James Horton, medical doctor and researcher, and writer of history; Samuel Johnson, a historian of the Yoruba; and others. Krio newspapers were read in much of West Africa, and many Krio operated businesses from Gambia to the Cameroons. This was indeed a high point in Krio history.

From the late 1890s, however, the fortunes of the Krios declined. In 1896 the British declared a protectorate over the hinterland of present-day Sierra Leone. This led to the Temné and Mendé wars to preserve their independence. Many Krio, considered by some Mendé and Temné as "black Englishmen," were killed along with Europeans. After the British won the war they decided to appoint British administrators in the interior and not to extend Western education but to preserve ethnic particularity among the Temné and Mendé. During the same period, Krio merchants received serious competition from European firms that were strongly backed by colonial policies; during the first decade of the twentieth century, the Krio were eliminated from administrative councils and other posts, which were filled by Europeans whose presence in the colony increased after the discovery of ways to control malaria and as the colonial powers entrenched their rule. Less useful to the British, therefore, Krio political, economic, and cultural influence declined. This new British policy seriously aborted the evolution of the Westernized society, proclaimed by the original founders of the colony, and heightened the distrust between the Krio and other Africans, and between the Krio and the British.

Nonetheless, Sierra Leone played a unique role in African history. It was a colony whose settlers' experiential background included life in Europe and the Americas. This plus the fact that the policy of the Sierra Leone Company and later the British government was to develop a "Westernized" African society in the colony had decisive consequences as the settlers migrated across West Africa as traders, missionaries, and searchers of their original home. They took with them various aspects of Western culture and learning. In addition, as Fourah Bay College became the only place in West Africa where a university education could be obtained in the nineteenth century, it emerged as a pool from which educated Africans were drawn by British officials, merchants, and missionaries to facilitate the extension of colonial control, trade, and Christianity. While the Sierra Leonean settlers were exploited to help establish and entrench European rule and culture, they nonetheless forged links in West Africa that broadened the horizons and expanded channels of communication beyond the local societies. In this way, therefore, Sierra Leone facilitated a growing awareness of and cooperation with various other African groups.

Liberia

In the United States, plans for repatriation took on a different dimension. As in England, whites formulated plans to settle blacks in Africa, but some blacks on their own initiative championed repatriation and developed plans for settlement in Africa. Several slave petitions for freedom prior to the American Revolution expressed the determination of the petitioners to migrate to Africa. But the real black repatriation thrust came in 1808 when Paul Cuffe, a successful black shipper in Rhode Island, inquired about conditions among the Sierra Leone settlers; in 1811 he sailed there to explore the possibilities of settlement for Africans from the United States. He organized the Friendly Society in Sierra Leone and appointed an ex-slave as director. In the United States he organized societies to assist in repatriation activities. Then, in 1815, he returned with thirty-eight settlers, brought at his own expense. Thus, the earlier British success in Sierra Leone and Cuffe's achievement demonstrated the feasibility of black repatriation in Africa. Within a few years, black colonization as a means of ridding the United States of "free" Africans became a serious concern of white Americans.

In the United States chattel slavery had become virtually synonymous with "Negro"; Africans were forbidden to practice their language, religion, or other customs; even the "free" black was denied rights of citizenship or human dignity and could be enslaved. There was no place for the African in the United States except as a slave, and from the 1790s, when the cotton gin was invented, westward expansion into richer cotton-growing areas created an even greater demand for slaves. Since the possible abolition of the slave trade had been set in 1787 for 1807, American planters sought ways of protecting and indeed expanding slavery itself. The smuggling of slaves from abroad and slave breeding were two ways of maintaining slavery; moreover, slavery was protected by a variety of laws, customs, and force. There remained, however, over eighty thousand "free" Africans in 1790. Some had secured that status through the performance of heroic deeds and services in the military; others attained it through wills, purchase, and escape. In any case, the "free" African was an anomaly in a country where the concept of black inferiority became a generally accepted "truth," where government and church leaders reinforced that belief and supported the institution of slavery, and where proponents of slavery explained that blacks were born for slavery and could not survive as free persons. Thus, slaveowners regarded the "free" blacks as a threat to their institution of slavery, not only in the sense that their mere presence proved the contrary to the proponents of slavery, but also because they helped to organize protest and resistance to the system. And with the independence of Haiti in 1804, many slaveowners in the United States and the Caribbean referred to that black state as the "black menace," which could encourage other New World Africans to revolt. For these reasons, therefore, Southern planters in the United States supported the idea of resettling "free" Africans in Africa, and white humanitarians who expressed disbelief that blacks could obtain freedom and justice in the country joined the Southern planters in organizing the American Colonization Society in 1816. This effort led to the founding of Liberia.

A large portion of the funds for the society came from Protestant churches that, as in the case of Sierra Leone, saw possibilities for evangelizing in Africa. Although the United States government did not directly organize the society, it gave benevolent encouragement. In the first place, prominent government leaders played key roles in the society, and in 1819 the federal government passed a bill authorizing the American navy to seize any American slave vessel and return the slaves to Africa. In order to carry out this project the society was appointed custodian and received government grants to finance its venture. Further, the involvement of Americans in such an international project so

similar to that of Sierra Leone carried with it at least the implication of American governmental support and protection.

The first group of settlers arrived in Liberia in 1821, and by
1867 nearly twenty thousand had settled there. Of that number
about thirteen thousand came from the United States, over forty-
five hundred of whom had been born "free." Approximately three
hundred and fifty came from Barbados. In comparison with
Sierra Leone, two points are noteworthy: First, although the overall number of Liberian settlers was much smaller, the great
majority of them had previously resided in the United States; second, although most of them were poor, several were educated and
had owned property in the United States. In Sierra Leone the
overwhelming majority of settlers were recaptured from slave
ships and therefore knew nothing much about England. The
Liberian settlers therefore retained a greater attachment to the
United States, in spite of their legitimate criticisms, and formed
many of their institutions after American ones.

The American Colonization Society governed the colony
through an agent who was also the United States government
official responsible for the recaptured Africans. But, as in Sierra
Leone, independent settlements sprang up across the country,
communications were poor, funds were limited, indigenous
groups periodically attacked the settlers, and disease took many
lives. Consequently, the settlers themselves took responsibility
for their own physical and social survival. They established their
own community churches under ministers from among themselves. These churches were supported by American missions,
which also operated schools. Land was allotted to settlers who
cultivated farms on their own initiative. As early as the 1820s
some of the colonists were trading in schooners along the coast
of West Africa, and by 1830 a few of them had annual sales worth
up to $70,000. However, by midcentury Liberian merchants had
to compete with European merchants who were supported by big
banks, shipping lines, modern equipment, and the diplomacy and

armies of European countries. In addition, several European countries refused to pay Liberian customs duties. Liberians thus increasingly felt the need for firm assurance for their political and economic security. For some time some of them, especially those settled in Monrovia, had agitated for freedom from the society, whose control was very tenuous and whose funds were limited. Finally, in 1847, the settlers declared their independence. Britain and France recognized the country almost immediately, but the United States, because of its racial and political climate fostered by the continued enslavement of Africans, delayed recognizing its "foster child" until 1862.

Liberia developed trade in palm oil, camwood, coffee, sugar, and molasses. But during the 1880s the European powers prevented Liberians from trading with their neighbors who were subjected to colonial rule. In addition, the United States began to increase its importation of Brazilian coffee and Cuban sugar (ultimately monopolizing the latter), and this had a very unfavorable impact on Liberia's economy. The country therefore secured European loans at high interest rates and on unfair terms. Finally, in 1912 some United States bankers provided a loan on condition that Americans assume control of Liberia's finances, similar to United States Caribbean policy at the time. The next few years were perhaps the nadir in Liberia's history.

With independence, Liberia devoted serious efforts toward devising a viable political structure, out of which emerged the one-party system that, it was hoped, would more effectively unite the people in the face of insults and aggression from the colonial powers. But real unity was a long way off. As in Sierra Leone, the repatriates, Americo-Liberians, assumed a superior attitude toward the indigenous Africans and naturally dominated positions in business, education, government, and the churches. Unlike Sierra Leone, however, Liberia was independent and its leaders had to formulate national policies. In contrast to Sierra Leone, one consequence was a greater tendency to assimilate some indigenous Africans through the policy of education. Although schools were not available throughout the country and compulsory education was not, indeed could not, be rigidly enforced, the school population became overwhelmingly indigenous, and this gradually opened up opportunities for non-Americo-Liberians. Increasingly in the early twentieth century, the Vai, Kru, Grebo, and other ethnic groups were represented in high government positions. Progress was slow, and some areas remained unaffected for years, but on balance, the Americo-Liberians assumed the mighty task of unification. That their progress was slow was due not only to their cultural difference from the masses, but also to powerful, unsympathetic, and sometimes conniving Europeans and Americans who sought to isolate and stunt Liberia's development.

Still, with independence, Liberia became a unique phenomenon in Africa. Not only did it result from the repatriation of Africans from abroad, it became the only internationally recognized independent African country except Ethiopia until well into the twentieth century. But precisely because of its unique status and history, Liberia became a symbol of hope for the regeneration of Africans at home and abroad. The Liberian Declaration of Independence noted that the Liberians had been inhabitants of the United States where they were debarred from all civil rights and privileges. Their coming to Africa therefore represented to them an opportunity to exercise their freedom, and within a few years Liberian leaders envisioned their country as destined to become a province of freedom for the uplift of all persons of African descent. The Liberian constitution noted that the object of forming the state was "to provide a home for the dispersed children of Africa."

Since Liberia was founded by Africans from the diaspora, links with overseas Africans remained strong. In 1820 Daniel Coker, a teacher and minister in Baltimore, declined the position of bishop for the African Methodist Episcopal Church in order to go to Liberia; Lott Carey left a successful position as minister in Richmond, Virginia, saying: "I am an African, . . . and I feel bound to labour for my suffering race." John Russwurm, who co-founded and edited the first black American newspaper, *Freedom's Journal,* believed that the "man of color would never find a place in the Western hemisphere to lay his head." Russwurm thus went to Liberia, founded the *Liberian Herald* newspaper, served as a superintendent of schools and governor of a county in Liberia. In 1830 John Day emigrated from North Carolina to Liberia as a missionary; he subsequently became a teacher and finally a chief justice. Joseph Roberts left Virginia and became Liberia's first president in 1847. These are only a few of the more prominent Africans who left the United States to help lay the foundation for Liberia.

A significant oversight of most studies is the role of women settlers. Over eight thousand black women from the United States, about two hundred from Barbados, and an estimated seventeen hundred women captured from slave vessels settled in Liberia. Although their greatest contribution was in educating the young, their impact was especially important in the formation of craft, benevolent, and literary societies. They also helped to bridge the gulf between the settlers and the indigenous people through their charitable work and adoption of village youths.

The greatest figure of the diaspora, one who literally linked Africans in the United States, the West Indies, and Africa, was Edward Wilmot Blyden, who came under the influence of the American Colonization Society. Born in St. Thomas in the West Indies, Blyden visited the United States where he was refused admission to Rutgers Theological College. He then went to Liberia in 1851 and completed a local school, of which he later became principal. In his subsequent Liberian posts—commissioner to Britain and the United States, ambassador to Britain, secretary of state, editor (of the *Liberian Herald*), professor and later president of Liberia College, and his assignments in Sierra Leone and Nigeria—Blyden constantly encouraged blacks "of every rank and station, in every clime and country" to support emigration to Liberia. He was particularly interested in attracting more blacks from the United States, where James Whitfield, James Holly, Martin Delany, Henry H. Garnet, Alexander Crummell, and other African-Americans organized emigration projects during the 1850s.

Because he believed that Liberia was destined to redeem all persons of African ancestry, Blyden accepted the challenge to prove "that black men, under favorable circumstances, can manage their own affairs." In part this was a reaction to conditions Blyden knew existed in the Western world, but it was also a manifestation of his belief that by providential design Africans had been taken to the New World, where they acquired elements of Western culture that could benefit Africa. In many of his speeches in Africa and abroad he advocated a synthesis of African and Western culture. This is further evidenced by his efforts, along with Alexander Crummell, an African-American, to develop Liberia College into a university oriented both to African culture and Western learning. The accomplishment of so great a mission required the migration of large numbers of educated and skilled persons. Thus Blyden's appeal to blacks: "Liberia with its outstretched arms invites all to come. . . . We summon them from the United States, from Canada, from the West Indies, from everywhere to come and take part with us in our great work."

In addition to many speaking engagements in the United States, Blyden had some direct contacts with influential blacks. In 1859 Martin Delany arrived in Monrovia from the United States and received a warm welcome. He reported that the "desire for African nationality has brought me to these shores." From Monrovia Delany went to Abeokuta in Nigeria where he and his associate, Robert Campbell, a black from Philadelphia, negotiated a treaty that gave them as "Commissioners on behalf of the African race in America, the right and privilege of settling in Abeokuta with the Egba people, on any part of the territory belonging to Abeokuta, not otherwise occupied." Delany regarded this as the first step toward establishing in Africa another nation based on the repatriation of blacks from the United States, this time on black initative. However, the intervention of British officials resulted in the nullification of the treaty. Furthermore, the Civil War in the United States persuaded Delany and other American blacks to believe that freedom and equality would follow the war. But Robert Campbell remained in Lagos and edited the first newspaper there, the *Anglo-African*.

Meanwhile, Crummell continued his appeal for emigration. In 1860 he wrote an African-American in New York about "the Relations and Duties of Free Colored Men in America to Africa." In that letter, which was published in 1861, Crummell spoke of the "natural call" to Africans abroad to develop the resources of Africa and prevent the European from denying him his "rightful inheritance." Crummell predicted an early repossession of Africa by her "scattered children in distant lands." Crummell, like Blyden, had an enduring faith in repatriation, but both were unable to stimulate the massive immigration necessary to achieve their goals.

The Freretown Community

Several histories have been written about repatriation in Sierra Leone and Liberia, but very little attention has been focused on the return and settlement of Africans in East Africa. There were, however, certain parallels and interrelationships between repatriation in East and West Africa. In both cases resettlement resulted mainly from European efforts to abolish the slave trade and engage in legitimate trade. We have already noted the Indian Ocean slave traffic and how the British negotiated treaties to end the trade in that area, and in East and West Africa the British employed several naval vessels to enforce abolitionist treaties. Britain also pressured several Asian sovereigns to prohibit the importation of African slaves. In addition, a number of refugee slaves sought haven in

British missions in Asia and on British ships. These two sources of Africans—those captured at sea and the refugees—led to the establishment of small communities of liberated Africans in various parts of Asia: on the Arabian peninsula and in Turkey, Persia, and India. Some of the liberated Africans were distributed as free persons to Asian and European families who assumed responsibility for housing, food, and education in return for domestic service. Others were employed on government farms, ships, docks, or wherever employment could be found. Most of the liberated children were enrolled in mission schools such as the Roman Catholic Sisters of Mercy and the Church of Scotland Mission, both in Aden, and the CMS African Asylum in Nasik, near Bombay, India. The mission schools taught English, Bible studies, and crafts, and the hope was that these schools would supply black missionaries for East Africa. In fact, nine from Nasik accompanied David Livingstone to East Africa in 1865; several others became missionaries in Ethiopia, Kenya, Mozambique, and Zanzibar.

From 1873 Britain's policy was to resettle liberated Africans in Africa, with the result that several small colonies emerged on the East African coast, most notably at Freretown (near Mombasa). In 1875, 150 arrived in Freretown from Bombay, thus the name "Bombay-Africans." Although the number of repatriated Africans in East Africa was never great, their impact was impressive. With their knowledge of English and Swahili, English customs, and crafts they were sought as catechists and teachers by European missionaries, agents for European merchants, and guides and interpreters for European explorers. They itinerated widely along the coast and in Zanzibar and were responsible for the establishment and conduct of several missions that catered primarily to ex-slaves. In 1880, for example, "Bombay-Africans" were training and caring for some three thousand ex-slaves at several locations. Moreover, many of the European reports on the social conditions and geography of Africa were based on reports and journals of "Bombay-Africans" like William Jones. As a group with Western training but denied opportunities equal to Europeans in mission stations, the "Bombay-Africans" became a source of protest against discrimination in the churches and missions.

Because of their small numbers and the lack of any consistent financial and political support, the achievements of the "Bombay-Africans" could not match those of the Sierra Leoneans or Liberians. But they did have an influence disproportionately greater than their numbers. They played especially influential roles as pioneer teachers, journalists, trade unionists, craftsmen, and civil servants during the colonial period. They also emerged as prominent politicians and many were ultimately assimilated into the wider African communities. Theirs was indeed a cyclic journey: Africa, Asia, Africa, and reintegration with their congeners.

Conclusion

It is important to note that during the era of the slave trade and abolition, and while Africans in Africa were confronting new challenges, organizing states and developing new institutions for the changing times, their congeners, who had been forced abroad into slavery, were also developing new ideas and projects for their survival and the uplift of black people in general. Thus the genesis of the back-to-Africa movement of the nineteenth century, which was engineered primarily by black repatriationists in America. That movement also coincided with the black renaissance in the United States that evolved during the early years of the nineteenth century and peaked between the late 1820s and 1860. That era reflected a deep consciousness of and identification with Africa. Whether through the names of their organizations, their participation in cultural, religious, or political activities in Africa and the West Indies, their writings and speeches, or their emigration activities, a sizable number of blacks in America sensed a historic, continuing relationship between Africans at home and abroad. The black renaissance in the United States thus supplied a group of educated, Afro-centric blacks to the Black World at a time when other African communities lacked the opportunity for such training. And, although strongly influenced by white churches, black churches in the United States provided the main opportunities for the establishment of enduring links joining Africa to blacks in the United States and in the West Indies in a triangular relationship which might be regarded as the seedtime of a pan-Africanist ideology.

The forced migration of Africans to various parts of the world via the slave trade has yet to be fully assessed, especially in Asia. While many of the physical aspects of the slave trade have been explored, too little attention has been focused on the ideological factors. The fact that large numbers of Africans settled abroad, cleared and worked plantations, toiled in mines, and labored in countless other ways to build great civilizations that not only refused to accept black people as equals but even denied the value of their African heritage meant that however much their blackness and Africanness were denigrated, blacks in fact had no other real identity. For many years in America, for example, they called themselves Africans, and centuries passed in the United States before they were recognized as citizens. During the interim many of them identified with Africa and even returned there to continue their contributions to civilization. In a real sense, therefore, African successes and failures abroad directly affected the position of Africans in Africa and vice versa. In addition, having witnessed centuries of physical and psychological derogation, Africans and their descendants continued to feel the need to "prove" their personal and historical worth. These factors became deeply embedded in the black heritage during the nineteenth century and led to the structuring of pan-Africanism under W. E. B. DuBois and others. In short, black men and women were deeply rooted in the African heritage and indeed are a vital part of Africa's heritage.

7

Politics and State-Building I: The Guinea Coast and Forest Regions

The African-European sea trade along the Guinea coast had far-reaching effects. West Africa became increasingly involved in international affairs, especially world trade, and this necessitated the development of different institutions to provide new solutions to new problems and demands. This occurred at a time when several African states were undergoing significant domestic change. Thus, as we have noted, the European trade, and especially the firearm, added to African problems of economic and political adjustment. In some cases law and order were disrupted and political tension and conflict ensued; but in other cases, old states became stronger and new states appeared.

Political expansion from about the seventeenth century witnessed the emergence of several prominent states, including Ashanti and Dahomey. They joined the ranks of Oyo and Benin, both of which remained powerful. However, both the alafin of Oyo and the oba of Benin had to contend with a host of rivals who were able to secure firearms, protect themselves, expand their states, and bargain independently with European merchants.

Oyo

Oyo reached its peak around 1650 and exercised great influence over most of the area between the Volta River and the Niger River. It also had strong influence over coastal trade. All of this was policed by a well-trained and much feared cavalry. At the center of this state was the alafin who ruled as a semi-divine king. His administration included the chief judge, the head of shango (a belief system which revered the alafin's ancestors), and a treasurer. The alafin was represented in each town, usually by a shango priest. The chief sub-rulers who comprised the council of nobles shared judicial powers in the capital, served as mediators in disputes between the alafin and a subordinate ruler, and appointed the army officers. Thus the alafin's rule was checked by the council, to which he had to submit his decisions. The council in turn was checked by notables of various great families. They too shared judicial functions and had religious powers; however, the alafin's representatives had considerable influence in this group. The same system appeared on a lesser scale throughout the state. This complex political system of checks and balances combined with Oyo's strategic commercial location, which linked the coast with the Sudan, enabled the state to exercise great control for many years over all trade (including the slave trade) along the southern Niger River, and to maintain considerable political power, though failing to unite all Yoruba under one central authority.

In time, however, neighboring and subject states acquired firearms and sought to establish and control their own politics and trade. The most serious challenge to Oyo came from the Fon people of Dahomey who had been paying tribute to the alafin.

However, during the eighteenth century the Fon sought independence. Although they did not succeed until the nineteenth century, they did lessen Oyo's hold on them. After the turn of the nineteenth century, Oyo also suffered and lost ground to the Fulani people of Hausaland. In addition, the cavalry depended on horses imported from the Hausa states. Not only were the horses costly, their life span was cut short by the tsetse fly; with the expansion of Islam in the Hausa states, Oyo found it increasingly difficult to obtain horses and to secure the necessary pastures for grazing. Finally, the great dependence of the state on the slave trade seriously challenged other economic activity, drained off needed labor, stimulated rivalry among rulers and merchants; the enforcement of abolition further complicated the situation as some Europeans continued to demand slaves while British patrols made the whole endeavor risky. The decline of Oyo during the nineteenth century, therefore, resulted from several key factors, and as it declined, rulers of some Yoruba towns lost power and others took advantage of the times to assert independence. Sometimes new towns were founded as some inhabitants of the older towns sought refuge. These new towns in particular emerged as successors to Oyo's greatness and leadership in Yoruba country: Abeokuta, Ijaye, and Ibadan. All of these changes were further complicated by European intervention in African politics from the mid-nineteenth century.

Dahomey

A principal subject area of Oyo was Dahomey, a thinly wooded coastal territory with a hinterland stretching about four hundred miles to the north. During the seventeenth century there existed several small states on the coast and in the interior, although most of the inhabitants recognized a common origin. The coastal states included Jakin, Whydah, and Grand Popo, and behind them was

Great Andrah. The coastal states naturally took advantage of the sea trade, including the slave trade. Local rulers fixed prices, levied taxes, and controlled bargaining with the Europeans. As the demand for slaves increased, the coastal states extended their raids deeper into the interior. This created serious friction with the inland Fon people who, like the coastal inhabitants, were also subjects of Oyo, whose cavalry took advantage of the open country to launch raids and collect tribute.

This double threat from Oyo and the coastal states caused the Fon to organize themselves around courageous and successful military leaders. Their state emerged from the town of Abomey around 1650, and in about fifty years, under King Agaja, who ruled over thirty years, Abomey captured the coastal states. Men and women participated in direct military service: indeed, Dahomean women formed units that often fought with distinction.

It was King Agaja who seemed determined to stop the slave raids into his country and terminate the export of slaves abroad. This was, in fact, a key stimulant to the formation of the state. However, Agaja's longer range objective was to establish direct access to the coastal trade. The coastal states, serving as intermediaries, had forced Dahomey to pay high prices for goods, and as the Fon began to unify themselves they had greater need for firearms and powder. By the middle of the eighteenth century, therefore, Dahomey had established firm control along the coast. Whydah became subject to Fon authority, which was represented by Dahomean officials, including one to supervise trade with Europeans.

At first the king limited European activity to the coast, where it was closely supervised. Special permission was necessary for a European to visit Abomey, but near the end of the eighteenth century there seems to have been a regular flow of Europeans between the coast and the capital. This was one indication of Dahomey's increased reliance on the slave trade, Agaja's earlier efforts to the contrary notwithstanding. Given the competition for firearms and other items provided by Europeans, the slave trade became a logical endeavor for Dahomey, which did not have the valuable gold resources of neighboring areas. Moreover, in an effort to abort Dahomey's growing power, the alafin of Oyo defeated Agaja's forces in 1726 and launched other attacks during the century. Dahomey thus engaged more vigorously in the slave trade to obtain more guns and powder, and therefore owed its rise and greatness largely to the profits of that trade. This activity became so vigorous by the end of the eighteenth century that King Kpengla organized slave-worked plantations to feed the increased population of the capital. These plantations eventually became a key economic base of the state after the termination of the slave trade.

Dahomey was also unique as one of the few absolute monarchies in the region. Although advised by a council, the king himself appointed and dismissed all state officials. He sanctioned the priests of religious groups. His top officials included a police chief, tax collector, minister of agriculture, and army commander. In addition to Abomey, the state was divided into six districts, each of which was supervised by an administrator. Paralleling the state officials was a group of women, often called the king's wives, each of whom was assigned to oversee the work of a particular official. Each woman in turn appointed workers to check on the reports of her assigned official. This system of inspection was designed to assure the loyalty and efficiency of all state officials. It was a unique system that gave women a very influential role in political affairs.

Dahomey was indeed evolving into a nation-state. The royal ancestors were related to the well-being of the country and were honored annually. The country's national symbol was a perforated calabash filled with water. Each citizen symbolically held a finger in a perforation to prevent the loss of water (national spirit and strength). Foreigners could become citizens by actually placing a finger in the hole of a calabash during a symbolic citizenship ceremony.

These several factors made Dahomey a strong nation, reaching the peak of its power between 1790 and 1850. After about 1800, even the alafin of Oyo lost political control of the state and only occasionally could collect tribute. In 1818 King Gezo declared his independence of Oyo. During the ensuing years Dahomey became a nation to be feared. Built on the fortunes of the slave trade, it eventually shifted to diversification in ivory and palm oil, but that was a different era, the era of colonial encroachment.

Ashanti

Sometime during the twelfth or thirteenth century, it seems that the ancestors of the Akan people migrated into the regions of modern Ghana and Ivory Coast. They probably sought refuge from the unsettled times following the collapse of the kingdom of Ghana, the conflicts over the trans-Saharan trade, and possibly from the pressures of Muslim rule. In any case, they settled southward and became ancestors to a number of small Akan states. They established control over the gold-producing area and maintained commercial contacts with the western Sudan; they also capitalized on the opportunities afforded by the coastal trade, especially after the arrival of the Europeans.

Several small states emerged in the area: Bono, Adansi, Denkera, Akwamu, and others. Denkera and Akwamu were the most powerful during the seventeenth century; the former expanded westward with its ally, Akim; Akwamu expanded eastward with its smaller ally, Ashanti. Akwamu's armies early in the eighteenth century occupied Whydah across the Volta River, bringing the Ewé and Ho areas under its influence. The motives behind these developments were to organize political systems that could take advantage of the commercial opportunities along the coast, and to maintain influence with the northern trade, which was dominated by Dyula traders. Unlike the savannah country of the Sudan, this region was characterized by dense forests, hills, and rivers, which restricted the size of the states. By 1710 Ashanti began asserting its power. At the same time the Fon were extending their control over the coastal city-states of Dahomey, and the Fante were emerging from Akwamu control. Out of this appeared a new locus of power—Ashanti, bigger than either Denkera or Akwamu and which dominated the commercial and political scene of the region for about two hundred years.

The capital of Ashanti, Kumasi, as a commercial center, became a meeting place for political and religious leaders. It attracted learned Muslims, priests of local faiths, and merchants from as far as Hausaland. This was the heart of Ashanti, whose legendary origin is as captivating as the kingdom was powerful. Traditions hold that Asantehene Osei Tutu, and his adviser and priest, Okomfo Anokye, were the founders of the Ashanti nation around 1695. Anokye declared that the Akan supreme god, Nyame, had instructed him to make Ashanti a great power. At a mass assembly called by Osei Tutu, Anokye caused a golden stool to appear from the sky and rest on Osei Tutu's knees. This stool was then described as containing the collective soul of the Ashanti people. The stool came to symbolize the Ashanti, and Osei Tutu was thus able to establish unity by forbidding the people to speak of former separate traditions. While those traditions were not forgotten, unity was achieved and the tradition of the golden stool became a powerful means of cohesion.

The practical factors behind the move to unite were the desire for security and prosperity. During the 1690s the most powerful state was Denkera, which through its control of the coastal trade secured a monopoly of European goods, especially guns and ammunition. For those goods, however, Denkera had to provide gold and slaves, and the victims of the latter were often Ashanti. To resist the Denkera and develop commercial links with the coast were powerful incentives to unite, and the skillful leadership of Osei Tutu and Okomfo capitalized on those factors.

Denkera was defeated shortly after 1700 and Ashanti proceeded to extend its power over the surrounding area. Hence, the Ashanti nation became a great empire similar to those of medieval western Sudan. Kumasi became a vigorous crossroads center for merchants, teachers, and politicians. Muslims were employed as clerks to keep government records and dispatch official correspondence.

The southward thrust of Ashanti brought them into direct contact with European merchants on the coast. Like the Denkera whom they defeated, the Ashanti developed a commercial partnership with the Dutch on the coast at Elmina. In the meantime, the coastal Fante were uniting in the area between Elmina and Accra. Because of their coastal location they developed trading relations with the British at Cape Coast. The competition between the Ashanti and Fante led to war in 1806 when the former were victorious. However, during the remainder of the century British power on the coast grew, their support of the Fante increased, and friction with the Ashanti mounted. When the Dutch left the coast in 1872, the British emerged dominant, and the final clash with the Ashanti was virtually inevitable.

Decentralized Societies

Historians have placed a good deal of emphasis on the centralized kingdoms and states like Oyo, the Futas, Ashanti, and Dahomey, largely because they appeared more unified, less complex, more familiar, and more "civilized." There are also more documents pertaining to centralized kingdoms that maintained royal repositories, oral and written. However, one of the unique political diversities of Africa is that several societies did not develop highly centralized bureaucracies with kings, ministers, and subordinate rulers; yet they formulated viable social systems with their own values, skills, and wealth; and they successfully maintained their societies. One such society was the Ibo who occupied fertile lands roughly between Benin and Igala to the west and north, the Cross River to the east, and the Niger delta states in the south.

The Ibos developed a complex system in which separate extended family groups balanced political relations within the larger Ibo unit. Although Iboland was one of the most densely populated areas in West Africa, the Ibos, unlike their Yoruba neighbors, did not found large cities; instead, they inhabited thousands of villages. Village government therefore became the basic political unit and consisted of a council of elders and a village assembly. The council included the heads of family units, but any adult male could participate in the deliberations. This assured that the council would always have the benefit of divergent viewpoints, especially when considering matters in dispute. The elders, in their capacity as judges, acted as arbiters and decisions had to be unanimous.

The village assembly characterized Ibo democracy. It was there that the elders presented issues to the people, everyone had a right to speak, and again decisions had to be unanimous. The village assembly therefore was a body in which the young and old, the rich and poor could be heard. Every citizen's participation was possible and important. Decision-making could often be time-consuming, but the slow procedure itself guaranteed greater individual participation.

In addition to the council and assembly, the Ibo political system was further balanced by age-set organizations, title and secret societies. These varied among the several groups, but in general an age-set included young people (male and female separate) initiated at a certain age who remained members all their lives. Each age-set selected a leader and organized competitive sports and community service. The age-sets thus provided discipline among the youth, kept the villages clean, helped maintain law and order, and assisted at the marketplace. As the members of the age-sets matured, their responsibilities changed, ultimately to embrace political power for the men as elders.

The title societies were open to any freeborn male who paid the initiation fee. With additional payments a man rose to a higher grade and eventually became eligible for a pension. Where secret societies existed, there were also initiation fees, titles, and pensions. There was also a secret ritual. Both the title and secret societies had social, religious, and political influence, and as such, they and the age-sets provided additional checks against unscrupulous village government officials. In the case of age-sets, there was occasional coordination of activities among several villages, thereby providing a wider Ibo link. Another link was through marriage, since the Ibo man was required to seek a wife from a neighboring lineage. This had the effect of minimizing disputes and warfare.

A major form of settling disputes was the oracle system, which also strengthened intergroup cooperation. Disputes between two villages could be submitted to an oracle, or elders of a third village. One of these was the Agbala oracle at Akwa. Since Akwa blacksmiths did business throughout Iboland, they became well-known and respected for their work. When they learned about disputes the Akwa blacksmiths would recommend that Agbala be consulted. A much more widely known oracle, however, was Arochukwa. Because the Aro traders engaged in business over much of the country, they like the Akwa would recommend their oracle. The oracle would sometimes levy fines in slaves who were said to be sacrificed to Chukwu. Some authorities hold that the slaves were not sacrificed but sold, as stated in chapter 4. The Aro were prominent in the slave trade, but also in the palm oil trade to the city-states of the Niger delta, notably to Bonny and Calabar. The Ibo of Aboh dominated much of the trade to Brass, another city-state on the Niger delta.

Thus, while the Ibo did not evolve a bureaucratic state system of government, they were indeed a dynamic and influential people. Their oracle system, the Ibo language, the recognition of ethnic loyalty and mutual obligation contributed to a cohesiveness within which the Ibo clearly emerged as a strongly egalitarian and competitive people, believing that all citizens had a right to be heard in their society. This fostered a competitive spirit between individuals, families, clans, and lineages, and contributed to a great adaptability of the Ibo, a factor of great consequence for the colonial era.

One may ask why some African societies developed centralized kingdoms or states while others remained stateless. This question has exercised the thinking and research of many scholars, with disputed results. For the most part, at least until recently, European writers have explained that the more complex, centralized political institutions were imported via the Hamites. It therefore followed that the stateless societies were of a lower civilization, as discussed in chapter 1. However, Professor Ogot of Kenya, in his research of the stateless Nilotes of East Africa, has very aptly noted that most historical inquiries have been most concerned with determining the origin of divine kingship instead of the more important question of what circumstances "produced the attitude of mind which regards kingship as divine." In the examples of Bunyoro and Shilluk, Ogot explains that the kingship system resulted from economic, political, and military factors. They evolved because, as a minority group, they imposed their authority over a disorganized majority. In that circumstance, kinship ties could not suffice. On the other hand, the stateless Nilotic Dinka and Nuer peoples, who inhabited one region for centuries, did not impose their rule over a disorganized majority, and therefore had less need to evolve kingships. This also may apply to the Ibo. In any case, the internal dynamics of societies greatly influenced the choice between a state or stateless system of social organization, and both types evolved meaningful, complex societies, which made creditable contributions to African history.

8

Politics and State-Building II: The Sudan

The period between the collapse of Songhai and the formation of the Islamic states beginning in the eighteenth century and continuing throughout most of the nineteenth was a time of general decline for Islam. Since it had been essentially a religion of the ruling elites of the great medieval kingdoms of the Sudan, the disruption of those states followed by the predominance of small competing states relegated Muslims to minority status with little real influence except as merchants. Bornu, which was powerful during much of the period from the fifteenth century, declined during the eighteenth century. The Hausa city-states remained active commercially, but they were not unified and Muslim influence there was diffuse. Along the bend of the Niger the Bambara people during the seventeenth century organized Segu and Karta as small non-Muslim states. The Mossi, who were long in contact with Mali and Songhai, nonetheless retained their political organization and remained a powerful, cohesive polity under non-Muslim rulers. In short, prior to the nineteenth century, Islam had little direct influence on most Sudanic peoples. At the same time, however, Muslims still resided in scattered areas throughout the region as traders and practiced their faith among themselves. In this way they in fact were passive agents of cultural change.

From about the first quarter of the eighteenth century a series of new states emerged under the leadership of the Fula (Fulani) people who, for the most part, had been cattle breeders but had begun to trade and settle down in towns. By so doing they established some influence among leading families who appointed local rulers. As traders, they encountered and accepted Islam and played a major role in the Islamic revival of the eighteenth and nineteenth centuries. They had become dominant elements among the people of Futa Toro, Futa Jallon, Masina, Kita, Sokoto, Bauchi, Adamawa, and Liptako. Those areas emerged as centers in which the Fula embraced Islam, established unity among themselves, won allies, and led revolutionary movements to revive and restore the power and law of Islam throughout much of the western Sudan. This dramatic and crucial epoch can only be surveyed briefly in the space allowed, and perhaps best by focusing primarily on a few of the movements.

By 1700 small communities of Muslim Fula settlers resided in Futa Jallon, where each village chose the most respected cleric, a karamoko (Muslim scholar), to serve as leader. As the communities grew, largely because of the fertile soil, lush pastures, and favorable location along trade routes, the Fula encountered resistance from their non-Muslim overlords. Grievances included land disputes between the cultivators and the Fula cattle breeders. In addition, Muslim Fula resented paying taxes to non-Muslim sovereigns, who thus regarded Fula efforts to spread Islam as an economic and political threat. Finally, in 1725 the Fula united in a jihad against all nonbelievers and within a few years developed the mechanisms of a state. The karamokos chose Karamoko Alpha as almamy (king) and organized a coronation ceremony in which each karamoko pledged allegiance to the almamy. Messengers were dispatched throughout Futa to inform the inhabitants and to win their loyalty to the new order.

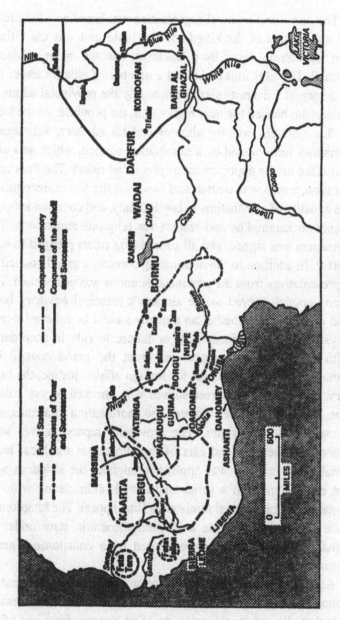

The Sudan in the Nineteenth Century

Legend:
- Conquests of Samory
- Conquests of the Mahdi and Successors
- Fulani State
- Conquests of Omar and Successors

Locations shown on map: Nile, Blue Nile, White Nile, Bahr el Ghazal, Sobat, KORDOFAN, BAHR AL GHAZAL, El Fasher, DARFUR, WADAI, CHAD, KANEM, Chari, BORNU, Kano, Zaria, Sokoto, FULANI EMPIRE, NUPE, BORGU, YORUBA, DAGOMBA, GURMA, Kong, Benue, Niger, YATENGA, WAGADUGU, MASSINA, SEGU, KAARTA, Tombuktu, Gambia, Senegal, Futa Toro, Futa Jallon, SIERRA LEONE, LIBERIA, ASHANTI, DAHOMEY, Congo, Ubangi, LAKE VICTORIA

0   500   MILES

The social and political organization was based on a hierarchical subdivision of the kingdom. The basic unit was the village that was administered by a headman, assisted by an advisory council. The next unit embraced a number of villages under the authority of a district ruler appointed by the provincial administrator, who headed the next higher unit, the province. At the head of this hierarchy was the almamy and his advisers. Subsequent almamies were named by a nominating council, which was also consulted on the appointment of provincial rulers. The Fula constitution, which was written and based on the Koran, recognized the equality of all Muslims in law and duty, and commanded obedience to karamokos and respect for religious regulations. The document was signed, and all subordinate rulers pledged to support it. In addition to the nominating council, a grand council of representatives from the provincial councils was established. The grand council served as the almamy's principal advisory body and could decide whether an almamy should be relieved due to physical or mental incapacity, or failure to rule in accordance with the Koran or constitution. From the grand council the almamy chose his ministers for foreign affairs, justice, the military, and provincial representatives who checked on tax collection, mediated disputes, assisted the coordination of armies, and consulted on land rights. The provincial representatives were essentially the eyes and ears of the almamy at the local level. Finally, Koranic law was applied throughout the kingdom with the establishment of a series of tribunals culminating with the almamy and his judicial minister as final appeal. The kingdom of Futa Jallon thus became a Muslim theocratic state under an almamy whose powers were limited by a constitution, grand council, and the Koran.

According to tradition, sometime around 1800 the nominating council succeeded in establishing a two-year alternate succession rule that allowed for the selection of an almamy from one of the two dynastic families prominent in the origin of the kingdom every two years. This appears to have been a tacit agreement that was frequently violated. Thus a series of conferences led to a specific two-year alternate succession rule around 1840. That arrangement seems to have minimized conflicts and rebellions over succession and remained in force until the establishment of French colonial authority in 1897.

During the course of the nineteenth century Futa Jallon extended its influence over much of the western Sudan both by launching jihads and by dispatching missionaries. Koranic schools taught the Arabic language, literature, and Muslim law, and made Futa Jallon a center for Islamic learning, attracting students from and dispatching proselytizers to neighboring regions. In this way the Fula of Futa Jallon played a major role in spreading Islam in much of the western Sudan. Moreover, the establishment of law and order along the trade routes and at the marketplace further enhanced Futa's influence.

The success of the Muslim movement in Futa Jallon inspired similar developments in Futa Toro. In the Senegal region of Futa Toro, Sulaiman Bal, who had studied in Futa Jallon, led a revolt in the 1770s and founded a Muslim state under the control of the Tukulor, a people closely related to the Fula. Included in the state were Wolof, Soninke, Bambara, and Mandingo peoples. The kings were chosen from among the founding families and their descendants. Another state was founded a little later between Futa Toro and Futa Jallon in the region of Bondu. The explorer, Mungo Park, passed through Bondu in 1795 and described it as prosperous, peaceful, and well provided with Koranic schools.

The impact of these developments was felt farther east in the Hausa states where many Fulas had settled in the commercial towns and had become prosperous traders and, because of their Muslim learning and outside contacts, occupied important positions as teachers, judges, and advisers. Indeed, many Fulas had married Hausa women and learned the Hausa language. But there were still nomadic Fulas who had difficulty securing pastures and using waterholes and streams for their cattle; they also objected to paying the cattle tax. Both the nomadic and urban Fula were joined by other Muslims, including some Hausa, in greivances against the Hausa rulers: They resented the wars against neighboring Muslims, the practice of impressing Muslims into servitude, heavy market taxes and luxury and corruption in the court. Thus, as Muslims they preached reform based on the Koran, and because some of their grievances appealed to oppressed non-Muslims, many of the latter were attracted into what became a decisive revolutionary movement in Hausaland.

The leader of the movement was a Fula from Gobir named Uthman dan Fodio (the Shehu, meaning "the senior") who, after having traveled and studied under various Muslim scholars, returned to Hausaland to teach and preach. Because of his knowledge and piety he won many converts and dispatched loyal disciples to carry the faith to the masses. The essence of his message was that Muslims should not willingly live in a country that did not believe in Islam, that such a country was one that had a non-Muslim ruler and was not governed in accordance with the Koran. Those Muslims living under Muslim rule should, according to the Shehu, wage a jihad against the unbelievers. These ideas were basic to Islam and were, of course, not new. But they illustrate the Shehu's determination to establish a Muslim state.

It was not long before the non-Muslim aristocracy attempted to abort the reform movement, even attempting to assassinate dan Fodio. Tensions increased and civil war became imminent. Thus in 1804 dan Fodio, his brother Abdullah, his son Muhammad Bello, and other Fulas and dissident Hausas launched a jihad against all unbelievers. The details of the war are impressive, but suffice it here to note that revolts broke out across Hausaland and in Bornu, at Nupe, Adamawa, and across the Niger in renowned Oyo, which was sacked and the alafin killed. In 1809 the capital of Sokoto was built by Bello, and by 1811 the Fula leaders had not only emerged as masters of Hausaland, they were also a major inspiration for other Muslim forces in the western Sudan.

After the conquests, the Fula leaders made determined efforts to win the loyalty of the Hausa. This was done by appointing Fulas and Hausas to trusted positions in the administration, encouraging nomadic Fulas to become farmers and settle near Hausas, assuring that justice in the courts was impartial, and by allowing non-Muslims to pay special taxes in return for assurance that they would not forcibly be converted to Islam. These and other factors reinforced efforts to unify Hausaland under the rule of the Muslim Fula. The territory was divided into self-governing emirates that chose their own emirs who were then confirmed by the sultan at Sokoto. Each emir demonstrated his loyalty through payments of tribute, the size of which brought prestige to the giver, and through annual holy wars, which continued until about 1880. Other officials of the state included the chief secretary, judge, police chief, and tax collector. Thus, for the first time in history, the Hausa states were brought under the authority of a single ruler and continued as a unified state for almost a hundred years, during which time it expanded the faith, spread Muslim learning, brought general peace and security to the masses, and prosperity from trade.

In neighboring Bornu, Islam had a long history. Mai Idris Alooma came to power in Bornu around 1580, and before his death in 1617 he had built a strong empire that for about half a century prospered from trade, developed friendly relations with the Turks in North Africa, constructed schools, and became a center for Muslim learning. The mai was semi-divine and had an elaborate court. He governed through a council of administrators who supervised tax collection, the recruitment of armies, and subordinate rulers. A central court of justices received appeals from lower courts. Due to this administrative system and because it dominated the great trade routes through the Fezzan to Tripoli where slaves and wheat were exchanged for salt, firearms, and luxuries, and also because it protected the pilgrim route to the east, Bornu became the most powerful kingdom of the central Sudan, enjoying relative peace, security, and prosperity throughout much of the eighteenth century.

While Bornu enjoyed its position of dominance, trouble brewed east of Lake Chad, where movements for Muslim conversion and reform appeared in Wadai, and as the century closed, the impact of developments in Hausaland threatened Bornu. Fula residents in the western dependencies were stimulated by the success of the neighboring Fula who around 1808 carried dan Fodio's jihad to Bornu, destroyed the capital, and forced Mai Ahmad to flee to Kanem, which resulted in several dependencies declaring independence. The mai then appealed to Al-Kanami, a Bornu Muslim scholar, who organized an army and regained the capital. Again in 1811 Al-Kanami repelled Fula forces and eventually recaptured some of the lost districts. He thus emerged as hero of Bornu and held the positions of chief justice and commander of the army. Because of his prestige and the loyalty of his Kanembu soldiers, he was able to initiate a number of reforms to win support of dissident factions. Muslim law was more carefully monitored for just application, schools were built, and the capital once again became a center of education. His exercise of power behind the throne was passed on to his son, Omar, who, as a consequence of civil war in 1846, ascended to the throne, thereby ending the thousand-year reign of the Sefawa dynasty. But, as noted earlier, the kingdom's success rested on its ability to control and regulate commerce, which increasingly during the nineteenth century witnessed competition from Wadai and other neighbors; in addition, European influence was closing in from the north and south. By the 1890s, therefore, Bornu's power and influence were only a shadow of its earlier role.

Rabih Fallullah led an armed band from the Bahr al-Ghazel through the eastern Sudan, defeated Bornu in 1893, and unsuccessfully challenged Sokoto. For a time he seemed master of the region of Lake Chad. Although he fought as a commander of the

Mahdi, he appears to have been motivated less by religion than by incentives of conquest and economic gain. Finally in 1900 his force was defeated by the French.

Northwest of Bornu, along the Niger bend, Fulas and allied people in the Masina plains launched an Islamic revolution under Hamad Bari, who studied under a noted Muslim scholar at Jenné, Al-Muktar, and possibly under dan Fodio. He did indeed consult with dan Fodio on the Masina jihad. Hamad Bari defeated Segu and established his control over the renowned cities of Jenné and Timbuktu. Several subordinate rulers declared in favor of Islam and invited Bari's authority. After conquest, he divided Masina into provinces, each under an emir. The state itself was governed by a grand council of Muslim scholars. Notable in this state was a censor to rid the state of immorality, but an unintended effect was to deprive the merchants of business that previously flowed in from the Sahara. However, the theocratic state did remain stable for a time, as succession passed on to Hamad II and Hamad III.

Near the middle of the nineteenth century there appeared another great Muslim leader destined to revolutionize much of the western Sudan. This was al-Haj Omar who was born in Futa Toro in 1794. Omar studied and traveled widely in Arabia and Egypt, where he could observe the effects of Mohammad Ali's efforts to adapt Egypt to modern industrial developments. He later visited Al-Kanami in Bornu, Muhammad Bello in Sokoto, Hamad Bari in Masina, and the almamy of Futu Jallon (probably Almamy Omarou Sori). During the 1840s Omar, with the almamy's permission, established his base in Futa Jallon at Dinguiraye, which became one of the leading centers of Muslim learning and missionary activity. Omar was therefore able to build a strong base of support with adherents proselytizing in several regions. In addition to his religious appeal Omar also preached a message of general social reform. During the early 1850s he launched several attacks against non-Muslim states.

Because Hamad III cooperated with non-Muslim Segu, Omar's forces swept across Masina, conquering Segu and Timbuktu. Much of this success resulted from the manufacture of firearms by blacksmiths in Omar's territory. Shortly after the fall of Segu in 1861, Omar lost his life in battle. He was succeeded by his son Ahmad, who had to contend with several revolts at the same time that French forces were penetrating the Sudan from Senegal. The end of Omar's creation was near at hand.

This Muslim resurgence in the western Sudan was matched by an equally great force in the eastern Sudan. As noted in chapter 3, when the Arabs conquered Egypt there were two Christian kingdoms south of Aswan: Makuria and Alodia. While the Arabs continued their advance southward, they were stopped by Makuria; but the governor of Egypt launched an expedition, which resulted in a treaty in 652, thereby bringing peace and allowing Arabs to settle and exploit the trade, especially in gold and slaves. The treaty of 652 remained the basis of Muslim–Nubian relations for about six centuries. The extension of Egyptian Mamluk authority to the Red Sea coast isolated the Christian kingdoms from the outside world, and this led to the foundation of a Muslim state by 1317.

In the case of Alodia the history is more obscure, though it probably disintegrated before the emergence of the Funj state around Sennar in 1504. Funj's favorable location along the Blue Nile attracted scholars, missionaries, and merchants. The kingdom expanded and established control over the region between the two Niles. But political stability was constantly threatened by waves of Islamic reform movements and economic competition. This general state of affairs was not really checked until the Turco-Egyptian conquest of the Sudan in 1820 brought the area into the Egyptian Empire. Muhammad Ali was determined to establish stability so that commerce could be revived. He particularly wanted to control the gold and the slave trade, the latter being one means of filling the ranks of his army. Following the conquest in 1820, therefore, the number of explorers and merchants visiting the Sudan increased, and this led to an intensification of the slave trade as European and Arab traders in Khartoum and other centers set up stations and employed armed groups to raid for slaves. When in 1860 the khedive of Egypt, Said, prohibited the trade in slaves, the government increasingly encountered resistance from the slave traders and their allies.

This policy culminated under Khedive Ismail (1863–1879) when international interest in Egypt was more marked. Ismail, like Said, was more responsive to Western influences and European advisers. Several expeditions were sent into the Sudan to suppress the slave trade, establish Egyptian authority, and encourage legitimate trade. The British explorer Samuel Baker carried the flag to Uganda territory, while another expedition was dispatched into the Bahr el Ghazal.

This was part of the general background to the resurgence of Islam in the eastern Sudan. When Muhammad Ahmad ibn Abdallah proclaimed himself the expected Mahdi in 1881 he found an atmosphere receptive to his call for justice and equality. As a former teacher, Ahmad had a base of supporters for Islamic reform. Other followers included Muslims who saw Ahmad as a fulfillment of the prophecy, the coming of the Mahdi; additional supporters were merchants whose livelihood was threatened by Egypt's efforts to suppress the slave trade and establish control in the south; a final group of supporters came from the ranks of ordinary inhabitants who resented misgovernment and high taxes. The Mahdi's appeals gradually gained momentum and coalesced the diverse groups into a strong reform movement that eventually reached parts of Ethiopia, Darfur, and southern Egypt. This revolt in the Sudan included Muslims and non-Muslims, northerners and many southerners, and in a sense launched an ostensible movement toward national unity. Whether or not this could have been accomplished is unanswerable. That it was not achieved, however, was due partly to the inability of the Mahdi's successor,

Abdullah at-Taaishi, to fulfill his predecessor's vision, partly to the ominous European developments in Egypt from 1882, and, most significantly, because of the diverse aims of the northerners and southerners. Muslims and non-Muslims never really solidified in an ultimate determination of national purpose. However, Abdullah did in fact succeed in maintaining a semblance of political and religious unity until he was finally defeated by Anglo-Egyptian troops in 1898.

For well over 150 years (from the founding of the state of Futa Jallon in 1725 throughout most of the nineteenth century) Islam inspired Muslim Africans to create large political states and empires based on Koranic principles, which provided an important measure of unity among the people. Muslim education and culture were extended across much of the Sudan, so that the faith was no longer just a religion of the elite but embraced many among the masses. Expanded trade brought greater prosperity and important links abroad. Heads of Muslim states more freely consulted on matters of common concern and the nature of social reform, as in the examples of dan Fodio, Hamad I, al-Haj Omar, and others. Indeed, the concern of these leaders for the social improvement of people attracted many converts and sympathizers and thus made government more sensitive to the needs of the people. In this process, Islam became more Africanized and proceeded to modify many parochial loyalties by providing more universal perspectives, which may well have brought even greater social consciousness and unity among the diverse groups had not the process been slowed down, limited, and in some cases redirected by the more powerful physical thrust of European colonialism.

9

Politics and State-Building III: Central and Southern Africa

From at least the fourteenth century through the nineteenth, the process of state-building in varying degrees occurred in the savannah region of the Congo, along the great lakes region, and southward into southern Africa. This great expanse of territory has not received anything like the research attention it deserves. In addition to the several obstacles to research in Africa referred to in chapter 1, central and southern Africa did not attract the attention of overseas scholars, especially in the United States, as did the early and more dramatic nationalist movements in West Africa and, to an extent, East Africa. In addition, most of central and southern Africa remained under colonial rule during the high water mark of 1960 when most African countries became independent. In more recent years, however, an expanded body of data has become available and will be surveyed in this chapter.

The Kongo

The kingdom of Kongo was probably founded in the fourteenth century. It had a hierarchical structure from the basic unit of the village, under a headman. Several villages were combined in a district under an official appointed by the king, who could also remove him. Several districts comprised a province under an official, also appointed and subject to removal by the king. At the center of the kingdom, of course, was the king, or manicongo. The selection of the king rested with an electoral council of elders who chose the most popular candidate from one of the two dynastic families. Once installed, the king had great power as a divine ruler who strengthened his position through the appointment of loyal officials. Although he had a council of advisers, his power was great, and the kingdom was marked by a high degree of centralization. The king maintained a royal fishery that provided shells as a medium of exchange. With this monopoly, the king could control monetary value in the state. Other income came from tribute, fines, and tolls paid in shells or in supplies. Although there was no standing army, the king did maintain a well-armed guard.

This was the kingdom the Portuguese found when Diogo Cao reached the mouth of the Kongo in 1482. Three years later he brought four Portuguese missionaries and took four Kongolese to Portugal. So impressed were the latter that on their return they persuaded the king to send an ambassador to Lisbon to request the assistance of technicians and missionaries. Several Kongolese were sent to Portugal for an education. Finally, in 1491 Portuguese missionaries, artisans, and explorers arrived and began a program of foreign aid to the African kingdom. Through this emerged a community of Portuguese living under the authority of the Kongolese monarch. The Portuguese built churches and began converting Kongolese, including the manicongo, the royal family, and some of the nobles. In the meantime, Kongolese stu-

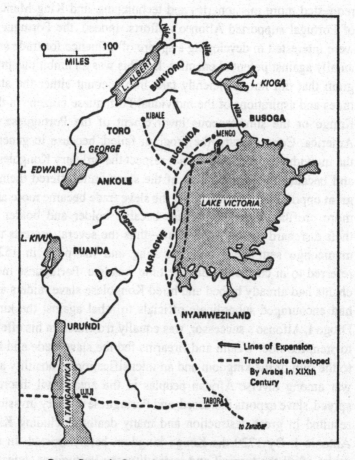

Bantu States in Central Africa in the Nineteenth Century

dents returning from Portugal further infused European values into the kingdom.

When Alfonso, a convert, ascended to the throne in 1506, he devoted his energies to the establishment of a Christian state. He requested more missionaries and technicians, and King Manuel of Portugal supported Alfonso's efforts. Indeed, the Portuguese were interested in developing a sphere of influence for trade and an ally against potential enemies. But this was an ambitious program that did not sufficiently take into account either the attitudes and aspirations of the individual Portuguese citizens in the Kongo or the simultaneous involvement of the Portuguese in America. Consequently, the program failed, because in general the individual Portuguese did not respect the ordinary Kongolese, and because the development of the slave trade offered them a great opportunity for wealth. As the slave trade became more and more profitable, the Portuguese became bolder and bolder in their disregard for the Kongolese—thus the several protests the manicongo sent the Portuguese king and the pope in 1526, referred to in chapter 4. But the time was late. Portuguese merchants had already bribed and hired Kongolese slave raiders and had encouraged subordinate officials to rebel against the king. Diogo I, Alfonso's successor, was equally frustrated in his efforts to stem the tide. Wealth and firearms fed the slave trade and led to the ruin of the kingdom and an intensification of hostility and war among diverse African peoples in the area. Civil disorder spread, slave exports increased, and Portuguese military invasions resulted in great destruction and many deaths, including King Antonio I. By 1720 the Kongo kingdom barely existed. In the midst of all the turmoil and instability, the Portuguese defeated the Ngola people and thus laid the base for colonial rule in Angola.

The Mutapa Empire

The empire of Mutapa emerged between the Zambezi and Limpopo Rivers and centered around the impressive stone buildings of Zimbabwe. Of the several structures, now in ruins, the main ones are known as the Acropolis and the Temple or Great Enclosure, names given by the first Europeans who saw the buildings in the nineteenth century and did not believe Africans had built them. Indeed, although today it is generally agreed that Africans constructed the buildings, there are still those who maintain that Arabs or Europeans were the builders, though there is no evidence to support the claim. The buildings appear to be the work of the Shona people in the fourteenth century. The Shona, a Bantu group, seem to have migrated from the Congo region during the early years of the fourteenth century and rose to power under kings of the Rozwi clan from about 1420. King Mutota embarked on a military campaign that brought large stretches of territory under his power and earned him the title of Mwene Mutapa (master soldier), a title passed on to his successors. Before the end of the century the Mwene Mutapa had extended his authority from the Zambezi to the Limpopo and over wide stretches between the Kalahari desert and the Indian Ocean.

The vigorous trade between the East African coast and Asia brought Zimbabwe into this great mercantile network. It was a major source of ivory, and rich in gold and copper. This trade was expanded and the caravan routes made more secure with the establishment of a more highly centralized regime under the Shona. While there is some question over how unified the kingdom became, there is little question about certain cohesive forces at work. One was the Shona belief that only the Mwene Mutapa could communicate with the spirits; thus he had ultimate religious authority and ruled by divine right. Second, cohesion was symbolized by the royal fire, which burned continually at court throughout a king's reign. Each subordinate ruler carried a flame to his district and kept a light as a symbol of unity. Each year the district's flame was relit from the royal fire to demonstrate continued loyalty. On the accession of a new king, the royal fire was extinguished, a new one ignited, and the procedure repeated. Third, subordinate rulers annually dispatched emissaries with tribute for the king, who organized a ceremony for the occasion. Clearly, therefore, the Mwene Mutapa and his advisers and officials were consciously pursuing a policy of unification and state-building. To be sure, internal rivalries seriously threatened these developments and, along with European interference, led to the eventual disruption of the kingdom.

The Interlacustrine States

Traditions in the interlacustrine states of Bunyoro, Ankole, Toro, Rwanda, and Burundi refer to a vague people as the Bachwezi, to whom is attributed credit for introducing a centralized monarchy and a hierarchical political structure. The Bachwezi are believed to have ruled in the region from about the middle of the fourteenth century to the sixteenth, when the Luo migrated from the eastern Sudan in search of pastures for their cattle. They settled along the lakes region and brought about the collapse of the Bachwezi.

Up to about the middle of the seventeenth century Bunyoro was the most powerful of the states, expanding at the expense of Ankole, Rwanda, Busoga, and Buganda. However, from the latter part of the century Buganda began to appear as a major competitor, and by the nineteenth century it was the most powerful state in the region. This position resulted from the development of a strong central government, which could assert its authority. Although the same pattern occurred in the neighboring states, Buganda's was more successful. The king (kabaka), whose position was hereditary, ruled with the advice of a council (lukiko) and adopted royal insignia of stools, drums, and spears as symbols of authority over his diverse subjects. He had a first minister under whom a hierarchical system of officials carried out the royal will. These officials were mostly appointed and subject to dismissal by the king, who thus achieved great power and influence through patronage at all levels of the state.

With this organization and the belief that the king ruled in accordance with the wishes of the ancestors who established the state, a strong sense of loyalty, and no doubt fear, permeated the kingdom and gave it unity and strength. This was the base that enabled Buganda to extend its authority to other groups, to establish control over trade routes and guarantee reliable market conditions, and to deal effectively with the early Arab and European arrivals. Indeed, so highly effective was the political system that in the nineteenth century the British helped to preserve it in the interests of colonial rule.

Southern African Peoples and States

The original inhabitants of South Africa were the Khoikhoi (better known as Hottentots, which has become a derisive nickname in South Africa) and the San or Saan (better known as Bushmen, another demeaning name). The Khoikhoi were herders and the San were hunters, and the language of both is characterized by clicks. Evidence of the early history of these people is limited mainly to travel accounts and other European reports, but archaeological finds in southern Africa have linked the Khoikhoi and San with Stone Age culture and rock art. Indeed it is remarkable that the San, hunters for whom the search for and supply of food was always a precarious and thus full-time vocation, should emerge as very prolific artists.

As hunters and food gatherers the San did not domesticate animals, except for the dog. They lived on wild roots, berries, honey,

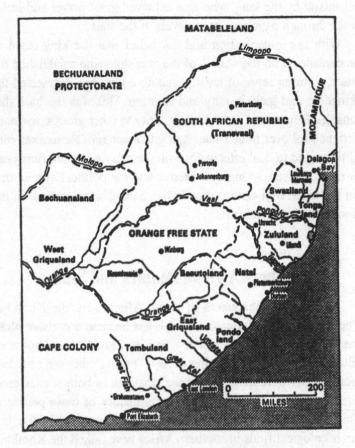

Southeastern Africa in the Nineteenth Century

fish, and wild game. The latter supplied their food and clothing, which was made of skins and furs. The San lived in small, independent bands, essentially isolated from most other people. This was especially true where land and game were plentiful, but as their population grew and as other people, Africans and later Europeans, settled nearby, there was more competition for both land and game. In this situation some of the San either migrated to remoter areas (such as the Kalahari desert) or attached themselves to farming communities. There were cases in which the San attached themselves to the Khoikhoi, for whom they hunted and herded in exchange for food. Over the years the San came to be known as cattle raiders and as such were frequently attacked, first by the Khoikhoi, later and more effectively by Europeans. It has been estimated, for example, that between 1715 and 1862, European farmers hunted and killed thousands of San, ostensibly to prevent future cattle raiding. But as the San were largely exterminated or pushed aside, white farmers occupied their land and made servants out of the captured children.

The Khoikhoi were a nomadic people who camped in small family clans under the senior clan head. This headman, assisted by a council, arbitrated disputes and passed judgments. The Khoikhoi, like the San, witnessed the first thrust of European settlers in southern Africa and became their competitors for land and cattle. In time they fell victim to the Europeans' power and many became servants. Out of this juxtaposition came concubinage and some intermarriage, which resulted in the emergence of a group of mulattoes called "coloreds."

Of the several other groups inhabiting southern Africa prior to European contact, the Nguni and Sotho are the largest. The Nguni comprise the Zulu, Xhosa, Pondo, Thembu, and Swazi, and together they number over seven million. They are widely settled in southern Africa, though most of them live between the Indian Ocean and the Drakensberg Mountains as east-west borders, and between the Fish River valley and Swazi as south-north borders.

Although the Nguni were herders, cultivators, and hunters, their major preoccupation was cattle. Their early weapons were the iron throwing spear and wooden club with hide shields. The famous longblade spear with a short handle appeared among the Zulu under Shaka. The Zulus were especially skilled in iron smelting, which enabled them to fashion iron hoes and arms in greater quantity sooner than their neighbors.

North of the Nguni are the Sotho who number about five million and include the Tswana. They relied mainly on agriculture but were also skilled craftsmen and metal and stone workers. In fact, some authorities believe a relationship exists between the Sotho and the Shona builders of Zimbabwe. Both the Nguni and Sotho have absorbed members from the other's ranks and have lived in symbiotic relationship with neighboring peoples. For example, in spite of local wars between them, members of the Sotho and Nguni intermarried with the San and have adopted words and click sounds from the Khoikhoi. Their homes and homesteads resemble each other, certain ceremonies are similar, and Xhosa dress resembles the Khoikhoi; the Sotho credit the San with teaching them circumcision. In short, while competition for land, water, and game sometimes led to wars and the dispersion of the San especially, there has been a long history of group and individual interaction among the several southern African peoples, and all of them made significant contributions to the cultural growth of the region.

This necessarily brief survey of key groups of people in southern Africa should enable one better to understand the political development of one group as a case survey during the nineteenth century, the Zulu. Sometime during the latter part of the eighteenth century Dingiswayo replaced his brother as ruler over a Nguni district and proceeded to build a state based on conscription of young men into military units designed to entrench an esprit de corps and heighten their competition. Within a few years Dingiswayo built a strong army, expanded his territory, and became the paramount ruler over a wide area. A commander responsible for much of this success was Shaka, who had been brought to the area as a child, but who was later conscripted and found to be a brave, intelligent, and effective leader. His military organization included the posting of an elder, loyal woman with each subcommander as a means of assuring support. He also introduced the short-handle stabbing spear for close combat and had his blacksmiths produce large quantities of the weapon. He enforced rigorous training and strict discipline, made widespread use of spies and surprise attacks, and followed the aim of complete destruction of the enemy. Shaka began these practices as a commander and perfected them as successor to Dingiswayo, who was killed in 1818. With an estimated army of approximately fifty thousand well-trained men, Shaka greatly expanded the kingdom.

Shaka established his headquarters at Bulawayo, though he moved about frequently. He maintained a small group of loyal councilors from different backgrounds. But he remained the source of power and decision because of his leadership ability, the loyalty of the army, his power to appoint and dismiss subordinate rulers, and also because he laid the basis for an evolving unity. This was manifested by Zulu becoming the basic language, and the absorption of outsiders as citizens, provided they swore allegiance to Shaka. In a sense, the trend was toward nation-building, albeit fear was also a cohesive factor. Because of this fear on the part of some, but mostly because neighboring states were disrupted by the rise of the Zulu kingdom, widespread migrations carried refugees in all directions. Many sought refuge nearer the coast where European power was increasing. Others broke away and founded their own states. The Nguni ruler, Sobhuza, organized a group that resisted Shaka for a time but eventually withdrew to more defensible terrain in the mountains overlooking the Pongola River. Here, during the 1820s and 1830s, Nguni and Sotho peoples laid the basis for the Swazi kingdom. Resistance also came from Mzilikazi, a subordinate who defied Shaka and fled with Ndebele people to the eastern Transvaal in 1823, and near Pretoria in 1825. There Mzilikazi and the Ndebele became a dominant kingdom including Nguni and Sotho peoples. The unsettled times also provided an opportunity for Moshweshwe to develop and demonstrate his military talents. He established himself and some followers in mountains near the Orange River, where he encouraged Nguni and other migrants to join him in what became the LeSotho state. Sobhuza, Mzilikazi, and Moshweshwe patterned their military after Shaka's and laid the basis for the emergence of national sentiments in small southern African states.

However, portentous developments had already appeared by the time of Shaka's assassination in 1828. Europeans were penetrating deeper and deeper into the interior, selling their wares and spreading their ideas. Shaka appreciated their gifts and recognized the value of their medical practices and their firearms. He welcomed the visitors, but made it clear that they were "his Europeans"; the latter appreciated the entrée and knew how much their lives and business depended on the great ruler. But Shaka's successor, Dingane, who was less effective as a military and political leader, became increasingly unable to contain the ominous European presence, if anyone could have. The other African kings faced the same dilemma: the extent to which they should accept the European infiltrators whose firearms and ideas were valuable assets for nation-building and economic strength, but whose links with the coast and nations abroad proved increasingly difficult to contain or control. This dilemma persisted throughout the nineteenth century, manifesting itself in protests, violence, and cooperation with Europeans, and finally was resolved by the imposition of colonial rule which is discussed in chapter 13.

10

Politics and Trade in East Africa

East African Coast and Early European Contact

The success of Vasco da Gama's first voyage around the tip of southern Africa set in motion a series of events that assured centuries of economic and political unrest as three forces sought dominance. These three forces were the Africans, Arabs, and Europeans. Rivalry between the first two was not new and was tempered somewhat by the fact of their historical, genetic, and cultural relationship, and relatively comparable technological development. Indeed, as we have noted, the rulers of the city-states in East Africa were for the most part of Omani Arab descent. This did not, however, preclude the struggle for Arab settler rule over both African and metropolitan Arab rule, which continued even after the Portuguese arrived.

On his second voyage to India in 1502, da Gama stopped at Kilwa and under threat of burning the town, compelled the sultan to acknowledge the supremacy of the Portuguese king and pay an

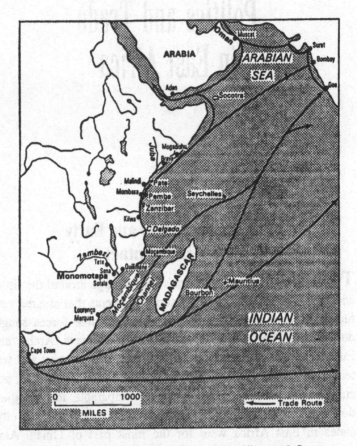

Eastern African Maritime Trade Routes in the Nineteenth Century

annual tribute. Zanzibar was the next victim, in 1503. Then in 1505 a fleet of over twenty ships left Portugal with orders to establish military settlements at half a dozen strategic points between Southeast Africa and Southwest India. The points in Africa were Sofala, the key to the gold supply; Kilwa, which was a shipping center and which had defaulted on the tribute; and Mombasa, which had a good harbor and was seriously challenging Kilwa as a great commercial port. Only Mombasa was able to mount serious resistance to the Portuguese. The Arab and Swahili townspeople were backed by mainland Africans in battle, but in the end Mombasa was defeated, looted, and burned by the Portuguese. A similar fate came to Lamu, Oja, and Brava in 1506, and the next year the town of Mozambique was taken, as a fort, hospital, church, and living quarters were established. It was hoped that Mozambique would thrive on trade from Sofala, but it emerged as a secondary trading center and after 1550 became the Portuguese East African headquarters.

By 1509, except for Malindi, which had accepted an alliance with Portugal to challenge Mombasa, all the chief coastal towns from Brava to Sofala and the islands of Zanzibar and Pemba had either agreed to pay tribute to the Portuguese or had been economically and politically destroyed by them. Mogadishu, Madagascar, and the Comoro Islands had escaped the conquest. Thus, the Portuguese within eight years of their arrival had established widespread control over the coast, had defeated the Muslim fleet in the Battle of Diu in India, and had seriously disrupted the Indian Ocean trade. However, control over such a wide coastal area remained tenuous as local resistance continued, and too few Portuguese were available to apply military rule.

On the coast north of Kilwa, small unofficial Portuguese communities settled in Zanzibar, Pemba, and Pate; but while tribute was periodically collected, the Portuguese could not seriously assert political control. Their main advantage lay in their advanced naval and military technology and the unity of purpose that were employed to exploit the political and economic divisions among the coastal states. The Portuguese thrust in the north, therefore, was primarily interventionist. Such interference between 1505 and 1512 hastened the decline of Kilwa. In 1541 a Portuguese military force intervened to help Ethiopia successfully repel a Muslim attack, but no political authority was established. However, Portuguese missionaries did remain there in vain efforts to win the Ethiopian Church's allegiance to Rome.

The most steadfast resistance on the northern coast came from Mombasa, which was attacked and plundered by the Portuguese in 1505 and 1528. Although it received assistance from two Turkish expeditions in 1585 and 1587, it finally lost its independence to the Portuguese in 1589. This represented a turning point for Portuguese policy in the area. The most powerful city-state had fallen, and in 1593 the Portuguese built the famous Mombasa citadel, Fort Jesus. The city thus became a headquarters for Portuguese officials and a main port of call for its vessels. However, during the years of the next century Portugal's power was tested by the Omani Arabs who periodically intervened on the coast. The imam of Oman assisted several of the coastal states and attacked Fort Jesus, which finally fell in 1698. Having been defeated in the Persian Gulf in 1622, the Portuguese were now forced to concentrate their efforts on the southern East African coast.

Official Portuguese settlements were planted in Kilwa and Sofala, in addition to the town of Mozambique, and systematic rule was applied. Trade monopoly was rigidly enforced, causing Arabs and Indians to migrate to Madagascar and elsewhere. In reality, however, although the Portuguese did establish their political authority, they were less successful in filling the Arab role of middleman. Like the Arabs, their influence only encompassed the coast, where over the years miscegenation resulted in a class of mulattoes between the mass of Africans at the lower level of society and the Portuguese colonizers. In the interior, African societies were hardly more affected than during earlier years. The Portuguese, like the Arabs, encouraged trade in the same general goods and seem not to have penetrated beyond the coast. Although Sofala was attacked in 1506 and periodic ambushes against Portuguese units occurred thereafter, generally tolerable relations developed between the coast and the interior.

The Portuguese had already established their position south of the Zambezi. In an attempt to secure greater control over the Sofala gold trade, they penetrated the interior to Sena in 1531 where a Swahili settlement already existed. A few years later they built a fort at Tete, farther up the Zambezi, in order to establish closer contact with the gold fields. None of these ventures proved very successful, but there did emerge the *prazo,* or plantation system, which included vast tracts of land administered by the Dominicans and Jesuits. These planters collected head taxes, dealt in slaves, and for years were the most powerful local forces in the region.

Portuguese dominance in overseas exploration, trade, and settlement did not long go unchallenged by other European powers. The first French ship rounded the Cape in 1529, the first English ship in 1580, and the first Dutch ship in 1595. These were the three powers who became the principal competitors of Portugal, not only in East Africa but in Africa generally, and in the non-European world. One should not forget that these were the years of the early slave-trading activities, which became an economic mainstay of several European powers.

The economic factor was clearly manifested in the similar approaches the European powers took in Africa and the world. The English initiative led to the organization of the East India Company in 1600, the Dutch counterpart was organized in 1602, and the French in 1664. With the regular dispatch of armed trading fleets from these powers, Portugal's political and economic influence collapsed in most East African areas except the southeast. The Dutch planted settlements in Mauritius in 1644 and the

Cape in 1652; they captured Portuguese forts in Angola and the Gold Coast in 1637–1648, but their main focus was the Orient. One result of the Dutch concentration on the Orient was that Britain and France became the principal competitors along the coast of East Africa between Ethiopia and Mozambique.

East Africa and the Omani Arabs

The expulsion of the Portuguese from Mombasa in 1698 inaugurated a new era for the northern coast of East Africa, which came under the domination of the Omani Arabs until the imposition of European colonial rule. Although the rulers of Oman could not immediately follow up their defeat of the Portuguese at Fort Jesus because of the pressure of wars in the Persian Gulf, they did take an increasingly direct interest in East Africa during the eighteenth century. Members of an Omani clan, the Mazrui, first went to Mombasa as representatives of the imam and became successful in organizing themselves into a dynasty of hereditary rulers from about 1735; they presided over the politics and economy of the city-state, and in 1746 they successfully declared their independence of Oman. For almost a century thereafter they maintained their sovereignty in Mombasa, though their fortunes began to wane when the imam, Sayyid Said, initiated a series of moves designed to bring East Africa under his control. Said made friends with the British, who were expanding their commercial influence in the Persian Gulf, secured naval materials from them, and gradually applied diplomacy and war to gain hegemony over the city-states. The principal resistance came from the Mazrui of Mombasa. But in 1837 Said's forces attacked and won the city; Mazrui leaders either fled or were deported. This was followed by the imam's change of official residence in 1840 from Muscat to Zanzibar, which had remained loyal to him during the eighteenth century while other coastal states asserted virtual independence. From

1840, therefore, Sayyid Said, sultan at Zanzibar, became the dominant sovereign on the coast down to Cape Delgado.

When Said moved his capital to Zanzibar he was followed by many of his compatriots who hoped to exploit the economic potentialities of the area. As already noted, cloves had been introduced successfully in 1818, and Said encouraged their cultivation for export; coconut plantations were also developed successfully to provide an export crop. Many Arabs therefore acquired extensive plots of land, developed plantations, and worked them with slave labor. Many of the African inhabitants of the islands fled to escape enslavement, thereby contributing to the expansion of the slave trade to the mainland. The Arabs thus established themselves as a ruling planter aristocracy based on slavery, marked by their acquisition of wealth, leisure, and disdain for the lower economic class, primarily the Africans.

In addition to Arab immigrants, Indian bankers or financiers were also attracted to Zanzibar. Said had patronized them in Oman and was no less interested in their input of capital and expansion of trade in East Africa. The sultan granted the Indians religious toleration, sought their commercial advice, and gave them control over finance, including the collection of customs. Through his control over customs the sultan received a large annual cash income to finance his administration and to launch commercial expeditions. By granting the supervision of customs to Indians, he was assured of financial expertise in a crucial slot and at the same time spared the expense of running it. Indians also controlled the large financial houses that extended credit to Arab and Swahili merchants who organized caravans to secure ivory and slaves. Only the rich Indian bankers could finance such risky ventures, which sometimes extended over several years.

Under Said, Zanzibar became the trading emporium in East Africa, and a power in world politics. The sultan negotiated commercial treaties with the United States in 1833, Britain in 1839, and France in 1844. Exports included cloves, slaves, ivory, copra, sesame, and cowry shells; imports consisted of rice, beads, gums, and gun-powder, and American, British, and Indian cotton. With this expanded trade the immigration of Asians increased. From a population of about two thousand in 1850 the Asian community grew to over five thousand by 1860, and many of these were permanent settlers.

Zanzibar's prosperity depended to a great extent on its relations with the mainland coastal settlements, each of which had its sheik, customs official, soldiers, Indian merchants, Arabs, and Swahilis to organize expeditions. Trade between the island and mainland stimulated trade between the coast and interior. Thus, Arabs, Indians, and Swahilis settled in greater numbers on the coast. As this occurred, Asian capitalization made loans available both on the coast and in the interior. Mogadishu and Merca were centers for cotton manufacture; Mombasa had a good harbor, became a distribution center for slaves, and produced sesame and coconut oil. Ivory, slaves, and rhinoceros horns were plentiful exports on the coast just opposite Zanzibar, including the Kilwa region. But as Zanzibar relied heavily on the coast, the latter relied on the interior; so the three areas—islands of Pemba and Zanzibar, the coastal cities, and the great hinterland—were joined by trade that strengthened their connections during the nineteenth century.

Interior Traders: The Yao and Nyamwezi

We have seen that the East African coast was characterized more by the establishment of great city-states than by powerful kingdoms. Those city-states, and at least some of the interior societies, were oriented toward the trade and politics of the Indian Ocean. In this context the Arabs and Swahilis played a dominant role and unconsciously began establishing a cohesiveness in East Africa based on Islam and Asian commerce. While the sheiks who ruled the coastal towns did not submit to direct control of the sultan of Zanzibar, they did share a common culture and economic interest. The sultan claimed authority over much of the coast but was not always able to enforce it; on several occasions, however, the towns did cooperate to protect their mutual vested interests, whether to resist the power of Omanis or the Portuguese. There was thus a basis for alliance and the possibility for future confederation or statehood along the coast.

This can hardly be said for much of the interior of East Africa, though coastal influences were having an impact at least from the eighteenth century. One of the areas in which that impact became visible was Yaoland, where the Yao were great long-distance merchants during the eighteenth and nineteenth centuries. Prior to their ascendancy as great traders the Yao were agriculturalists, hunters, and fishermen inhabiting the areas of Mozambique primarily, though some lived in southern Tanganyika. Yaoland was rich in iron, and the Yao thus became major suppliers of iron hoes and other implements that they exchanged for cloth, salt, beads, and other goods available on the coast. Coastal merchants increasingly sought greater supplies of ivory to meet the demand of Asians. Consequently, the much more lucrative possibilities of the ivory trade resulted in great changes among the Yao, who became the major suppliers. From the eighteenth century the expansion of the slave trade also provided great commercial opportunities for the Yao. As elsewhere, the exploration of this lucrative trade required greater organization and control, and led to the growth of towns in which the prominent merchants lived. People were attracted to the towns by employment opportunities, and in search of protection from slave raids. Since the demand for ivory remained high, life in these towns never deteriorated to the point of focusing only on slaves for trade. This is not to imply that towns were not raided and devastated; they were, but many Yao towns seem to have grown during this period. David Livingstone and others commented on the large Yao towns.

Unlike some of the other people we have considered, the Yao's expanded involvement in trade did not lead to the formal organization of bureaucratic government. Power and status centered in the village around those Yao who could command support of the inhabitants. Although kinship was important, it alone did not suffice. Wealth and military power were the key factors of control. Local affairs remained essentially a local business as rulers could command only the village headmen in their territory. Intermarriage was sometimes a bridge of alliance and cooperation; but Yaoland, though prosperous, remained un-united when colonial rule came.

Among the dominant traders around Lake Tanganyika were the Nyamwezi, who expanded their business to the coast. They, like the Yao, were especially prominent as iron hoe merchants, though they also engaged in trading copper ornaments, ivory, and salt. Most of this was very likely interior trade, but the growth of the ivory trade and later the trade in slaves stimulated more direct trade with the coast. At least by the middle of the nineteenth century the Nyamwezi traders also traveled to the Congo and north. By that time also, Arab and Swahili merchants had emerged as important commercial competitors, bringing a new supply of goods and guns from the coast. In order better to organize and service their wider field of operations, Arab and Swahili merchants established settlement bases. In 1852, for example, they organized in Nyamweziland a settlement later called Tabora. Although the immigrants did not found a political state there, they did become strong enough in some cases to establish reciprocal relations with some Nyamwezi rulers to win exemption from local taxes in exchange for maintaining a reliable flow of goods and weapons into the country.

The Arab and Swahili merchants provided real opportunities for local rulers not only to gain wealth but also to establish and entrench their economic and political power. Through the collection of tolls, more ivory and slaves were obtained and sold for more firearms for defense, for protection of the trade routes and markets, and for territorial expansion. A number of leaders, Msiri for example, built up a big business, secured weapons, and established a political kingdom. Another example of this is Mirambo, who during the 1860s built up a small army and exercised political control over a small area. Eventually he secured control of the trade between Tabora and Ujiji, defeated the Arabs in Tabora, and obliged them to pay tribute. Mirambo dispatched agents to Buganda and to Zanzibar. He welcomed Europeans whom he knew would attract trade, provide him with information about the coast, and in a sense help him maintain contact with the world outside. Although he did not found an enduring kingdom, Mirambo did play a significant role in developing trade and facilitating the reciprocal flow of ideas that stimulated cultural innovations and modifications among Africans both on the coast and in the interior.

While it is easier to document the flow of cultural innovations from the coast to the interior, the flow of ideas was indeed a two-way process. The nineteenth-century trade, for example, stimulated the Yao to build dhows like those of the Arabs; they planted crops introduced from the coast; and one Yao ruler, Mataka, is reported to have built a village that he said resembled the coast and would provide him with fruits eaten on the coast. Houses in Ujiji reportedly represented Indian and Arab architectural styles. Moreover, the spread of the Swahili language was not a single, direct line from the coast by Arabs and Swahilis, but as one community learned it, it was passed on, consciously or unconsciously, to another as a trade language providing greater cross-cultural communication. On the other hand, interior Africans affected the coastal communities as Africans from various interior areas settled in neighboring and coastal regions, carrying with them their songs, dances, and beliefs. The flow of ideas and culture was thus reciprocal and laid the basis for change and the development of a wider consciousness and potential unity by the time of European penetration.

Ethiopia

Centuries before the Europeans rounded the southern tip of Africa, Ethiopians had begun the process of state-building and the development of a distinct culture of their own, as noted in chapter 3. Its rulers continued efforts to unify the country and to spread Christianity through the establishment of churches and monasteries. There were many setbacks, however. The reign of Lebne Dengel (1508–1540), for example, was marked by several Muslim invasions, which resulted in widespread destruction and looting and which were followed by many conversions to Islam in several provinces. Finally in 1541 Emperor Galawdewos defeated the Muslims with assistance from Portuguese troops. But the country continued to suffer from invasions by Turks on the Red Sea coast, the Oromo (Gallos) in the southern districts, and revengeful Muslims. In addition, a Jesuit mission under a Portuguese priest arrived and sought to convert the country to the Roman Catholic faith. In this time of great crisis Ethiopian kings, though the extent and wealth of their realm were reduced, continued to exercise vital political power. Invaders were resisted, and in 1669 Emperor Yohannes I proceeded to expel Roman Catholics from his kingdom. Political and economic stability was not established, however. Indeed, within about eighty years Ethiopia entered one of its darkest periods.

The century from about 1750 to 1855, known as the era of the princes, was a time of great conflict. The country was wracked by conflicting claims to power; widespread and almost continuous warfare devastated Ethiopia and brought great frustration and suffering to the people. This period of chaos and decentralization continued until 1855 when one of the greatest Ethiopian rulers appeared. Not being a member of the royal family, Kassa ascended to the throne by first rebelling against the rulers in Gondar, solidifying support, and then proclaiming himself Emperor Theodore II in 1855. During his reign he attempted to unite the whole country under his rule, to establish peace and security, and to manufacture arms for his army by attracting craftsmen from Europe. This was all cut short, however, when the emperor arrested the envoy from Queen Victoria of England, who subsequently dispatched a military expedition that defeated Theodore's army and led to his suicide in 1869. Thus, it was left to Yohannes IV to continue Theodore's plans for unification and reform. However, although Yohannes defeated an Egyptian unit in 1876 and an Italian force in 1887, Ethiopia, like the rest of Africa, had entered a new era characterized by the increasing extension of European military and political power.

11

The Scramble and Partition

The establishment of European rule in Africa resulted from the culmination of efforts on the part of many people and organizations, which laid the basis for the more dramatic conflicts, conferences, and decisions with which is generally associated the inauguration of colonial rule in Africa. This necessarily brief discussion will attempt to bring into sharper relief the activities of several people, organizations, and events functioning at different levels in various African and European societies and paving the way for the ultimate application of European authority over most of Africa during the late nineteenth and early twentieth centuries. The precursors of that development were missionaries, explorers, and merchants, sometimes operating within the narrow limits of those labels but frequently combining both the perspectives and practices of others. In short, the functions of a given explorer, missionary, or merchant were often interrelated parts of several interest groups.

When the British African Association was founded in 1788 a new force emerged with great consequences for the future of African history. The association inaugurated the era of systematic exploration of the continent. After three expeditions to determine the exact location and direction of flow of the Niger River failed, the association sent Mungo Park on a similar mission in 1795–1797 and again in 1805. These expeditions greatly expanded European knowledge about the Niger, but about twenty-five years elapsed before the river's outflow into the ocean was established by John and Richard Landers. During that interim, Walter Ondney, Dixon Denham, and Hugh Clapperton were sent out in 1822. Denham visited Bornu and the Lake Chad region; Ondney died; and Clapperton visited Kano and Sokoto. The reports of Denham and Clapperton provided Europeans with their first reliable accounts of the caravan routes between Tripoli and Bornu, and the peoples inhabiting the area between Sokoto and Lake Chad. Other prominent explorers in West Africa included Gaspard Mollien who visited the sources of the Senegal and Gambia Rivers; René Caillé who visited Timbuktu, 1827–1829; Heinrich Barth who in the 1850s traveled from Tripoli to Agadés and visited Katsina, Kano, Bornu, Sokoto, Say, and Timbuktu.

John Ludwig Krapf and John Rebmann, CMS missionaries, went to East Africa to spread the gospel, but became well known for their explorations and reports of Mt. Kilimanjaro, Ethiopia, Zanzibar, Mombasa, and other points of European interest. Richard Burton and John Speke explored the East African lakes between 1856 and 1859, and wrote about several places and people, including Mtesa's court in Buganda, and the town of Tabora. Speke ultimately reached the source of the Nile River. Samuel Baker and Joseph Thomson also explored East Africa. But the most widely known explorers of the area were David Livingstone and H. M. Stanley. Livingstone began his travels in South Africa in 1842. He named Victoria Falls, where the Zambezi River falls from a great height. Livingstone visited many parts of the area and was met by Stanley at Ujiji on Lake Tanganyika in 1871.

Nineteenth-century missionary activity also had a slow growth but accelerated during the last half of the century. Although propagators of Christianity had been in tropical Africa since the Portuguese arrival, little was achieved in the way of African conversions during the early centuries, the Congo experience notwithstanding. However, a new sense of popular and emotional religion emerged in Europe during the eighteenth and early nineteenth centuries and resulted in the establishment of several overseas missions by Methodists, Baptists, the London Missionary Society, Church Missionary Society, and others in the United States and Britain; several protestant groups (Rhenish, Berlin, Bremen, and Paris evangelical societies) in continental Europe; and later by the Catholic Church, e.g., the White Fathers in 1868.

Antislavery activity directed the attention of many Europeans to Africa. The resettlement projects in Sierra Leone, Liberia, Freretown (Kenya), and a smaller settlement effort by the French in Libreville led to efforts at rehabilitation, and this, among other things, stimulated projects for the expansion of Christianity and commerce. By 1870 various mission stations had been set up from the Gambia River to the Cameroons to help Africa recover from the effects of the slave trade. In South Africa the London Missionary Society took up the cause. And in East Africa, David Livingstone caught the imagination of many Europeans and thus spurred vigorous efforts among missionaries.

While abolitionism and the general humanitarian conscience played an important part in this European interest and activity in Africa, political and economic considerations were also vital forces in the movement. Countries and mission societies naturally favored sending their missionaries to those parts of Africa where their nationals were already residing. The earlier European residents were mostly traders and a few missionaries of the pre–foreign mission era; although small in number, these groups became crucial links in the nineteenth-century penetration of Africa. The European traders and missionaries were significant contacts for explorers planning adventures into the interior, and the explorers' accounts of resources and activities in the interior stimulated projects on the part of traders to tap those resources. Without a doubt, the publicity attendant upon the visits and reports of the several explorers made various parts of Africa attractive to merchants eager to extend their economic spheres of influence. Explorers, for example, showed that the Senegal and Niger Rivers were suitable for the shipment of goods to and from the interior. Between 1832 and 1834 an English merchant, Macgregor Laird, sponsored an expedition in two steamships to attempt direct trade north of the Niger delta. A larger expedition was sent during 1841–1842. In addition to trading, the expedition was supposed to construct a mission station and develop a model agricultural farm near the confluence of the Niger and Benue Rivers.

The rationale for expeditions like the Niger one was probably best articulated to the public by David Livingstone. He believed that the only way to abolish the slave trade was through cooperative ventures of traders and missionaries in the African interior. Settlements of Christian merchants and farmers around a mission station, Livingstone thought, would convince Africans that the slave trade could be profitably replaced by trade in legitimate produce (cotton, for example); that this combination of agriculture and trade would teach industriousness and form the basis for a stable community; and that Christianity would provide the spiritual cohesion for that community. Although the Niger expedition and Livingstone's Zambezi project failed to achieve those aims, European merchants and others recognized the economic potential of the African interior and continued to seek ways of tapping it.

In 1849 a British consul for the Bights of Benin and Biafra was appointed to assist British merchants. In 1851 the British captured Lagos, partly to pursue the abolition of the slave trade and partly to increase protection of British traders; in 1853 a consul was appointed to Lagos, which was finally annexed to the crown in 1861. The British were thus poised to exploit the interior when the time became appropriate. A major breakthrough occurred when Dr. William Baikie's expedition of the Niger and Benue Rivers in 1854 demonstrated that the use of quinine could overcome the fever that had taken so many European lives on earlier expeditions. This discovery paved the way for more effective penetration of the interior by Europeans in general, and in particular the British along the Niger. Farther to the west, in the Gold Coast, the British consolidated their economic interests, negotiated the takeover of Dutch forts, turned down the Fante constitution and efforts for independence, defeated the Ashanti, and established colonial rule in 1874. These actions, explained in greater detail in chapter 12, were the culmination of many years of trade, missionary activity, and conflict with the Ashanti, and cleared the way for a monopoly of commerce that would help cover the costs of British colonial rule.

In East Africa British efforts to abolish the slave trade increasingly forced the sultan of Zanzibar to rely on British diplomatic and military power. At first reluctant, and always concerned that his subjects might rebel over his decisions leading to abolition, the sultan by the 1870s was virtually at the mercy of the British, who had appointed John Kirk as consul at Zanzibar in 1866. Kirk assured the sultan that the British navy would enforce the abolitionist treaty of 1873. At the same time, missionaries and explorers were trying to interest merchants and shippers in East African trade. The appeals of Livingstone had great effect. In 1872 the Glasgow shipowner and member of the Free Church of Scotland William Mackinnon began having the ships of his Steam Navigation Company stop at Zanzibar. In 1874 some Glasgow merchants subscribed to put a steamer on Lake Nyasa; in 1876 Mackinnon decided to begin construction of two roads from the coast to Lakes Nyasa and Victoria; and two years later some Glasgow merchants formed a company to run more steamers on Lake Nyasa. Some Hamburg merchants established trade in local produce. While Britain, as the world's greatest naval power, was primarily interested in keeping the sea lanes open for trade, and although prevailing economic theories held that colonies were uneconomical, the fact that European, mainly British, missionaries and traders had established what to them were satisfactory spheres of influence and London had appointed a consul to watch over its citizens meant a political and economic involvement deeper than a desire to abolish the slave trade.

While these developments in West and East Africa were occurring, the situation was fast approaching a climax between Egyptian rulers and Europeans, and the results of this had serious repercussions in other parts of Africa. With the opening of the Suez Canal in 1869, Egypt became vitally important to European, especially British, interests in Asia. In 1875, Benjamin Disraeli, British prime minister, purchased Khedive Ismail's shares in the Canal Company; European private investments increased in the country; and European officials received posts in the Egyptian administration. This reflected the khedive's policy of attracting European aid in the modernization of Egypt. Samuel Baker was appointed governor-general in the Equatorial region of the Nile in 1869, and within three years he had pushed to the Lado Enclave in an attempt to stop the slave trade, encourage legitimate commerce, and control the source of the Nile. Baker arrived in Bunyoro in 1872 and sought to establish an Egyptian protectorate there, but was forced out by the king's army. Baker's successor, Charles Gordon, also attempted to establish control over Bunyoro. He convinced the khedive to occupy a post on the east coast and establish a series of stations connecting with Uganda. Such a landing was made, but British pressure forced its withdrawal in the interest of Sultan Barghash of Zanzibar, still nominal ruler on the east coast. In exchange, on the urging of Kirk, Barghash agreed to organize his army under a British officer and accept arms from the British government. He also accepted Mackinnon's road-building scheme. Britain had indeed established unofficial indirect rule over the sultan.

Back in Egypt inefficiency and corruption in the administration and high interest rates by European bankers brought bankruptcy, which led to British and French plans to occupy the country in the interest of European investors. After considerable political maneuvering the British landed troops in Alexandria in 1882, defeated nationalist troops, took control of Egypt's finances, pledged to reform the administration and withdraw. The French, unable to intervene because of domestic problems, were apprehensive of Britain's unilateral move. Indeed, economic and political considerations led to this occupation, which further accelerated European penetration of other parts of Africa.

French efforts in Africa had suffered during the Napoleonic wars when Britain gained control of the seas and occupied some of the French posts in Africa. In 1817, however, France reestablished control over Saint-Louis, Gorée, and other posts along the Senegal River. This was followed by attempts to develop plantations on the lower Senegal, to tap the goldfields of Bambuk, and to engage in trade with surrounding regions. Exploratory expeditions into the interior, by Mollien and Caillé in particular, revealed the existence of strong, organized states in the Sudan, the presence of gold, cotton, and other products, and the existence of a vigorous trade with northern Africa. In the 1840s the French fortified posts at Assinie and Grand Bassam on the Ivory Coast, Whydah in Dahomey, and in Gabon to check the expanding influence of the British, to protect French trade, and to provide stations for the French navy. In addition, French occupation of Algeria in 1830 had stimulated interest in an empire comprising northwestern Africa and Senegal.

Under Napoleon III's government, Louis Faidherbe was appointed in 1854 to pursue the expansion of trade along the Senegal. From the headquarters in Gorée, Faidherbe established forts along the Senegal, where he imposed control over Futa Toro and checked the advance of al-Haj Omar. After 1860, the development of the peanut trade and the interest of Marseille and Bordeaux firms in the cultivation of peanuts and coffee around the

Rio Nunez river led Faidherbe to envision the grand design of empire. Dakar had been occupied in 1857 and missions were dispatched in the 1860s and 1870s to Futa Jallon and points east. Although Faidherbe failed to achieve his empire, he did pave the way for the strategy of his successors.

Meanwhile portentous developments were occurring along the Congo River. The king of Belgium, Leopold II, had convened an international conference in Brussels in 1876, ostensibly to discuss means of cooperative action for scientific exploration, to abolish the slave trade, and to develop legitimate commerce. When the conference broke up into competing national groups, Leopold proceeded with plans to explore the Congo under his own auspices. He secured Stanley, who returned to the Congo with instructions to negotiate treaties with African rulers. The dissident French branch of the international conference sponsored the explorer Pierre Savorgnan de Brazza to the Congo where in 1880 he began negotiating treaties with local rulers. When de Brazza returned to the Congo in 1883, he was a government commissioner with instructions to organize a colony. By that time, in the wake of the French defeat by the Germans in 1866 and the subsequent unilateral British occupation of Egypt, French public opinion made a national hero of de Brazza and accelerated official interest in other African projects. Within a few months other missions were dispatched to the Niger and Benue region, Porto Novo, and other commercial ports in West Africa. In short, French tariffs began eliminating other nationals, and there was renewed official consideration for constructing a railroad connecting Algeria, Timbuktu, and Senegal.

This chain of events set in motion by King Leopold's efforts to carve out an empire in the Congo represented a culmination of years of efforts by missionaries, explorers, merchants, and others to map out and assess various areas in Africa. Indeed, the Congo events dramatized and climaxed the conflicting interests of Portugal, France, and Britain, and led to the convening of the Berlin

Conference in 1884–1885. At that conference, the powers agreed that traders and missionaries of all countries should have free access to the African interior, that the slave trade should be abolished, and that European morality should be "brought" to Africans. It was also agreed that the Congo and Niger Rivers should be open to all nationals. But more important than that was the stipulation that no new European colony would be recognized unless they were effectively occupied, which meant that European officials had to establish visible and effective power in the areas claimed. The results of that provision were predictable. Those spheres of influence built by European merchants and missionaries now required their government protection to be valid in international law. Thus, the scramble was intensified, and partition was now inevitable. Even before the signatories left Berlin, German officials were negotiating agreements with Africans in the Cameroons, Togoland, and South-West Africa, which became protectorates in 1884; the German East African Protectorate, based on Carl Peters's treaties with Africans, was proclaimed in 1885. The several other powers, with a longer presence in Africa, accelerated efforts to consolidate their spheres of influence and meet the terms of the Berlin Conference. Not that the conference had any enforcing powers but it offered a peaceful way of legitimizing "the rape" of Africa.

The situation in southern Africa was somewhat unique in that the Dutch had settled at the Cape in 1652 and had proceeded to attempt to construct a society in which Africans and Europeans would be separated geographically, politically, and socially. The first legal step was taken in 1779 when they proclaimed the Fish River as the eastern border of the colony. Then during the French Revolutionary and the Napoleonic Wars a number of French Huguenots migrated to the Cape; during those wars, the British occupied that area, an action that was sanctioned by the Congress of Vienna in 1814. In 1820 the British government provided free passage and land to potential settlers of the Cape. This resulted in some five thousand British farmers, artisans, and professionals settling the Cape colony. In the 1850s Britain arranged for the settlement of about three thousand Germans who agreed to serve in the British Foreign Legion; they gradually became assimilated into the British community. Smaller numbers of Irish settlers also arrived in the 1850s. All of these settlers reinforced the British settlements, which retained their language and culture apart from the Dutch descendants.

Much of the nineteenth century in southern Africa was marked by the conflict among the Africans, Boers, and British. Dissatisfaction with the extension of British culture and rule not only antagonized Africans, but also aroused resentment on the part of the Boers and led to their migration north. This advance has been characterized as the Great Trek, but was in fact a great aggression inland—an organized migration of several thousand Boers across the Fish and Orange Rivers from 1835. By 1845 an estimated fourteen thousand had left the Cape. They founded the Transvaal and Orange Free states in the area where Bantu-speaking people had lived for centuries and, as seen in chapter 9, had established political units. When the Europeans discovered diamonds in Kimberley (1867) and gold in Transvaal (1886), conflicts intensified between the Africans and Europeans, the Boers and the British. Britain finally annexed Transvaal in 1877, but war with the Zulus led to the defeat of British troops at Isandhlwana in 1879.

Meanwhile, Cecil Rhodes, who had made a fortune in the diamond and gold mines, sought to extend Britain's influence. In 1888 his agents persuaded Lobengula, the Ndebele king, to grant mining rights in return for a subsidy, arms, and a steamboat. The following year Rhodes formed the British South Africa Company which spearheaded the occupation of Matabeleland and destroyed Lobengula's power.

Political and economic conflicts continued to hamper relations between the British and Boers and finally exploded into war in 1899. The result of that war sealed the fate of Africans until 1994.

The Union of South Africa was established in 1909 and each of the component regions—Cape, Natal, Transvaal, and Orange—retained its autonomy in regulating African rights. No common franchise for elections to the Union parliament was provided and no African was assured the vote outside the Cape where the "colored" people had the vote, which itself was whittled away over the years. Blacks in South Africa thus became a colonized people in their own land under a small but wealthy and powerful minority-resident European government. More fortunately, Basutoland (LeSotho), Bechuanaland (Botswana), and Swaziland became High Commission territories under the direct authority of the British government, but they were small and weak islands in the sea of South African suppression of blacks.

Although, aside from the early Portuguese claims in Africa, partition may be regarded as commencing with the French occupation of Algiers in 1830, it remained for the final chapter of the era of partition to be written in northern Africa. France assumed control over Tunisian finances in 1881 and the entire administration in 1883. In 1904 Britain supported France's sphere of influence in Morocco in exchange for a "free hand" in Egypt, and France was obliged to recognize Spain's control over the principalities of Ceuta and Melilla on the northern coast as well as Italy's claims to Tripoli. Then in 1912, after considerable military and diplomatic maneuverings between Germany and France, the Treaty of Fez granted France a protectorate over Morocco, with Spain keeping her possessions. This rounded out the era in which Europeans arbitrarily partitioned Africa among themselves. It thus remained for them to secure their hold on the territories and develop policies to control the African people.

12

African Diplomacy, Resistance, and Rebellion

Much of the history of Africa prior to contact with Europeans was characterized by diplomatic and military struggles to gain and maintain control over fertile land, trade, and trade routes. Kingdoms and city-states had risen and fallen in these struggles. The nineteenth century witnessed a continuation of that tradition, but the struggle for power reached a higher level of consciousness among many African societies. The preceding chapters have shown the tremendous efforts to extend and centralize political organization across ethnic and geographical lines. Without denying the presence of ethnic particularity in the centralizing trends, there is abundant evidence that political movements in the eastern and western Sudan, Ethiopia, parts of central and southern Africa, and the Guinea coast were tending toward a broad consolidation of smaller entities under centralized power, in order to develop different methods and institutions to resolve problems of economic growth, increased population concentrations in towns, and to deal more effectively with other problems, including external relations.

Simultaneous with these centralizing trends was the determined efforts of Europeans to expand and entrench their power in Africa. These developments provided additional options for the Africans and thus diverted and further divided African leaders. While the ultimate objective of centralized self-government was not altered, the attainment of that objective required a reliable source of modern weapons, which Europeans were best prepared to supply. African dependence on European arms and other goods, however, obviated the development and maintenance of black self-rule. Some Africans recognized this, but saw no viable alternative to cooperation with Europeans. What often happened, therefore, was that African leaders broadened the scope of their political operations to include Europeans to further local political objectives. In exchange for trading rights, Africans won promises of European friendship, arms, consumer goods, and protection. It is within this context of divergent interior and external forces that African diplomacy and wars between the 1880s and World War I must be viewed. They were essentially a continuation of struggles for a balance of power among African states and ethnic groups, but at various points they merged and became indistinguishable from wars of resistance to European control. In this sense, the European factor became an added obstacle to the achievement of a broader political base for Africans.

This was no even match. African leaders were in the process of building states and nations to meet the needs of their societies when the European intrusion came. Africans lacked comparable technology and broad experience in international affairs. Thus, few of them at the outset could perceive the interrelationships among the European powers even in Africa, not to mention the global aspects of Western imperialism and colonialism at the time. Not only were Africans generally unfamiliar with the European languages, they were mostly pre-literate and without swift means of communication—telegraph, locomotives, etc. Nonetheless, Africans responded to the challenges with dignity, sometimes as collaborators, sometimes as resisters, and sometimes as both, but always in the hope of guaranteeing African self-determination. This will be illustrated by examples from diverse and widely separated regions of the continent.

The Ashanti

By the early nineteenth century Ashanti embraced an empire of approximately 125,000 to 150,000 square miles with probably three million to five million inhabitants. In addition, the area was rich in resources, especially gold, and engaged in a profitable trade with Hausaland, the western Sudan, and with Danish, Dutch, British, and French merchants on the coast. When the British began to extend their influence, they met fierce resistance from the Ashanti. With guns and ammunition acquired in trade from European merchants, Ashanti forces engaged British forces in seven battles (1806, 1811, 1814–1815, 1823–1826, 1863, 1873–1874, and 1895). But it was the battle of 1873–1874 that set the stage for British ascendancy and led to the establishment of the Cape Colony in 1874. British troops marched into Kumasi, burned the town, blew up the asantehene's palace, and dictated the Fomena Treaty, which provided the following: The Ashanti should pay an indemnity of 50,000 ounces of gold; renounce claims over Denkera, Akim, Elmina, and some other territories; promise to keep the Kumasi road open to trade; and abolish human sacrifice.

This humiliation of Ashanti, the British monopoly of trade, and the proclamation of a colony over the Gold Coast prevented serious conflicts with Ashanti for about twenty years. And the Ashantis continued their efforts at state-building. The asantehene regained allegiance and prestige, and a movement to recover the non-Ashanti states was launched. In 1893 Prempeh I became the asantehene and two years later, 1895, the British decided once again to intervene. They charged the Ashantis with failing to honor the Fomena Treaty and called for the acceptance of a British protectorate. Prempeh I refused, and asserted that Ashanti would remain independent. That Prempeh assumed or hoped the British would not attack is confirmed by the Ashantis' unpreparedness when in 1896 a British expedition entered Kumasi unopposed. Prempeh, his relatives, and his chief supporters were deported, and the Ashantis were forced to accept a British protectorate.

The next four years were tense. Ashanti leaders felt tricked because they had not been defeated in battle, yet their leaders were exiled. Finally, when in 1900 the British governor on the coast demanded the Golden Stool—the symbolic soul of the Ashantis—hard fighting ensued, but the British won and annexed the territory as a colony in 1901. Thus, after almost a century of intermittent war, the British broke Ashanti resistance and diverted the thrust of Ashanti history from that of a proud, state-building people to that of a defeated, colonized people. But Ashanti leaders had won the hearts of their people, who successfully pressured Britain for the return of Prempeh. Under colonial administration Ashanti retained a measure of autonomy and unity, due no doubt to their traditions and the determined stand of their leaders.

Mahmadou Lamine and Samory Touré

When al-Haj Omar died in 1864, his son Ahmadou confronted several revolts: The Fula and Bambara in Masina were in arms; Aguibou, Ahmadou's brother, was being challenged in Dinguiraye; and Samory Touré was expanding his conquests around Kankan. The French captain J. S. Gallieni had the responsibility of establishing contact with Ahmadou and developing trade along the Niger River and therefore had to decide whether or not to support the desperate Ahmadou. Gallieni tried to play the Tukulor leader against his enemies. Indeed, the French refrained from military confrontation in exchange for the freedom to develop allies and trade.

A potential ally was Mahmadou Lamine, who emerged as a Muslim political leader at a time when the Sarrakole people in Senegambia and Karta were resisting the rule of the Tukulors of Segu, which Omar had conquered in 1861; this was also the time of the aggressive expansion of the French into the western Sudan. These two alien forces, Tukulor and French, greatly accelerated the Sarrakole unity movement, which Lamine led on the basis of ethnic solidarity and Islam.

As a pious leader, Lamine organized the Sarrakole and established commercial relations with the French, who provided arms in the hope that the Sarrakole would limit their attacks to the common foe—the Tukulor Ahmadou, Omar's successor. But the situation changed perceptibly when the French sought to ensure their influence in neighboring Bondu by installing a replacement for the deceased almamy whom they had kept in power. Lamine responded by occupying Bondu and assuming control. Realizing that Lamine was attempting to build a state at the expense of their imperial interests, the French succeeded in allying with Ahmadou against Lamine. Finally, confronted with the French-Ahmadou alliance and their larger, better armed, and more highly disciplined force, Lamine was defeated in 1887. Thus a nascent nationalist movement that began to unfold before the colonial era was aborted.

Samory Touré represented a much more dramatic instance of nascent nationalism. His early life is somewhat hazy, but he was a merchant and won fame as a soldier. During the 1860s he had a loyal group of men around him, and in the 1870s he established a base of operations in Kankan, assumed the title of almamy, and proceeded to appeal to Mandingo solidarity in the task of state-building, not only in the geographical region of medieval Mali but also in the tradition of Islam as a unifying ideology. His control during the 1880s reached as far as present-day Sierra Leone, Liberia, and Ivory Coast. He established a bureaucracy to assist in administering the provinces of his state, but he alone had ultimate power, which was based on his success as a military leader and the prestige of Islam manifested in his title, almamy.

Since Samory's ascendance coincided with creeping European colonial rule, he had to decide on his options. As long as his independence appeared safeguarded, he seemed as prepared as any sovereign to trade and negotiate friendship agreements with the Europeans. But like the Europeans, he pursued a policy to secure as much power and influence as possible in surrounding areas. Samory's army thus became the key to his success. When in 1881 his forces expanded their occupation in parts of the Sudan, the French regarded him as a threat to their attempts to establish a series of forts along the Senegal River where they had fought Omar. A brief military skirmish followed in 1882, Samory's first real challenge from Europeans. A second encounter occurred near Bamako in 1883 when French forces again tried to limit Samory's activities.

Both sides wanted to avoid war. Samory recognized the superiority of French firepower and did not want to jeopardize his state-building efforts by risking war. The French preferred to negotiate and build allies in the area. Under these conditions Samory attempted to develop relations with the British and Krios in Sierra Leone where he had major commercial contacts, especially for arms. Other supplies for arms came from Assinie and Grand Bassam in Ivory Coast, and from Liberia. At the same time the Mandingo king negotiated with the French. In 1886 the two sides recognized Samory's state on the south of the Niger, with the implication that French influence would prevail on the north side. This agreement was followed by one in 1887 when the king agreed to abandon the gold of Bouré to the French and, according to them, he accepted French protection. Samory, of course, did not have that interpretation. The follow-up was a treaty in

1889 reaffirming the Niger as the border. Both sides bought time through these negotiations. Samory concentrated his efforts on attacking a neighbor, Tieba, who, the king discovered, was receiving French aid. The Mandingo thus declared the treaties with the French broken. But Samory did not defeat Tieba, whom the French won as an ally.

In 1890 Samory signed with a British commissioner a treaty promising not to grant territory to another power except with British approval. The king was desperately trying to balance the power relationships with himself, the British, and French, but time had run out. London had decided to accept the French versions of the treaties and to accede to partition of Samory's territory. It only remained for the French to give practical value to their claims. They finally decided that the elusive hit-and-run, burn-and-retreat tactics of Samory required massive encirclement. Troops from its neighboring colonies participated in this scheme, which in 1898 resulted in the defeat of Samory's forces after nearly twenty years of intermittent war—one of the most determined and dramatic examples of African struggles to maintain freedom from European domination.

As a military commander, Samory was one of the greatest. His alternation between negotiation and war, his all-out warfare and guerrilla tactics made him feared by all who were threatened by his infantry and cavalry. As his supply of arms was gradually cut off by both the more effective European observance of the Brussels Convention (for arms control) of 1890 and by the later French encirclement, the Mandingo king increasingly relied on his own firearms industry where hundreds of blacksmiths regularly manufactured guns and cartridges. But in the end, Samory's struggle to maintain independence was incompatible with superior firepower and the determination of the French to subjugate his state. He was thus captured in 1898 and deported to an island off the coast of Gabon where he died in 1900. But the memory of his state-

building efforts and resistance to European domination continued and fired the movement of later nationalists.

Alpha Yaya and the Fula of Futa Jallon

Resistance to the establishment of French colonial rule in Futa
Jallon came in the form of protests and unsuccessful plots,
mainly from Alpha Yaya, whose rise to power in Labé province
coincided with the determined penetration of the French into Futa
Jallon. The extent to which the Labé ruler supported the establishment of the French headquarters in Guinea in 1891 is not
clear; by 1896, however, his position ostensibly was indeed pro-
French. In that year he wrote the French governor promising his
support as a friend of the French and recognized his dependence
on the governor. It was because of this pro-French stance that
Yaya's son proclaimed his father dethroned and led an army
against him. However, loyal forces rallied behind Yaya, who
defeated and killed his son in battle. Yaya then proceeded to
launch attacks against other rulers in Futa Jallon and received the
praise of the French, who rewarded him with the title of permanent chief of an enlarged Labé province and granted him personal
access to the provincial headquarters at Timbo. Thus, at least up
to 1897 when the treaty of protection was signed between the
French and the king (almamy) of Futa, Alpha Yaya seemed
aligned with the French.

Although Yaya did cultivate a close relationship with the
French he did not long submit to their authority, which indicates
that he sought their support of his own interest for power. Until
1904 there was little conflict between him and the colonial
administration, but after that time he and the French administrator quarreled over tax collection, from which Yaya received a
commission. The administrator accused the Labé ruler of falsely
reporting taxes. Another source of grievance was the extent of

Yaya's political autonomy. The Labé ruler interpreted his power as permanent ruler to include the appointment of subordinate rulers, but a French regulation of 1898 required that all appointments be approved by the administrator. The refusal of Yaya to accept this procedure led him to take an openly hostile stance against the French. Finally, when the colonial administration transferred part of the Labé district to Portuguese Guinea without consulting Yaya, the latter began plans for violent resistance. The Labé ruler began stockpiling arms and dispatching emissaries throughout the region to intensify anti-French sentiment. Before the scheme could be executed, however, the French arrested Yaya, relieved him of his title, and deported him. This was possible because the Labé ruler had made several enemies among the Fula, and the French had cultivated good relations with some of them, who, after Yaya's arrest, were appointed administrators over a partitioned Labé province.

While imprisoned in Dahomey, Alpha Yaya maintained contact with loyal followers in Labé. Consequently, when he was released in 1910, several of his supporters organized celebrations throughout Futa Jallon and neighboring areas in Portuguese Guinea. In order to minimize Yaya's political influence, the French made him promise not to engage in any political or administrative activities, in exchange for an annual subsidy. Alpha Yaya accepted those terms but continued to carry out clandestine activities for the liberation of his people. He developed contacts and acquired arms in Sierra Leone. But again, an African spy in the employ of the French informed the administration of Yaya's plans. The result was a second arrest and deportation in 1911.

Although Alpha Yaya's plans never materialized, rumors of them struck fear among the French, who intensified their efforts to cultivate collaborators in Futa. In addition, the colonial administration sought to meet some of the more general complaints—the lack of schools, jobs, and reform of police treatment. In this context, therefore, Yaya's threats of violence brought some immediate results. And in the long run he became a symbol of pride and a hero of Guinean nationalists, who interpret his actions as a means of freeing his people from French rule.

The Ethiopians

The best example of an African state consolidation and modernization during the nineteenth century is Ethiopia. Emperors Theodore II and Yohannes IV laid the foundation for modern Ethiopia, and Emperor Menelik II became its immediate founder. Menelik was king of Shoa for twenty-four years and in 1889 became emperor of the whole country. He proceeded to reconquer several provinces and to establish control over others. He founded his capital at Addis Ababa.

This occurred after the opening of the Suez Canal, the British occupation of Egypt, the rise of the Mahdi and his war with the British in the Sudan, and during the period of the Berlin Conference; all of which made Ethiopia strategically important in the calculations of the major European powers, which sent diplomatic representatives to Addis Ababa.

In order not only to resist European conquest but also to establish his country's viability and dominance over neighboring areas, Menelik employed both military power and shrewd diplomacy in playing off the powers against one another. He received weapons and duty-free privileges at the port of Massawa from the Italians, who had established themselves at Assab on the Red Sea coast and expected Menelik to accept a protectorate over Ethiopia; he received similar privileges from the French at Djibuti as a means of offsetting the Italians; and he duplicated the process with the English to counter the other powers and maintain influence for negotiations over the Blue Nile. Indeed, Menelik capitalized on these diplomatic rivalries by importing large quantities of weapons, mainly from France but also from Russia. In short, it was a scramble in northeast Africa.

Italy had formed a colony in Eritrea and anticipated bringing Ethiopia within its sphere of influence. In 1889 Ethiopia and Italy negotiated a treaty of peace and friendship, the Treaty of Uccialli. The Amharic text stated that the emperor could use Italy's services in relations with foreign powers. The Italian text made it compulsory that the emperor conduct his diplomatic affairs through Italy, which therefore claimed a protectorate over the African country. While these differences were under discussion the Italians were advancing into northern Ethiopia. Menelik thus realized that he had to fight to preserve his country's independence. The confrontation occurred at Adowa on March 1, 1896, when the Ethiopians defeated the Italians in the first major African victory over a European country since Hannibal's time two thousand years earlier.

Italy thus temporarily abandoned its claim of a protectorate, and Ethiopia's position as a power was enhanced in the eyes of the world. Menelik had used European technology and trade both to help unify his country and to defeat European encroachment. He is credited with the establishment of a national currency, a mint, and a bank; the development of a postal service; the installation of telegraph and telephone systems; the introduction of a national newspaper and printing press; the construction of the Djibuti–Addis Ababa railroad by the French. Menelik also inaugurated a modern system of education in 1908, thereby paving the way for the emergence of a strong core of Western nationalist elite.

Ethiopia's prestige was on the ascendancy not only among the powers of the world but also among descendant Africans abroad who saw the country as a symbol of African achievement and a source of inspiration for the redemption of black people throughout the world.

The Maji Maji

World trade played a significant role in change in East Africa. On the Tanganyika coast the Omani Arabs had established control by the 1840s and commercial ventures expanded deeper and deeper into the interior. Insofar as a centralization of political power was concerned, the locus was in Zanzibar, but this was gradually undermined by the British through their abolitionist treaties. Although there was not much unity among the coastal Africans, they did periodically cooperate to resist Omani authority. When the Germans declared the protectorate, immediate resistance was minimal. In 1888, however, an Arab, Bushiri bin Salim, who opposed the sultan at Zanzibar, and an African, Bwana Heri, organized a force that defeated a German unit in 1889. This revolt was aimed at both the Germans and their Omani collaborators. The uprising, however, did not spread. The Germans negotiated peace and employed Arabs and Swahilis as government administrators. Progressively the Germans continued their occupation by pushing farther inland. Here they met the Hehe under Mkwawa. The Hehe state had emerged in the 1840s to resist the Ngoni invaders and had continued to unify the several clans. Mkwawa's forces attacked and killed some Germans in 1891, and the Germans retaliated and captured the Hehe capital in 1894. An uneasy peace followed, as rumors of revolt continued in 1905, when the big uprising—the Maji Maji—came in Matumba Hills, northeast of Kilwa, and spread to the coast, the Rufiji Valley, the Kilombero Valley, and to Lake Nyasa. While guerrilla action was sometimes fierce, the Germans finally defeated the uprising, and by 1907 the war was over.

The reasons for the outbreak seem similar to other rebellions: taxation, forced labor, brutality, insult, a general loss of freedom, and disrespect for European rule. What made the Maji Maji so important was that it incorporated traditional religion to support an ideology of solidarity and resistance. The belief in the Kolelo faith was widespread, with shrines scattered throughout the Rufiji Valley. Consequently, religious leaders were able to build on the faith. In addition, unity was assisted by an appeal to blackness: "Be not afraid, Kolelo spares his black children." In this way, Africans could unite against Europeans or whites.

The belief that a water-medicine—maji, from which the rebellion got its name—would prevent injury from bullets or spears provided a continuity in traditional beliefs and implanted an idea similar to that of the master-race concept. Psychologically, these ideas were effective as a pan-Africanist movement that engulfed people of several ethnic and geographical areas. The realization of the need and the efforts for unity are the legacy of the Maji Maji in Tanganyika. Although the revolt failed, German officials were so impressed by it that reform of colonial policies followed (see chapter 13), once again showing that African activities affected European rule. The outbreak remained as a symbol of resistance to colonial rule and nascent unity of purpose among diverse peoples.

The Zulu

When Dingane was defeated by one of Shaka's brothers, Mpande, in 1840, he fled to Sobhuza's country where he was executed. Mpande maintained cordial relations with both Englishmen and Boers, and many Zulus migrated to Natal where they worked for Europeans. In 1873 Mpande was succeeded by Cetewayo, under whom the Zulu reemerged as a powerful force in Southern Africa. Although Cetewayo, like his predecessors, wanted to avoid conflicts with the white settlers, this proved impossible because the latter were still determined both to acquire the Zulu's good grazing lands and to eliminate any African threat to European hegemony. Thus in January, 1879, a British regiment marched into Zululand, but Cetewayo's forces stood firm and destroyed the regiment at Isandhlwana. But that was the last great victory of the Zulus. Six months later the British won a decisive victory over the Zulus and deported Cetewayo. This marked the end of the Zulu kingdom. Dinizulu, Cetewayo's son, was placed on the throne of part of the kingdom; another part was annexed to Transvaal. Then in 1887 the remainder was annexed to the crown. The last great Zulu rebellion broke out in Natal in 1906, but it too was suppressed. The conclusion of the Boer War assured white rule for a time, but Shaka and his successors had created a sense of pride and identity that continue.

The Shona and Ndebele

Throughout much of the nineteenth century Zulu immigrants from southern Africa settled among the Shona cultivators in the area of Zimbabwe. Among them were the Ndebele under Mzilikazi. Unlike the Shona, the Ndebele were not primarily farmers but depended largely on the raising and raiding of cattle. This made the Shona and other neighboring people vulnerable to the strong, militarily disciplined Ndebele under the supreme authority of their king, Mzilikazi, who was succeeded by Lobengula in 1868.

Both the Shona and Ndebele felt the persistent pressure of European penetration from the 1880s when the Portuguese dispatched expeditions into the area to negotiate treaties to be used as proof of "effective occupation." British pressures came from the south where the discovery of diamonds and gold accelerated a northward thrust in search of rich minerals and fertile land. Lobengula became especially concerned over these expeditions because he, unlike his enemies (Lewanika in Barotseland and Khama in Bechuanaland), did not seek British trade or protection against neighbors. Indeed, the Ndebele were strong enough to discourage attack by a neighboring African state and, not being primarily traders, did not seek commercial agreements.

Cecil Rhodes masterminded the British penetration under the cover of the British South Africa Company (BSAC). Although Lobengula played a delaying strategy, he was no match for Rhodes and the resources of the BSAC. The Ndebele king probably thought he had protected his prerogatives when he secured a verbal agreement that only up to ten Europeans would enter his country to work in the mines and that those miners would abide by Ndebele laws. This was only a verbal understanding, however; it was not included in a written agreement providing the mining concession. Thus, in 1890 the famed Pioneer Column of ninety men entered Mashonaland and was received by the Shona as temporary visitors. But an Ndebele raid on the Shona in 1893 was used by BSAC officials to organize an armed force, promising the men land and cattle. This led to the invasion of Matabeleland in October. The Ndebele assegai was no match for the machine gun; the Matabeleland kingdom was crushed, and Lobengula died in hiding in 1894.

The defeat of the Ndebele nation in 1893 resulted in great humiliation: The state was disrupted and the king lost, the cattle were confiscated and the land alienated. And there was no provision for a redress of grievances. This might well have spelled the end of the Ndebele threat to European rule, but the Ndebele had little to lose; they thus resumed their armed resistance in 1896. This uprising is noteworthy for two other reasons: It was a major attack on Europeans in the 1890s, and it resulted in a significant degree of African unity.

The Shona, who had regarded the European intruders in 1893 as temporary immigrants, realized by 1896 that their freedom was also curtailed. Shona rulers began to refuse and protest European demands for taxes and labor, but important as these grievances were, the Shona had to overcome their loose political organization, and effect unity. This was achieved by resorting to traditional religious beliefs, the Mwani belief system. This system had also spread among the Ndebele and provided a strong

potential for a united Shona-Ndebele front against white domination. Mwani represented a supreme power or force that manifested itself in natural phenomena like lightning. Shrines were
established and a priesthood spread the word and served as
guardians of the faith. This organization and political consciousness facilitated the development of resistance by the Shona and
Ndebele in 1896. But appeals to the past and slogans of African
invincibility were no match for the power of the European settlers, backed by South Africa and Britain. The rebellion was thus
crushed, but at a high cost in money and European and African
lives.

Although they lost the battle, the Ndebele improved their lot
over what had been the situation prior to the second uprising.
They reoccupied some of their land (though they did not receive
European title to it); some rebel leaders became salaried administrators, unlike before. These gains were small, to be sure, but
they were an improvement that helped to ease the lot of some
Ndebele and paved the way for acquiring skills to employ later
against colonial rule.

In the case of the Shona, the situation differed. They surren-
dered unconditionally, and many of their leaders were executed.
Largely leaderless, many Shona eventually went into missionary
work; some took menial jobs for whites; others migrated to
neighboring areas; and a few continued to resist. But although
European power had established itself, the African resistance was
not forgotten. The Europeans now knew they could not take the
Africans for granted; and the Africans remembered the European
oppression and the African leaders who became heroic resisters.

Chilembwe's Rebellion

European missionaries arrived in the Shire Highlands of
Nyasaland in 1876, a British protectorate was declared in 1889,

and around 1890 the Blantyre Mission of the Church of Scotland enrolled John Chilembwe, son of Yao and Cewa parents. A few years later he met Joseph Booth, a British missionary who criticized the treatment of Africans by European missionaries, preached equality, articulated the idea of Africa for the Africans and thus attracted a following among Africans, including Chilembwe. In 1897 Booth and Chilembwe planned an African Christian Union to encourage and develop education and economic opportunities for Africans, to secure a fair settlement of land disputes with Europeans, and to pursue an independent African Christianity. Later that year the two men visited England and the United States. Chilembwe remained in the United States and attended the Virginia Theological College and Seminary in Lynchburg.

'For about three years Chilembwe witnessed American life firsthand: He lived among American blacks and shared experiences of racial segregation, insult, and violence. He was in a position to observe, discuss, participate in, and assess the precarious situation of blacks in the United States at a time when African-Americans were being denied rights as citizens, when all branches of the government supported that denial, and when lynchings were at their peak.

Chilembwe could not have avoided consideration of Booker T. Washington's philosophy and practices of black self-help, DuBois's assertion of black pride and achievement, AME Bishop Henry M. Turner's constant emphasis on African culture and the possibilities of reunion. While it is impossible to determine the extent to which Chilembwe understood and was affected by these and other currents in the United States at the time, his position as a student and his contacts with African-Americans in various walks of life had to relate in some manner to those currents. Indeed, after his return to Nyasaland in 1900, Chilembwe was assisted by African-Americans in the opening of mission stations and schools. He often spoke favorably of his black "fellows" in the United States. Chilembwe was also favorably impressed by the work of the martyred American abolitionist John Brown, with whose raid he reportedly compared his own. But Chilembwe was also a student of the Bible and a preacher whose sermons frequently included examples of the Jews and their struggle for freedom.

These were all critical ingredients of the man who in 1915 led a group of Africans in a violent attack against Europeans in Nyasaland. Harsh treatment, discrimination, labor exploitation, and taxes by the Europeans were specific causes of the uprising; the general desire for freedom and dignity was the ultimate aim. An investigative commission later reported that Chilembwe sought to establish a state with himself as head. Others said he wanted to be king of Nyasaland, and some writers believe he only wanted to assert a physical protest to demonstrate pride and cause change. Chilembwe may even have sought the martyrdom of a John Brown. In any case, the rebellion was poorly planned, the insurgents poorly armed and disciplined. Within three days it was over, with three whites killed and two wounded. Chilembwe was shot, and forty of his supporters were later executed. In one sense, the rebellion was small scale; in another, its potential was great and thus struck fear among the settlers. Memory of the event remains, and Chilembwe is revered as a nationalist hero.

Conclusion

Many other examples could be examined: the Lozi's diplomatic efforts to ward off the British in Rhodesia, the forceful resistance of the Yao, Makua, Ovimbundu, and Chokwe against the British and Portuguese. Indeed, the Chokwe against the Belgians in Congo, the Ovimbundu against the Portuguese in Angola, and the Chikundu against the British in Rhodesia during the late nineteenth century had acquired sufficient quantities of arms to support fierce resistance. In some cases a number of ethnic groups formed alliances. The Lunda and the Chokwe in the Congo Free State and the Cuanhama and Cuamato in southern Angola are good examples. The latter repelled the Portuguese on several occasions up to 1915. African resistance to European penetration and control is long and impressive.

All of the European colonial powers confronted resistance from Africans, and in several cases the resistance was violent, long, and costly to both Africans and Europeans. That the two sides were willing to pay the price for their actions is some indication of the stakes involved. For the Europeans the stakes included economic gain and local and international political power. For Africans the stakes were nothing less than the preservation of their institutions and way of life, indeed, their freedom from European encroachment and control. Of all these cases of African resistance and rebellion against European aggression in the nineteenth and twentieth centuries (and not all cases are covered in this book), only the Ethiopians, with their unity and developing technology, were able successfully to forestall their European adversaries.

This has been a limited discussion of a few cases in which African initiatives in diplomacy and war had a significant long- and short-range impact on African lives, the lives of the European colonizers, and by extension, many Europeans in Europe, where decisions were made regarding investment in Africa, the import and export of goods to and from Africa, the dispatch of troops to meet military demands there, and the role of the colonies in overall diplomatic policy of the European countries. It is clear that once the European powers decided to establish their rule, the Africans were forced to react. Their actions were not always responses solely to the European factor, important though that was, but usually were part of such broader concerns as state- and nation-building. Thus, the question of collaboration or resistance is only a secondary issue, a question of means rather than objective. All the great African leaders—whether a Samory, Menelik,

Msiri, Nzinga, Lobengula, Alpha Yaya, Ja Ja, Khama, Shaka, Cetewayo, Lewanika, Behanzin, Lat Dor, or a host of others, known and unknown to outsiders—were guided by their assessment of what means best served African interests of survival, and in this sense contributed to the establishment of a heroic trend for future African freedom-fighters.

13

The European Colonizers: Policies and Practices

Historically, much of Africa has been the scene of a long series of migrations and invasions of foreigners from the Phoenicians, Greeks, Romans, Arabs, Indians, Turks, to the Western Europeans. Each group was attracted to the continent by self-interest: economic, political, military, prestige; and Africans to varying degrees accepted that presence. The influx of increasing numbers of European explorers, merchants, and missionaries brought a significant new tide of forces from Europe: industrial expansion and mercantilist concepts, abolitionist sentiments and projects of foreign missions, doctrines and practices of racial superiority, the fervor of European nationalism, and the dissemination of firearms. Such forces as these made the Western European presence ominous because it represented a greater potential power than any previous alien group, and appeared in numbers at a time when racism was popularized as "scientific" truth by reputable Western scholars and statesmen. In short, the inquiring explorer, the benevolent missionary, and the well-meaning merchant were all products of that European milieu and thus served as precursors of colonial rule.

The Berlin Conference of 1884–1885 legitimized the creeping European economic and political dominance in Africa and accelerated the shift from informal to formal involvement in African societies. This led to the drawing of artificial boundaries that more precisely defined areas claimed by European powers, but which also divided historically contiguous and closely related, sometimes kinship communities, and obstructed the normal historical thrust and continuity of African societies, whether in cultural developments, economic growth, or state-building.

No European power seems to have embarked on the partition and occupation of African territories with any fixed or preconceived monolithic policy. Only after territorial claims were made and resistance reasonably controlled did colonial policies begin to take shape. Three factors had great weight in determining the nature of those policies: (a) the prior colonial experience of the European power, (b) the state of the African society, (c) the assessment of local administrations in terms of politics and trade.

In terms of previous colonial experience, one must remember that Britain and France had already constructed colonial empires in Asia and the Americas before undertaking similar ventures in nineteenth-century Africa. Indeed, long before the Berlin Conference convened, some of the colonies in the Americas had rebelled and gained independence (the United States and Haiti for example). The two major imperial powers in Africa therefore had learned from their earlier colonial experiences and developed attitudes and policies they believed should apply in Africa.

French Policies

The French had developed a highly centralized system that was as bureaucratic and direct as any. During the nineteenth century the policy was dominated by the theory of assimilation that stemmed from the era of the Enlightenment and the French Revolution when the idea emerged that men were born free and equal. Those principles were extended to the French colonies and intermittently applied during the nineteenth century. In 1848 the French-inhabited settlements in Senegal were granted a seat in the Chamber of Deputies in Paris, and over the next three decades citizens of Saint-Louis, Gorée, Rufisque, and Dakar could elect their own councils. Although citizenship rights were primarily intended for the resident Frenchmen and mulattoes, they applied to all men born in those four towns or communes. It was not until 1914, however, that a Senegalese, Blaise Diagne, was elected to the Chamber of Deputies. While this experiment in Senegal was not seriously extended to other French colonies, except Algeria, until 1946, the idea of ultimate integration into French culture remained a distant possibility.

The French divided their colonies into two blocs: French West Africa under a governor-general and council with headquarters in the capital, Dakar, and French Equatorial Africa with a similar arrangement in the capital, Brazzaville. Each individual colony had a lieutenant governor and an appointed advisory council. This organizational structure facilitated a more centralized approach for governance and coordinated economic and military support, but it failed to take into account the diversities of peoples and structures contained therein. But colonial rule was not established primarily for considerations of Africans or their institutions.

The educational opportunities (the necessary means for assimilation) were designed for advancement within the French system, but these opportunities were extremely limited. French was the medium of instruction from the beginning, unlike the case in British territories where the vernacular was used in the lower grades. By 1920 only two lycées, both in Senegal, provided easy access to institutions of higher learning in France, and only a minority of Senegalese students were enrolled in these. Clearly, therefore, the French did not provide the means for achieving assimilation of the African into French society and culture. It should be recognized, however, that most Africans preferred their own culture anyway, including those who received French citizenship. This is illustrated by demands that led to the passage of a law of 1916 allowing Senegalese citizens of France to retain their Muslim private status if they chose. In effect, this law allowed for cultural duality in Senegal, a situation repugnant to many Frenchmen.

Both the British and French had to recognize the state of African societies over which colonial rule was established. This was more difficult for the French, whose highly centralized system was less flexible. However, the French did attempt, in some areas, a decentralized policy of indirect rule. After they captured Segu, French officers installed Mari-Diara, heir to the Bambara dynasty that Al Haj Omar had overthrown. It was hoped that this return to "legitimacy" would win local support. But within a few weeks the French executed Mari-Diara for alleged conspiracy and replaced him with a more willing subordinate, Bodian. The French explained to Segu rulers that a French resident would be appointed to help maintain order by providing advice and military support to the Bambara ruler, who was prohibited from making war or entering diplomatic relations without the resident's approval. Bodian could collect taxes but he had to share them with the French. Otherwise, he was reasonably free to govern his area without French interference.

Another situation involved the Mossi, one of the societies whose basic social and political structure survived until well into the twentieth century. In 1905, the French supported Saidou Congo, a member of a traditional dynasty among the Mossi. Although the Mossi electoral council opposed Saidou because of his youth and immaturity, the French secured his election through bribes because they believed they could easily control him. Backed by the French, Saidou had a measure of internal power, except that the French policies regarding taxation, labor supply, and the military were not negotiable. Again, in Futa Jallon the French supported Alpha Yaya as permanent ruler of Labé province. Yaya had some local autonomy but no power over taxes, the military, or foreign affairs. When Yaya sought to install a subordinate, the French intervened, installed their own candidate, and subsequently removed Alpha Yaya. These examples characterized much of French rule, showing a great proclivity for interference in local affairs even of bureaucratic societies.

Mariage à la mode du pays was practiced by colonial officials of the several powers, but France gave it official sanction. The French *Practical Guide for the European in West Africa* (1902) recommended temporary unions "with a well-chosen native woman." Two of the justifications for this policy were to assure a medically approved female who would be faithful, and to help cement relations with Africans. After completing a tour of duty the French official sent his African mistress back to her family, realizing that "former wives of Europeans are in great demand among the Negroes." Nothing more dramatically illustrates the contemptible disregard for African women and culture. Again, the French were not alone in this behavior, but they publicized official sanction of it.

Another distinctive characteristic of French rule was the *indigenat,* a system introduced in 1887 and modified in 1888 and 1924, whereby a commandant could summarily punish Africans for certain offenses, such as refusal to pay taxes or to do public work, disrespect for French authority, or giving refuge to offenders. No trial was necessary, there was no appeal, and the victim, immediately after serving one sentence, could be punished for another offense. In addition, while serving a sentence, the African could be required to do public work, thereby providing a source of bonded labor for the administration. The *indigenat* did not, of course, apply to French citizens, black or white. And in 1924 various exemptions were announced: veterans, some "chiefs," some merchants, and employers of the administration.

The French also placed particular emphasis on enlisting Africans in their armed forces for duty throughout the empire. In 1857 General Louis Faidherbe organized a standing force drawn from among Senegalese, and in time recruitment brought African soldiers from various parts of the Sudan. Many recruits were liberated slaves beholden to the French for their freedom. The force, known as *Tirailleurs*, greatly strengthened the French position not only as a fighting force but also as a politically divisive unit whose knowledge of local languages and customs, political organization, and geography became crucial to colonial officials. By the 1880s the *Tirailleurs* had become a well-trained and -armed unit under French officers (there were a few African junior officers); in time, the force distinguished itself not only in victories over African resistance, but in French battles overseas.

While French policy was generally characterized by a high degree of centralization, there clearly were deviations that took into account variations in African societies. The French obviously failed, for various reasons already mentioned, to adhere to their policy of assimilation, but one should note that such a policy was in fact an arrogant reflection of French assumptions of black inferiority and their commitment to "civilize" an elite above the masses. The direct and disruptive results of this divisive policy remain embedded in many continuing conflicts in French-speaking Africa.

British Policies

Britain, which had already developed a decentralized colonial policy leading to the commonwealth of nations, never envisioned African assimilation into British culture and institutions as black Englishmen. Not even the European settlers in America were granted seats in the British parliament. It was more natural, therefore, for the British to adjust, within limits, of course, to the state of African societies. Because of their greater flexibility, British policies varied more markedly than other powers' policies.

The kingdom of Buganda in East Africa and the emirates of Nigeria in West Africa provide the British models of indirect rule. British merchants were attracted by the resources and trade of Buganda. In addition, Protestant and Catholic missionaries at the kabaka's court had witnessed the effective bureaucracy at Buganda; the missionaries also had cultivated some European influence. Indeed, the competition of Christian factions, Protestant and Catholic, on the one hand, and both against Muslims, weakened the authority of the kabaka, who vacillated from one side to the other in attempting to maintain power and reap the commercial benefits the religious factions attracted to the kingdom. It was into this state of affairs that British authority penetrated in the 1890s. After military engagements, British officials succeeded in reducing the kabaka's authority, and in 1894 declared a protectorate over Buganda. In the Agreement of 1900, therefore, the kabaka undertook to collect taxes for the colonial administration in exchange for the continuation of the traditional ruling hierarchy, which was subject to ultimate colonial authority. Land was divided between the British crown and several thousand Buganda rulers. Thereafter, the British laid down general policy, while the day-to-day regulations remained with Buganda. This model was gradually extended, with Buganda assistance as officials to other areas—Bunyoro, Toro, Ankole, Busoga, and others—comprising what became the Uganda Protectorate.

In West Africa the British model for indirect rule was northern Nigeria. The extension of British power over that area was largely the work of the Royal Niger Company formed by George Goldie. Two French companies, the Compagnie Française de l'Afrique Equatoriale and the Compagnie du Sénégal et la Côté Occidentale de l'Afrique, were competitors along the Niger, but the stronger financial backing of the National African Company (predecessor of the Royal Niger Company) forced both French firms out by 1885. Goldie pressed for a government charter while also negotiating treaties, which formed the basis for British claims at the Berlin Conference. In 1886 the British government granted Goldie a charter, which launched the company as a spearhead of colonial rule. By the charter the Royal Niger Company was authorized to administer justice, to maintain order, and to levy taxes. The company was forbidden to interfere with African laws and customs (an impossibility in terms of the authorities mentioned above); it was also prohibited from establishing a commercial monopoly.

The company failed to honor its charge of maintaining free trade. Not only were German and French merchants eliminated, African traders were harassed and forced to pay taxes on their long-established trade. This led to an attack on the company by merchants of Brass in 1895. In 1897 the Fulani of Ilorin and Nupe fought the company. Because of the African attacks and the threats of battles with the French in Dahomey and the Germans in the Cameroons, the British government in 1897 organized the West Africa Frontier Force of African conscripts, and three years later, the British assumed control over the region and appointed Frederick Lugard to formulate the administrative policy for the region. The result was indirect rule.

A new emir was enthroned at Sokoto, but the Muslim courts and bureaucracy continued to function. A British resident, supported by troops, was appointed to advise the emirs on pursuing colonial regulations. Since the Fulani had already established a bureaucracy, the British had only to secure the cooperation of the emir in much the same way as was the case with the kabaka of Buganda. The assurance of his rule and economic benefits won his support. By agreeing not to interfere with the Muslim culture, the British thus isolated the area from European settlers, and, for that matter, greatly minimized the presence of British officials. While this seemed to be an African advantage at the time, such a policy had the effect of greatly restricting meaningful relations

with the southern provinces of Nigeria where European education, trade, and religion accelerated change and set in motion
several developments in social and political life that led to self-
government. The unification of Nigeria in 1914 did not change
that situation.

The British did not always support strong rulers. The experiences of Ja Ja in the Niger delta provide an example in which an
African leader attempted to cooperate in commerce with the
British, but within the context of freedom for his people. Ja Ja, by
1870, had emerged as head of the "house," or trading association,
in Bonny, but subsequent fighting forced him to flee with his supporters to Opobo where he founded a new trading settlement.
Through skillful diplomacy he succeeded in having the area's
palm oil flow through Opobo. He thus won the respect of British
merchants who hoped to benefit from his policies.

When, in 1885, the British declared a protectorate over the
lower Niger and Oil Rivers, Ja Ja questioned the meaning of a
"protectorate," and refused to accept provisions for free trade.
Because of his influence and good relations with British merchants, these provisions were not included in the treaty Ja Ja
signed. Inevitably, however, the British consul interpreted the
protectorate as including the aim of developing trade on British
terms, while Ja Ja insisted on maintaining his monopoly. In order
to retaliate, several British firms organized the African Association and decided to pay less for Opobo's oil. When Ja Ja induced
one firm to accept his terms, the die was cast. Invited to visit the
consul, Ja Ja was arrested and deported, and direct rule was
applied.

Although direct rule in Africa is generally associated with the
French, the state of several African societies caused Britain to
resort to a more direct policy. This occurred in Iboland, where
neither a strong central ruler nor a centralized bureaucracy
existed. Even the British-established rulers could not control the
individualistic tradition embodied in the Ibo town or village

councils. Colonial administration thus took the form of direct rule by British officials.

Kenya provides an example of both direct administration and the influence of white and Indian settlers. Located just next to Uganda, Kenya was traversed to reach Buganda. Between Buganda and the coast lived the Luo, Masai, Nandi, Somali, Turkana, Kamba, and Kikuyu, who were organized primarily along kinship lines and came to be regarded, like the Ibo, as stateless societies. When in 1895 the British declared the protectorate (the East African Protectorate, later Kenya), the imposition of Western laws, collection of taxes, recruitment of labor, and many other necessary components of the colonial administration required the formation of a central bureaucracy. The British thus appointed officials whose success depended on their direct involvement in African states.

The key to the successful extension of British rule over Kenya was the policy toward the Masai, whose power in the interior could have seriously obstructed British penetration toward Uganda. But the Masai were preoccupied with raids, epidemics, and famine, the latter two providing an opportunity for British assistance, which impressed the Masai. In addition, British firepower also impressed the Masai. The British, moreover, were not yet prepared to force the issue of control because of limited personnel, funds, and the havoc Masai raids could cause on the construction of the Uganda railroad. Both sides therefore saw gains in cooperation.

The highlands of Kenya, like those in central and southern Africa, led to deliberate colonization schemes in which the British supported the apportionment of land to white settlers, the recruitment of cheap African labor, and blatant racial discrimination. As farmers and herders, the Africans suffered greatly from land alienation, which reduced their subsistence agriculture and forced them to work that land or in the urban areas for Europeans. In this situation British policy favored white settlers, who eventually came to regard Kenya as the "white man's country," as was the case in South Africa and Zimbabwe (Rhodesia).

In addition to the European settlers, the position of the Indians posed a great problem after the completion of the railroad in 1901. Some Indians had helped to build the railroad; many others accompanied the construction as traders. Indian troops were also used by Britain to suppress African rebellions. European and Indian settlements were encouraged by the British commissioner until about 1902 when the European settlers forced him to reverse the practice for Indians. But Indians in Kenya, and also in Tanganyika, began to have visions of an Indian empire in Africa.

In 1910 A. M. Jeevanjee, an Indian in Kenya, advocated annexing the territory to India; in 1919 Indians meeting in Nairobi passed resolutions calling for the colonization of German East Africa by Indians. Support by Indians came from Tanganyika and England, and in 1921 an Indian publication in Kenya foresaw Indian administration of the territory. These, of course, were only dreams. The European settlers not only resisted that pressure but demanded and received a greater measure of local rule, the reservation of the highlands as settlement areas for whites, ordinances for contract African labor, and segregation of public facilities.

Direct rule in Kenya therefore was characterized by a growing number of European settlers who asserted their influence for advantages from London. As they won those advantages, their local power increased, thereby greatly alienating them from the Africans, forcing the Indians into middle ground locally, and causing British policy to become a vain attempt to balance all groups to maintain stability and control.

The central African colonies of Northern Rhodesia (Zambia), Southern Rhodesia (Zimbabwe), and Nyasaland (Malawi) were affected by two powerful European influences, British and white South African. Missionaries in the area during the nineteenth century had sought British government support to abolish the slave trade, to limit the Arab influence, and to protect missionary interests. When Lord Salisbury appeared doubtful, Cecil Rhodes offered to pay for the administration of the territories. With this incentive Britain declared a protectorate over the Shire Highlands of Nyasaland in 1889. Rhodes, under the cover of the British South Africa Company, spearheaded British advancement into the Rhodesias in 1890. Of the three colonies, the largest number of whites settled in Southern Rhodesia where they received representation on the legislative council as early as 1898. Largely because of that and the fact that the British South Africa Company had promised that self-government would come to the settlers, Britain, when it assumed control from the company in 1923, granted the colony internal self-government. But the smaller number of settlers in Northern Rhodesia preferred to become a crown colony with a legislative council, which in fact occurred in 1924. Nyasaland remained a protectorate.

Self-government in Southern Rhodesia provided the constitutional authority for white domination of blacks. African land was alienated, reserves were expanded, contract labor became common, and discriminatory legislation assured whites the better jobs and higher wages. Segregation in public accommodations also received legislative support. This approach was less stringent in Northern Rhodesia, where most whites were discouraged from settling because of malaria and the appearance of economic poverty. But during the 1920s better prospecting techniques revealed large quantities of copper ores. After the depression of the 1930s, production increased, and by 1945 Northern Rhodesia was one of the world's leading producers of copper. This development quite naturally attracted many white settlers who received the skilled jobs. It also attracted Africans, in the form of migrant labor, which was unskilled. Although the migrant labor was essentially short term, the settlers feared the possibility of emerging African communities, especially since the government neither included Africans nor provided them with suitable housing or other amenities of urban life. The situation was further aggravated by the fact that the migrants were single men, but after World War II mining companies increasingly provided accommodations for the families of migrants, though the quality was usually substandard.

The third colony, Nyasaland, lacked the economic incentives to attract many white settlers. While this did not promise much in the way of economic development, it did assure less racial friction in the colony, although Africans had no voice in the colonial administration. But migrants from Nyasaland did work in the Rhodesias and South Africa, and thereby gained a higher awareness of problems affecting themselves and others.

After 1945, federation became a major preoccupation of whites in central Africa. Settlers in Nyasaland and Northern Rhodesia wanted union to protect their small numbers against rising pressures for freedom by Africans in and outside the colony. Southern Rhodesian settlers favored union as a means of sharing the wealth of the northern copper mines, and as a step toward a broader-based white rule in central Africa. Many Britishers and settlers argued that federation would facilitate coordination of Southern Rhodesian skills and capital, Northern Rhodesia's copper, and Nyasaland's labor. Thus, over vigorous African protests, the British established in 1953 the Federation of Rhodesia and Nyasaland (Central African Federation). In the federal legislature Nyasaland and Northern Rhodesia received eighteen seats, while Southern Rhodesia received seventeen. Each territory elected two Africans and one European to represent African interests. This amounted to nine representatives for Africans (six blacks and three whites) and twenty-six for the settlers. This was indeed an ominous beginning: The settlers hoped the Federation would solidify settler control, while in fact it became a signal for more aggressive political action by Africans.

Although the British usually responded to African pressures and demands, there was never any question about ultimate power or the status of Europeans over Africans. So long as changes did not seriously threaten those prerogatives, the British could compromise; when the "winds of change" blew more intensely, British flexibility made accommodation more palatable.

Belgian Policy

Prior to World War I Belgium had only one colony in Africa, the Belgian Congo. Up to 1908 the Belgian Congo was known as the Congo Free State, and it was unique both in the way it originated and in its early administration. In 1876 the king of Belgium, Leopold II, launched the International Association, which negotiated the treaties that provided the basis for international recognition of the Congo at the Berlin Conference in 1884. Leopold II thus acquired not only a huge, rich piece of real estate, he was also invested with private sovereignty over the territory. The administration was direct, absolute, and worked closely with the Church and big business. Raymond Buell in his *Native Problem in Africa* noted in the 1920s that the density of administration in the Congo was unequaled in Africa, except for the minor cases of Mauritania and Dahomey. Indeed, most regions of the Congo Free State, rural and urban, felt colonial rule directly.

Leopold II believed that the colony should contribute directly to the interests of the imperial country. He therefore sought to extract maximum profits from the Congo, and instructed colonial officials to follow that policy. The state was declared proprietor of all lands not occupied or being exploited by the Africans. The result was that what became the territory's most valuable products, ivory and rubber, came from those "vacant" lands and could be collected only by the state. Compulsory cultivation and public work became common and led to great abuses of Africans. Local Belgian officials were charged with seeing that work was performed and harvests, mainly rubber, were collected. Because their position and pay depended on the quantities collected, the officials made harsh exactions from the Africans. To help achieve the desired results, varying degrees of force were applied: Hostages were taken, floggings were common, and military expeditions were launched. Africans were even mutilated and killed as punishment for falling short in crop collection.

In addition to state lands, concessions were granted to companies that received government permission to collect crops and taxes. Concessions were also granted for railroads and mining. The state, in exchange for concessions, received shares in the companies, and in several instances retired colonial officials assumed more lucrative positions with some of the companies. In short, the urge for profits and position by the officials and the overall philosophy of Leopold led to dehumanizing and extensive exploitation of Africans, especially those who inhabited the rich rubber areas.

Partly because of the Congo's rich endowment of resources, which were in great demand by the industrial European countries and the United States, and partly because of Leopold's belief that colonies existed for the benefit of the metropolitan country, Belgium benefited immensely from the Congo's economy. But the brutal means to that end became known internationally and created such great pressure that in 1908 Leopold was forced to transfer his personal rule over the Congo to the Belgian government, which meant that colonial policy became a prerogative of the constitutional monarchy and a minister of colonies. Obligatory cultivation for the state was abolished and other reforms were made.

On the missionary front the Congo was largely a Belgian preserve also. In 1906 a set of regulations laid the basis for cooperation between the administration and missionaries. Catholic mission schools and missionaries were subsidized, and land grants were made to the missions. Colonial administrators were expected to give full support to the missions. With this kind of support, non-Belgian missions obviously could not effectively compete.

After 1908 Belgian policy in the Congo was paternal. The government and the great concessionary companies, notably Union Minière du Haut Katanga and Huiteries du Congo Belge, concentrated on looking after the economic well-being of African workers. While the colonial economy rested primarily on wild rubber, ivory, and oil palm prior to World War I, by the 1920s large-scale mining in Katanga (copper and tin), Kasai (diamonds), Kivu and Orientale (gold) was becoming the key industry. Government and company accommodations for African families, while below that of the Europeans, were probably better than elsewhere in colonial Africa. Food, clothing, medical care, and other amenities were provided to maintain a satisfied labor force. Primary education was available, and secondary education was geared to training clerks, nurses, and others not destined for the liberal professions or university education, except priests. The theory was that this paternal approach would assure contented Africans, and the skewed educational system would prevent the rise of political activists who would agitate against black inequality. Segregated facilities were justified on cultural rather than racial grounds. This system prevailed with a minimum of violent resistance and a maximum of censorship of the communication media until the late 1950s.

German Policies

German colonial administration in Africa was highly centralized and carried out by a hierarchical bureaucracy of colonial officials responsible through the chancellor to the kaiser. Like the Belgians, English, and French, the Germans granted concessions to companies. There were, however, some variations in policy from one colony to another. This resulted mainly from African initiatives and responses as well as prior German interests in certain specific areas.

In South-West Africa (Namibia), for example, the long struggle for political supremacy between the Herero and Nama peoples made it easy for the Germans to play one against the other. In addition, the Berg-Damara (or Damaras) for many years confronted the pressures of white advance from the south as well as the stronger African groups, the Herero and Nama. In all of these cases the Germans met with resistance that sometimes caused them serious losses. Thus, mindful of their losses in battle with others, the Germans shied away from the Ovambo, known as well-armed and disciplined soldiers. Indeed, in 1906 the Germans forbade entry into Ovamboland, except on the governor's approval.

South-West Africa was not Germany's largest colony, but portions of it were suited for white settlement. However, those suitable areas were already inhabited by Africans. This fact led to the eviction of Africans for settlement on reserves so Europeans could acquire the better lands. This action not only deprived the Africans of pastures for their cattle and land for their subsistence, it also meant that they had to submit as laborers on many of the European farms. With the development of mining, labor recruitment became more critical, and Africans were forced to seek employment in European establishments. Then following the rebellions of 1906–1907, Africans were required to carry passes and forbidden to acquire land or animals without official permission. By that time the Africans were scattered, weak, and under the strong hand of the German conquerors.

Togo was small in size and had little accessible mineral wealth. These factors and the climate made Togo less attractive to European settlers. Thus, no great companies or plantations emerged there. The colony did produce palm oil, and Africans were encouraged to grow coffee, cocoa, cotton, coconuts, and corn. Except among the Fulani of the north, German officers and appointed African assistants directly supervised colonial affairs. African labor was conscripted for road building and other public works, and traditional laws were subordinated to German codes.

A similar policy obtained in Cameroon. In the northern region the Fulani were employed in the system of indirect rule, while more direct administration occurred in the south. Compulsory labor was practiced, with laborers being rounded up, shackled together, and marched to work for Europeans. Africans were also forced to collect wild rubber and transport ivory. The European cacao and rubber plantations and other cash crops encouraged the development of railroads and port facilities. Official German schools were established in Cameroon from 1886, and Christian missions with their schools were active in the south, while the northern section maintained its Muslim schools in somewhat the same way as the Muslims in northern Nigeria.

The German East Africa Company was responsible for the administration of German East Africa (Tanganyika) from 1885 to 1890, when the state assumed direct responsibility. There was physical resistance by the coastal people from the beginning, and it culminated in large-scale uprisings from 1905 to 1907. In addition to the general desire for freedom, the local inhabitants resented taxation, physical brutality, forced labor, and the exploitation of African women by some German officials. The German response to the rebellions was an attempt to redress grievances in all the colonies. But in Tanganyika the settlers, some of whom came from South Africa, resisted reform and continued to exploit the territory's human and material resources. Ivory remained important as an export. Plantations grew coffee, cotton, tea, tobacco, and sisal among other crops, and African labor was conscripted to work them.

In its East African colony the Germans made use of the *akida*, Swahili or Arab administrator, who helped to supervise colonial administration. Swahili thus became more widely disseminated and deeply entrenched as a vehicular language. In addition, newspapers and other tracts, secular and religious, appeared in Swahili. Indeed, missionaries, traders, and the colonial administration facilitated the development of Swahili as a language of the people of Tanganyika.

With its defeat during World War I, Germany lost its colonies, which became mandates technically under the Mandates Commission of the League of Nations. In fact, the colonial powers that occupied the German colonies during the war became mandatory powers and generally administered the mandates as if they were colonies. Britain and France shared Togo and Cameroon; South Africa received South-West Africa; Britain received Tanganyika; and Belgium received Burundi and Ruanda. While the Mandates Commission was charged with overseeing the administration of the mandates, it had no executive powers. It thus sought in vain to hold on-the-spot investigations, to hear oral petitions, and to require that mandatory powers submit regular annual reports. These powers were not assumed until after the Trusteeship Council was organized in 1945.

Portuguese Policy

The tenacity of Portugal's hold on colonies in Africa was remarkable. An impoverished country that lost Brazil in the nineteenth century, Portugal also lost to King Leopold's Congo Association at the Berlin Congress of 1884–1885, but it did retain its claims to Angola, Mozambique, a portion of Guinea, and some offshore islands. Whereas distance, lack of swift communications, lack of funds, and the slow growth of Portuguese settlements were great problems, the opening of the Suez Canal in 1869, the establishment of the telegraph cable in Mozambique in 1879, and the European discovery of gold and diamonds in southern Africa raised the economic prospects of Portugal's colonies and inspired a resurgence of national interest in them, and thus a greater concern for Portugal's administrative policy in Africa.

The Portuguese had regarded their rule as paternal, bringing civilization to Africans. But the means of extending their civilization followed a slavelike path. Into the twentieth century

Africans had no political rights, were sent "on contract" to sugar and cocoa plantations in São Thomé, in French Indian Ocean colonies, and in the mines of South Africa. Many Africans were required to collect rubber and could be leased to plantation managers. This, in effect, was a form of slavery and was criticized as such. However, during the 1930s, Portugal began to articulate and apply a more coherent policy that aroused greater interest in Portugal. The government began to emphasize the unity between the colonies and Portugal. This, of course, reemphasized the need for centralization and direct application of Portuguese customs and law. In theory, the new policy stressed the integration of the metropolis with the colonies and the assimilation of Africans in some distant future. Thus, Africans in Portuguese colonies were divided into assimilated and unassimilated categories. The former could hope to enjoy rights and privileges of Portuguese citizenship if they could speak and write Portuguese fluently, had become Christians, had sufficient income to support a family, received testimonials of good character, paid taxes, and remained loyal. Only a few Africans acquired that status—some fifty thousand of over seven million by 1950. The great majority of Africans were treated as children; they were frequently disciplined with a hippopotamus hide whip (the cikoti) and a wooden paddle (the palmatoria) with holes in it to raise welts. Portugal was a small and poor country, but its rule in colonial Africa was as strict and harsh as any, if not more so.

The Christian Factor

It was during the eighteenth century, when religious revivals in Europe appealed more to the masses, that the trend of establishing overseas missions began in earnest. Especially after the abolition of slavery in England and the mounting support for abolishing the slave trade, European evangelicals focused serious

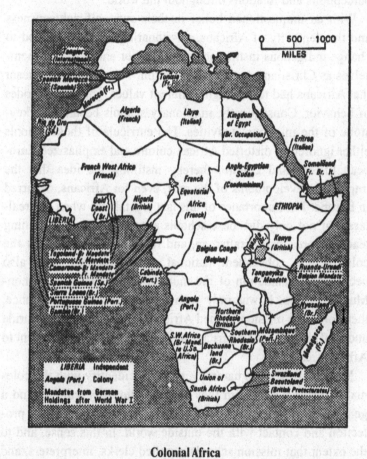

Colonial Africa

attention on Africa as a place for African repatriation and prose-lytization. This European initiative, emanating among people whose cultures historically demeaned things African, had a deci-sive impact not only on Africa and Africans but on black-white perceptions and relations throughout the world.

With an unquestioned belief in their own self-righteousness and the depravity of Africans, missionaries were determined to change indigenous institutions and behavior and thus saw them-selves as Christian agents of civilization. This conclusion meant that Africans had to be taught different values, goals, and modes of behavior. Consequently, missionary schools became the key-stone of the missions' activities. The curricula of those schools either ignored or distorted African culture and emphasized Euro-pean history and culture, thereby instilling the idea that the important developments of the past, even for Africans, occurred in Europe. The importance of this fact crystallizes when one real-izes that not only did these schools assume the task of training teachers, preachers, craftsmen, and future civil servants for the colonial and subsequent national administrations, they also became the foundation of the modern schools in most of non-Muslim Africa. It was only with the greatest of perseverance, therefore, that mission-trained Africans retained a sense of pride and confidence in their heritage and people, and a commitment to African freedom.

Missionaries, quite naturally, tended to identify with the colo-nial officials with whom they shared nationality, culture, and a general way of life, and on whom they frequently relied for pro-tection and contact with the outside world. In this sense, and to the extent that mission schools supplied clerks, interpreters, and others for the government, missionaries often became allies of the colonial administrations. And in at least two instances missionar-ies became directly involved in the extension of colonial control: Bishop Tucker of Uganda helped to induce Britain to declare a protectorate over that territory, and François Coillard played an active role leading to the British protectorate over Barotseland in today's Zambia. However, given the fact of colonial rule, missionaries within that context often sought to limit administrative oppression. Their vigorous campaign against atrocities in the Congo led to the transfer of that territory from Leopold II to the more responsible Belgian government; they criticized the exploitation of African labor (especially in the Congo, Rhodesia, South Africa, Mozambique, and Angola); they often voiced opposition to the imposition of heavy taxes. And in several colonies missionaries were appointed to legislative councils and became unofficial voices of African discontent, short of advocating freedom.

Missionaries established hospitals, clinics, health centers, refugee camps; they studied and provided curative and preventive medicines for tropical diseases; they studied and supplied a script for several African languages; they encouraged the development of legitimate trade to replace the slave trade; and a few of them provided useful accounts of African life. It should be stressed, however, that African assistants contributed to each of these endeavors, though they received little credit in the records.

Had the missionaries not gone to Africa as a censor, not sought a deliberate destruction of African values and customs, not attempted to teach the worthlessness of the African past, not supported white superiority, all of their contributions would have had greater meaning and would have led to more positive race relations. As it turned out, however, from about the last decade of the nineteenth century, some mission-trained Africans began to demand greater religious responsibilities for themselves, a greater respect for African culture (music, dance, language, beliefs, customs), and racial equality. These concerns launched the independent church movements whose objective was to develop separate African churches that would be Christian while identifying with African cultural and physical needs. These churches are found in most of the countries where Christianity was established. The two largest and best known are perhaps the

Kimbanguists in the Congo and the Lenshina sect in Zambia and environs.

While the independent churches vary considerably among themselves (some of them are very similar to the mission churches), they are alike in their independence from white control. In this sense they represent a dimension of the African liberation movements. The independent churches also established programs of self-improvement and the reaffirmation of African values. They also unified diverse ethnic groups; unlike the traditional mission churches, the independent ones sought converts among those persons previously unsought or denied the Christian faith because of deep attachment to ethnic behavior. In sum, the Christian factor in Africa, with few exceptions, is becoming Africanized even in the mission churches, and has responded more positively to the nationalist movements. Christianity has thus entered a new, more African-centric stage in African developments.

Colonial Economies

The demography of Africa suffered immensely, though unevenly, as a result of the slave trade in several areas of the continent. In addition to the global redistribution of Africa's population, the trade also led to a population redistribution within and between regions of the continent itself. In addition to the involuntary displacement of people, there were migrations of voluntary laborers, farmers, and traders seeking stability and employment as economies were being transformed to legitimate export trade. The increased immigration of Europeans and Asians as merchants, missionaries, and government officials during this period of instability and transformation added to those uncertain times.

The colonial state, often through chartered companies, played an important role in establishing European-controlled farming, both by trying to eliminate African competition and by providing settlers with extensive support. Taxation and rents as well as discriminatory practices in general were designed to reduce African self-sufficiency and competition in agriculture and trade.

The situation in North Africa was somewhat different. Nineteenth-century European bondholders and creditors were the leading forces behind the colonial conquest and occupation of that region. North African governments sought to modernize their armies and economies in order to safeguard their political autonomy and satisfy the needs of Europeans for markets, sources of raw materials, and outlets for investments and European settlement. Essentially these demands by Europeans led to local and national broad-based organizations that eventually galvanized into nationalist movements.

There obviously was great diversity in African economies, from the less complex village communities to more complex political systems. In addition, economic development was tied to patterns of rainfall and drought, soil types, crop disease, and other ecological changes, and as the export trade expanded, African economies became more and more monocultured with less emphasis on the food sector, with drastic consequences for the future. Trade swelled, the money economy became dominant, credit institutions grew, and transport systems developed. But this development was uneven and inequitable. The slave trade had weakened African societies demographically, economically, socially, and politically while strengthening western European countries in the reverse. The slave trade thus paved the way for colonial rule.

Conclusion

The establishment of European colonial rule in Africa placed ultimate power in the hands of aliens who came from a cultural background that traditionally had denigrated African people. Thus the dominant long-range force became the colonial state that emphasized modern forms of economic development and bureaucratic rule. Indigenous political and economic structures lost their legitimacy and authority.

Although colonial policies differed, all colonial administrations pursued efforts for economic self-sufficiency to make the colonies "pay their way." These efforts included pressure and force to establish an economy based on cash crops and mineral extraction. African economies thus became export-oriented, largely dependent on a single product (rubber for Liberia, cocoa for the Gold Coast, peanuts for Senegal, copper for Zambia and Katanga, etc.), with ultimate dependence on the colonial power.

Colonial authorities developed infrastructures to serve exports: roads and railroads from plantations and mines to coastal harbors, and storage and shipping facilities. These activities not only provided employment for Africans but stimulated urban growth. Consequently, rural-to-urban migration accelerated, and caused a greater need for social services and employment, increased the demand for Western products, promoted individualism, and increased pressure on the African extended family, marriage, religion, sex roles, etc. And the European presence in those urban areas heightened racial sensitivities and conflicts.

African women suffered special colonial oppression because they were both African and female. Many of them were sexually exploited, and all of them were victimized by colonial regulations and practices that entrenched male dominance. Not that women were equal partners prior to colonial Africa, for they were not in general either in indigenous or Islamic societies; however, there were notable exceptions. Queens, female chiefs and spiritual leaders with political influence, village councillors, and so forth existed in a number of pre-colonial societies. Moreover, women were prominent in pre-colonial economies as market women and producers of specialized crops. But colonial administrators sought men for bureaucratic positions, which provided the base for political and economic power after independence. In addition, higher education, though limited, was restricted generally for males. And as new forms of technology were introduced (tractors and typewriters, for example) men became the primary beneficiaries of these skills.

Issues of race, culture, class, and gender were thus exacerbated by the colonial experience in Africa and would remain major challenges during nationalist struggles and independence.

14

The Struggle for Independence

By 1920 colonial control was pretty well established in Africa. The Chilembwe uprising, in a sense, marked the end of an era, for increasingly after World War I many Africans diverted their energies to working within the colonial context. They accepted European domination as a temporary situation from which they could acquire certain skills needed to survive and to advance their societies. Europeans interpreted this reprieve as indicative of their superiority and testimony to the righteousness of their cause to "civilize" Africans. Officials of the colonial powers thus proceeded to strengthen their contacts with African rulers, merchants, and the mission-trained by involving them in the administration. All the colonial powers sought Africans to assist in local government. Many traditional rulers accepted judicial, police, financial, and public works responsibilities, which were performed with varying degrees of autonomy. This led to a gradual, sometimes unconscious transformation of traditional rulers into de facto civil servants. Those new responsibilities (1) provided a means for acquiring a knowledge of how the colonial system worked and how it might be used to advantage for Africans; (2) facilitated the development of political and economic links with influential Europeans who aided in the growth of educational and political institutions; (3) enabled Africans, especially rulers, to share the wealth, however disproportionately, through government grants, tax commissions, salaries, and commercial arrangements.

Reliance on indigenous participation in the colonial administrations meant that the governments had to train Africans for a variety of tasks. Largely because of their longer presence in the territories and because governments sought to economize, missionary schools played a major role in training not only catechists, but also teachers, medical assistants, craftsmen, interpreters, translators, and clerks. These trained personnel were obviously vital to colonial administrations. Britain during the early days of colonial rule subsidized mission schools and gradually increased expenditures on education generally. The French devoted more attention to government schools, which developed alongside mission schools. The Dakar Medical School, Lycée Faidherbe, and William Ponty Normal School were key institutions the French established in Senegal between 1910 and 1920. By 1940 government schools operated in several of the French colonies. Both Belgium and Portugal gave a privileged position to the Roman Catholic mission schools through special subsidies and official statements of support. In addition, a sizable number of Africans received a university education in British and French universities, and a few were trained in Belgium, mostly in religion. In these ways the colonial government created a class of evolués from which were drawn African personnel for administrative work. It was largely from this group of Africans that the core of the emergent nationalist elite appeared.

The nationalist elite also included members from labor groups, whose history may extend back to a strike in Freetown in 1874. A clearer case for unionization, however, occurred with the formation of the Nigerian Civil Servants Union in 1912. But it was the era of the 1920s and 1930s that witnessed a great organizational flurry of trade unions: the Nigerian Mechanics Union (1921), Association des Anciens Elèves des Pères de Sheut (Belgian

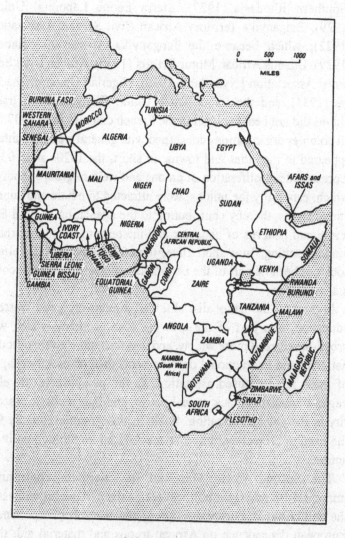

Independent Africa

Congo, 1925), Industrial and Commercial Workers Union (Southern Rhodesia, 1927), Sierra Leone Laborers' Union (1929), Tanganyika Territory African Civil Service Association (1922), which became the Tanganyika African Association (1929), Uganda African Motor Drivers (1930), African Civil Servants' Association (Nyasaland, 1930), Nigerian Union of Teachers (1931), and the Labor Trade Union (Kenya, 1937); trade unions did not become legal in the French colonies until 1937. In all colonies organizations concerned with general welfare matters appeared in the cities and towns. In short, the 1920s and 1930s represented a proliferation of unions and welfare groups, both of which, especially the unions, were attracted to ethnic and supra-ethnic issues, thereby contributing to the adaptation of rural and traditional patterns of behavior and interests to the more urban, modern setting. In a short time, therefore, unions and welfare societies became part of the nationalist vanguard in several colonial territories.

In general, the nationalist elite had a relatively good Western education, was part of the growing cash economy, which was urban-based, read more widely, and was thus more aware of local, national, and international developments than other Africans; all of these factors raised aspirations to the point where the elite began to realize its lack of real power, and thus its basic insecurity in the colonial situation. In short, this group eventually felt the need to protect and improve the African lot through political action.

The Second World War and its aftermath contributed immensely to emergent political nationalism. Africans witnessed the fallibility of Europeans during the war; they experienced European dependence on African troops and material aid; they learned new technical skills and gained a wider perspective on world affairs; they met and exchanged ideas with Asians then engaged in ridding themselves of domination by the same powers ruling Africa; they also were influenced by African-American soldiers; some of them experienced better social treatment in Europe than in Africa. Africans with these kinds of experiences would not submit to a continuation of the status quo in their countries, and they were encouraged by the post-war sentiment that supported political self-determination. The great symbol in this connection was the United Nations, whose anti-colonialist, anti-imperialist, and anti-racist posture became more vocal as new Asian nations joined the communist nations on issues of self-government for colonial territories. All of these forces influenced the trend toward national liberation in the African countries after World War II. Much of the success of that resurgent nationalism stemmed from the pioneer efforts of the African people in Africa and in the diaspora between 1900 and 1945.

The visual and expressive arts, built on age-old traditions, also played a major role in this epochal transformation to independence. Historical and decorative reproductions of African life and leaders gave a deeper meaning to nationalist movements while poetry and story-telling by the griots, songs of praise, work, protest, and inspiration, as well as dance energized those movements and added to the vision of independent societies. The arts indeed remain a vital and integral part of African history.

The quest for African independence was thus a mosaic of various uneven forces that will be more closely scrutinized first in a discussion of pan-Africanism, and second in an examination of specific territories.

The Pan-African Movement

The development of significant cross currents of mutual influence between Africans in Africa and the diaspora that developed during repatriation in Sierra Leone and Liberia continued in a variety of less dramatic ways. The great United States repatriationist of the 1850s, Martin Delany, who was persuaded that the

American Civil War would bring freedom and equality to African-Americans, became frustrated over the persistence of racism and cooperated in launching the Liberian Exodus Joint Stock Steamship Company to encourage emigration to Africa. The American Colonization Society continued to send an annual average of one hundred African-Americans to Liberia during the late nineteenth century. Bishop Henry M. Turner of the African Methodist Church spoke widely in the United States and Africa about African culture and the advantages of repatriation. His newspapers reached readers in the United States and Africa, and he was instrumental in securing opportunities for Africans to study in the United States; several separatist churches in South Africa sought links with his AME church. John Chilembwe's links with African-Americans during the 1890s have already been discussed. "Chief Alfred Sam" from the Gold Coast established offices in the United States to facilitate emigration to Africa. And although Booker T. Washington was neither a reunionist nor advocate of African culture, he became a vigorous critic of Belgian atrocities in the Congo, and sent several teams from Tuskegee Institute to develop cotton plantations and experimental agricultural stations in Togoland, Belgian Congo, and the Anglo-Egyptian Sudan. Several African schools, notably Achimota College in Ghana, the Zulu Christian Industrial School, and the South African Native College at Fort Hare, were modeled after Tuskegee. These were efforts on the part of United States blacks to maintain physical and spiritual links with the homeland.

In 1900 Henry Sylvester Williams, a Trinidadian lawyer living in London, took steps to solidify those cross currents of mutual influence between Africans and their descendants. London had long been a place where blacks from the West Indies, United States, and Africa had become acquainted as businessmen, journalists, scholars, and travelers. Thus Sylvester Williams's appeal for a conference to discuss common problems met with an encouraging response. Blacks from Africa, the United States, and the West Indies met and agreed to coordinate their actions against racism and to protest the alienation of African lands. "Pan-African" seems to have been used for the first time to describe this type of coordinated activity at an international level. Although this first effort did not establish any firm organizational structure for maintaining itself, it did lay the foundation for the development of a unified ideological movement in the interest of African people.

This pan-African conference of 1900 must be viewed in the context of the times: African-Americans were being denied their rights as citizens and were suffering the physical terror of lynchings; Europeans' aggression in and their partition of Africa had received international sanction by the Berlin Conference; European settlers had already alienated land and were fighting a war to entrench white supremacy in South Africa; the United States had established a colonial empire in the Caribbean and Pacific and was about to launch the "big stick" policy toward its southern neighbors. The black response to these developments locally alternated between violence and nonviolence, while at the international level several key blacks sought to rally support through their writings and organizations.

In Africa there was J. E. Casely Hayford, a Ghanaian lawyer, political theorist, and practitioner, and author of *Ethiopia Unbound* (1911), in which he appealed to African people to defend their culture, institutions, and racial integrity. In 1919 he founded the Congress of British West Africa (CBWA) as a united effort to achieve those goals. At its first annual conference in 1920 the Congress attracted delegates from Sierra Leone, Gambia, Nigeria, and Ghana and passed resolutions calling for the vote, more and better schools, and equal opportunities. Protests were made and deputations were sent to London, and in the 1920s Britain extended a limited franchise to several of the principal cities in West Africa, and in 1926 Achimota College was founded. Limited though these gains were, they resulted in part from the pressure of organized elite Africans seeking unity.

The significant increase in the black student population in Britain during the interwar years created a sizable reading constituency for works by Casely Hayford, Amy and Marcus Garvey, C. L. R. James and George Padmore of Trinidad, and DuBois of the United States. The following list of organizations formed in Britain at the time illustrates the great activity on behalf of pan-Africanism: British Guiana Association, League of Colored People, UNIA, Gold Coast Student Association, Gold Coast Aborigines Protection Society, Somali Society, Kikuyu Association of Kenya, etc.

The most active and successful of the organizations in Britain at the time was the West African Student Union (WASU), which appeared in 1924 out of the coalescence of several student groups. Led by the Nigerian Ladipo Solanke in London, the WASU began as a social group and eventually became a center for the discussion of political ideas and action. Solanke visited several West African cities where he collected funds and set up branch offices as local channels of communication and support. Not as many Africans were studying in the United States at the time, but in 1927 a Trinidadian named George Padmore, who had arrived in the country in 1924 and attended two African-American colleges, sought the assistance of Nnamdi Azikiwe, a Nigerian student then at Howard University and later at Lincoln University in Pennsylvania, to help in organizing an African student group. Although important, this movement remained small until during World War II, when African students in the United States formed the Association of African Students in the United States and Canada in 1941. Over the years, therefore, these student organizations in Europe and the United States became a gathering point not only for students but for politically conscious African people from Africa, the West Indies, and the United States. Several of the present African heads of state and other leaders were affiliated with student organizations.

Pan-Africanism took a dramatic turn in the United States when

Marcus Garvey, a Jamaican, arrived on the scene in 1916. He had traveled widely in the West Indies and in Central and South America, where he had protested against white exploitation of blacks; he had spent two years in England agitating against racial injustices. In London, Garvey met Duse Mohammed, a Sudanese pan-Africanist publisher of the *African Times and Orient Review,* who reportedly inspired the Jamaican toward more radical agitation for black pride and freedom. Finally, Garvey read about Booker T. Washington's self-help efforts and the establishment of Tuskegee. He wrote Washington and planned to consult with him, but Washington died before Garvey arrived in the United States. In any case, Garvey believed that the black man should go beyond self-help programs, and develop economic, political, and military power at an international level. He thus organized the Universal Negro Improvement Association (UNIA) with branches throughout the black world. His newspaper, *The Negro World*—a weekly that appeared in English, French, and Spanish—made a strong appeal for black unity, pride, and organization. He established the Black Star Line for the purpose not only of transporting blacks in the diaspora to Africa but also to initiate commercial relations between the diaspora and Africa. Garvey organized several businesses and cultural and social groups to make blacks independent of whites. He adopted a flag (black, red, and green) and negotiated for land in Liberia. Garvey's radical program and enthusiastic reception among blacks in the diaspora and the possibility of establishing a base of operations in Africa that might undermine European colonialism and commerce caused the United States, Britain, and France to bring pressure on Liberia not to grant land to Garvey's organization. Finally, Garvey was convicted in the United States of using the mails to defraud; he was deported in 1927.

While Garvey's projects failed, his impact on African peoples was enormous. He contributed immeasurably to the development of a consciousness of Africa in the diaspora, and to race pride and organization in the diaspora and Africa. Kwame Nkrumah and Azikiwe, both of whom attended African-American colleges in the United States, have paid tribute to Garvey's influence on nationalism in Africa. Nkrumah named Ghana's fleet of ships the Black Star Line and placed a black star in Ghana's flag. Garvey's influence reached members of the West African Student Union whom he addressed on several occasions, and for whom he provided hostels in London. A branch of the UNIA was organized in Lagos in 1920, and subsequently in Sierra Leone, Senegal, and South Africa, among other African countries; not only did news of Garveyism reach eastern and southern Africa, but according to one of Garvey's contemporary critics, W. E. B. DuBois, the Jamaican's movement penetrated even Asia.

In the United States W. E. B. DuBois, who had also played a major role in the pan-African conference of 1900, also continued his efforts to sensitize and organize leaders in the black world. A prolific writer of books, DuBois, for about twenty-five years (1910–1934), edited *The Crisis,* the journal of the National Association for the Advancement of Colored People in the United States. He interpreted his role with the journal as one of educating blacks on the conditions of the black world and protesting white aggression and exploitation of black people. He also convened four Pan-African Congresses (1919, 1921, 1923, 1927), which called for African local self-government, educational opportunities, freedom to practice their customs, and the protection of their land rights. Petitions of this nature were presented to the League of Nations. Mutual support was established with Casely Hayford's CBWA, underscoring the common concern and approach of the two organizations and symbolizing the unity among black men and women in Africa and the diaspora.

A consciousness of African links was also manifested in education. Pioneer efforts in research and teaching about Africa were undertaken by Carter G. Woodson in 1916; the inauguration of an African studies program was begun at Howard University by

William Leo Hansberry in 1922; participation with DuBois in the pan-African conferences of the 1920s was combined with teaching and research in African history by Rayford W. Logan and William Leo Hansberry at Howard University. Lincoln University in Pennsylvania pioneered in educating Africans while the Howard and Meharry Medical Schools trained most African physicians in the United States before independence. Although conducted largely in academia, these and similar activities by other African-Americans helped to prepare the way for future leaders with a full awareness of the continuing links between Africa and the diaspora.

The great depression stalled but did not kill the pan-African movement. Indeed, some United States blacks and others resident in the country from Barbados, Jamaica, and Trinidad emigrated to Ethiopia between 1930 and 1934. They had hoped to reestablish their roots on the continent. However, budgetary constraints and the Italo-Ethiopian War forced most of them to return to the United States.

The invasion of Ethiopia by Italy in 1935 ignited a pro-Ethiopian reaction among many Africans and in diaspora communities in Europe and the Americas. Organized groups of persons of African descent in the United States and Britain in particular mobilized efforts to rally blacks worldwide and to contribute money and supplies, and to send advisers to assist the Ethiopians. Several efforts also were mounted to send military volunteers to that embattled country.

These sentiments and activities heightened the pan-African consciousness of Africans and African-Americans and contributed to greater efforts by them to seek political responsibility for their communities. An example of greater political assertion in the United States came with the organization of a lobby, the Council on African Affairs in 1941 under the leadership of Max Yergan, Paul Robeson, William Hunton, and W. E. B. DuBois. In international bodies and the United States, this group addressed issues that affected African people at a time when few agencies existed for this purpose. Such groups kept African issues alive and helped to sustain the pan-African tradition.

In 1945 Nkrumah, Padmore, Makonnen, and others organized the fifth Pan-African Congress in Manchester, England. Although DuBois was elected president, continental Africans and a few West Indians were in control. Resolutions passed by this conference called for freedom and self-determination for Africans, reflecting the critical involvement of a new generation of Africans influenced by Casely Hayford, Garvey, DuBois, and others in the tradition of pan-Africanism. This new generation became the leaders of the independence movements in Africa during the 1950s and 1960s.

The cultural component of pan-Africanism made a dramatic appeal, especially among French-speaking Africans whose reverence for DuBois and Garvey was tempered by the French assimilationist policy, which caused them to pursue the cultural rather than the political route. The greatest impact on French-speaking Africans, therefore, came from the Harlem Renaissance of the 1920s and Negrismo in Cuba. Writers like Alain Locke, Countee Cullen, Langston Hughes, DuBois, and others from the United States, Claude McKay from Jamaica, Eric Walrond from Guyana, Nicolas Guillen of Cuba, Jean Price-Mars from Haiti, and others represented the international group of black writers who had a particular influence on their French-speaking brothers, especially on Leopold Senghor.

Two blacks from the diaspora, Aimé Cesaire of Martinique and Leon Damas of Guyana, joined hands with a continental African, Leopold Sedar Senghor, to found the negritude movement and its periodical, *L'Etudiant Noir.* This movement thus became the dominant force among descendant Africans in the French-speaking world. It focused on physical and cultural exile but did not call for independence. Two more radical voices in France came from Kodjo-Tovalou Hovenou of Benin and Tremoko

Kouyata Garan of Mali. Each founded his own publication and became a militant challenger of the colonial regime. Both men were in contact with Garvey and DuBois.

Senghor and his colleagues published in 1931 *La Revue du Mond Noir*, a monthly journal about African people throughout the world. He, Damas of Guyana, and Aimé Cesaire of Martinique emerged as leading proponents of the concept of negritude, or cultural pan-Africanism. A landmark was reached in 1947 when Alioune Diop of Senegal founded *Présence Africaine*, which ranked as the major international journal in English and French about African peoples. This venture led to the formation in 1956 of the International Society of African Culture with headquarters in Paris; Richard Wright and James Baldwin from the United States were part of that endeavor. The Society has published many outstanding volumes; translations of books by DuBois and Padmore have also been published. African-Americans in the United States founded an affiliate, the American Society of African Culture, and published the *African Forum*. These and other cultural currents paved the way for the World Festival of Negro Arts, which convened in Senegal in 1966 with President Senghor as host. Three years later the Pan-African Cultural Festival convened in Algeria, the adopted home of the late Frantz Fanon, the Martinican pan-Africanist ideologue for African liberation. These conferences represented the high point of cultural pan-Africanism, complemented the political pan-African conferences, and dramatized the fact that slavery and colonialism did not sever the links between Africa and the diaspora.

The pan-African initiative from the diaspora was in fact planted in the homeland when Nkrumah, Azikiwe, Jomo Kenyatta, and other nationalists carried the struggle onto African soil. This transition from the diaspora to Africa symbolically occurred when Nkrumah returned to Ghana in 1947 and began his political campaign, which he regarded as the beginning of the liberation of all of Africa.

Western and Equatorial Africa

British-Controlled Territories

Nationalist sentiment had manifested itself in the Gold Coast as early as 1871 when the Fanti agreed to a constitution that attempted to combine African and European ideas of government to insure Fanti freedom and independence after the anticipated British departure, which did not come. The wave of colonialism cut short that freedom thrust, but it continued to survive in other forms, mainly in the coastal area among a growing educated elite whose income came from participation in the cash or Western-style economy. An example in Ghana was the Gold Coast Aborigines Rights Protection Society (1897), and in Nigeria, the People's Union in Lagos (1908). In 1919, as we have noted, J. E. Casely Hayford and others organized the Congress of British West Africa (CBWA) in an attempt to unify and coordinate the political activities of the West African political elite.

Herbert Macaulay, a grandson of Bishop Samuel Crowther and participant in the CBWA, became more involved in local Nigerian issues, and when Britain revised the colony's constitution to allow for elected representatives in 1922, Macaulay formed the Nigerian National Democratic Party (NNDP), which won elections during the 1920s. But, although both the CBWA and NNDP reflected accelerated nationalist sentiment, both were reform-oriented, and once elected to office the leaders began to develop rapport with the administration.

Women too were part of the protests and struggle for freedom. They too resented the derogation of their culture, the usurpation of legitimate authority, the imposition of taxes, and arbitrary and unfair economic opportunities. Perhaps the best known challenge by women to these kinds of grievances occurred in southeastern Nigeria. In 1925 a group of women began to protest against the colonial administration and in 1929 some ten thousand women marched to the administrative center, where troops fired on them. When the confrontation ended, over fifty women had been killed. The situation was temporarily resolved but deep-seated resentment remained.

A more radical nationalist movement was the several youth leagues of the 1930s. This youth movement reflected the growing influence of young people with a territory-wide concern. The Nigerian Youth League appeared in 1932 to seek reform in education; the Nigerian Youth Movement (1934) in Lagos clearly articulated a national concern for economic and social issues. It established branches in various cities and in 1937 won Nnamdi Azikiwe's support. Isaac Wallace-Johnson, a trade unionist, formed the West African Youth League in Sierra Leone to help bridge the gulf between the Krios and the indigenous inhabitants. Also in 1938, J. B. Danquah established the Gold Coast Youth League to discuss colony-wide problems. In each of these leagues, the political focus of Africans was elevated to the higher level of national consciousness, and this was made more effective, in the case of Nigeria, when Azikiwe used his *West African Pilot* (newspaper) as a vehicle to disseminate national sentiments (Azikiwe had previously served as a reporter for the Baltimore African-American newspaper and participated in protest groups while attending school in the United States); the *African Standard* in Sierra Leone had a shorter duration but served a similar function.

Clearly, therefore, contemporary nationalist movements were evolving in West Africa prior to World War II. It also seems apparent that although colonial governors and other European officials held that only traditional rulers had the support of the people, changes that not only took account of the "new voices" but also included them in the political structure were taking place. Direct election to the legislative council came in Nigeria in 1922, in Sierra Leone in 1924, and to the Gold Coast in 1925. Although this franchise was limited, and included only coastal towns (where traditional influence was less decisive), and while the Africans still had no real political authority, a trend toward greater African involvement was set in motion and probably would have continued even without the influence of World War II.

During the years immediately following World War II Britain pursued its policy of gradualism by promulgating new constitutions for the Gold Coast and Nigeria in 1946 and Sierra Leone in 1947. Although regional advisory councils and representation of the north was provided for the first time in the legislative council of Nigeria, and while Ashanti obtained a voice in the Gold Coast legislative council, and greater representation was provided for Sierra Leone's indigenous inhabitants, the constitutions came too late and met resistance in Nigeria from the National Council of Nigeria and the Cameroons (NCNC) founded by Azikiwe in 1944, the United Gold Coast Convention (UGCC), organized in 1947 by Danquah and others in the Gold Coast, and the Sierra Leone People's Party (SLPP) under Milton Margai in 1951.

Kwame Nkrumah, whom Danquah appointed as secretary of the UGCC in 1947, proceeded to build a strong nationalist base under the slogan of self-government. After a series of protests and a successful boycott of European goods in 1948, Nkrumah left the UGCC and in 1949 founded the Convention People's Party (CPP), which appealed more to the masses. In 1950 he called for a general strike and boycott, which ended in violence and led to his imprisonment. Thus martyred, Nkrumah led his party to victory in the elections in 1951, and became prime minister. Although the British remained in ultimate control, power was shifting to the nationalists. This culminated in a more liberal constitution in 1954 and, finally, independence in 1957.

In Nigeria, opposition to the 1946 constitution led to a second one in 1951 that attempted to balance the regional diversities nourished by earlier colonial policies. At the same time, however, regional and ethnic consciousness deepened and was manifested in the Pan-Ibo Federal Union, the Ibibio State Union, Yoruba Egbe Omo Oduduwa, and the Northern Peoples' Congress (NPC), each expressing an ethnic nationalism that had to be accommodated within the artificial borders of Nigerian nationalism. Consequently, the 1951 constitution further entrenched regionalism and ethnic particularity as the NCNC dominated in the east, the NPC in the north, and the Action Group (AG, 1951) among the Yoruba in the west. The federal legislature with ministers chosen from the regional assemblies did not have the appeal of the regional governments, which were in closer touch with their constituencies. That was where the major leaders—Azikiwe (NCNC), Awolowo (AG), and Ahmadu Bello, the Sardauno (NPC)—assumed power. Another divisive factor was the aim of the NCNC and AG for early autonomy, while the NPP delayed out of fear that the southerners' longer exposure to European institutions and ideas would dominate the larger, more populous northern regions (see page 211). However, greater cooperation and unity were achieved in 1957 when a new constitution provided for a federal prime minister to choose his own cabinet. Abubakar Tafawa Balewa of the NPP was agreed on as prime minister and the NCNC joined the NPP to form the government. Although each region was granted autonomy, the way was open to independence, which came in 1960.

Political activism in Sierra Leone was also accelerated by British constitutional reforms after World War II. The National Council of Sierra Leone (NCSL) was formed in 1950 through the merging of several semipolitical groups of Krios under H. C. Bankole-Bright. The program of the NCSL, therefore, very naturally reflected the Krio interest in preserving their elevated status in the country's modern or western sector. The Sierra Leone People's Party (SLPP), on the other hand, was organized in 1951 to represent indigenous inhabitants of the protectorate, but Sir Milton Margai insisted that it take a territorial approach. In spite of Margai's insistence, the SLPP, which in fact comprised semipolitical organizations of protectorate Africans who greatly outnumbered Krios, was dominated by the Mendé and Temné, whose key attributes were large numbers and educational and commercial opportunities acquired during colonial rule. Largely because of that background and the fact that the SLPP initially appealed primarily to traditional authorities, the nationalist movement in Sierra Leone lacked much of the militancy seen in neighboring territories. The party did succeed, however, in fashioning several coalitions, and in 1960 was joined by the NCSL. Independence was achieved in 1961. With independence for the tiny territory of Gambia in 1965, British colonial control in West Africa became history.

French-Controlled Territories

In 1914 Blaise Diagne, an educated Senegalese who was elected to the French Chamber of Deputies to represent the four communes in Senegal, became a symbol of black achievement as the first African to fill such a position. Diagne played a key role in recruiting Africans to fight with the French during World War I; in 1916 he secured passage of legislation conferring citizenship on African inhabitants of the communes while at the same time retaining their traditional customs. But Diagne was a product of a French assimilation policy that committed him to conviction of the superiority of French civilization. He is reported to have remarked, for example: "I am first of all a Frenchman, and secondly an African." Little in the direction of African freedom could be expected, therefore, from Diagne. When he died in 1934 his seat was filled by Galandou Diouf, who was followed by Lamine Gueye, founder of the Senegalese Socialist party, which affiliated with the Socialist party in France. Diouf and Gueye also accepted the idea that Africans should assimilate into French culture.

In fact, the thrust for independence in French-speaking Africa did not really emerge until the 1950s. There were, however, certain post–World War II factors that paved the way for that thrust.

When France fell to the Germans in 1940, Felix Eboué, a black man from Guyana who was governor of Chad, declared support for de Gaulle. Eboué, therefore, played a key role in the Brazzaville Conference (1944), which convened to reconsider the relationship between Africa and Free France. The delegates to the conference were all European except Eboué, but the decisions taken there had a decisive impact on the resurgence of nationalism in French Africa. The conference delegates supported administrative and economic decentralization, the establishment of territorial assemblies, programs of economic development, and the suppression of the repugnant policies of forced labor and the *indigenat*. The details of these proposals were to be worked out by a constitutional assembly in which Africans and Europeans would be represented.

The Brazzaville Conference of 1944 was both a plus and a minus for African nationalism. Not only did it refuse to consider independence as a legitimate option, it went on record as recognizing that "the aims of France's colonizing mission in her colonies preclude any thought of autonomy or any possibility of development outside the French empire." On the plus side, however, in addition to the reforms proposed, African political parties emerged to chart the way to the future.

In October 1946, the constitution of the French Fourth Republic was approved by referendum and included a number of provisions pertaining to a redefined relationship between France and its African colonies. Citizenship was conferred on all inhabitants of the empire; the *indigenat* and forced labor were abolished; the colonies became overseas territories of an "indivisible" France and could elect representatives to the national assembly and the consultative assembly of the French Union in Paris; and elected assemblies were provided for each territory. The Investment Fund for Economic and Social Development was established to finance social and economic projects. These were substantial reforms, but most Africans in the French territories could not meet the property and educational qualifications to vote. Moreover, only the national assembly in Paris had any real power, and the main concern in that body was metropolitan France. As a small minority, the African representatives had to seek allies in order to secure support on African issues. In short, terminology, procedures, and perhaps some attitudes had been modified and Africans had a measure of representation in Paris. (Several Africans became ministers of state in Paris: Felix Houphouet-Boigny, for example, held a prominent post in each cabinet from 1956 to 1959.) Real power, however, remained in the hands of the European French, and the great majority of Africans continued to live in a colonial situation largely uninfluenced by the recent changes.

However imperceptible at some local levels, times were in fact changing. In the Ivory Coast, for example, cash agricultural production (cocoa and coffee) increased rapidly and created problems over such issues as prices, government subsidies, and labor. These and other grievances led to the formation of the African Agricultural Syndicate (1944) under Houphouet-Boigny, son of a royal Baoulé family, a medical doctor, and a wealthy farmer. In 1946 he was elected to the constitutional assembly. From that base, and his status as an affluent and educated African, Houphouet-Boigny played a key role in convening a conference of West and Equatorial African leaders in October 1946 to unify their political action for liberal reforms. The result was the formation of the Rassemblement Démocratique Africain (RDA), an interterritorial (French West and Equatorial Africa) party under Houphouet-Boigny's leadership. With the exception of Senegal, the RDA dominated the political movements in the French tropical African colonies. In Senegal, where the Socialist party was strong, Leopold Senghor, born outside the four communes, led a drive that resulted in the formation of the more militant Senegalese Democratic Bloc (1948), which relied primarily on the rural voters. Senghor sought one or at the most two strong federations within the French Union. The RDA, however, remained the dominant party, especially after it ended a brief alignment with the French communists in 1950. The party became more amenable to the French government, and Houphouet-Boigny became minister of health in Paris. As an interterritorial party and with increased support through Houphouet-Boigny and the socialists in Paris, the RDA's appeal mounted and it assumed the leadership of the nationalist thrust.

External forces had a great impact on political evolution in French Africa. Especially significant was the French defeat in Dien Bien Phu and the commencement of the Algerian revolution, both in 1954; independence for the French protectorates of Tunisia and Morocco in 1956; nationalist advance in Ghana; the integration of part of Togo into Ghana (1956), the demand for a unified Togo, and subsequent political reforms in Togo. It was becoming clear by the mid-1950s that self-government for Africans would alter the framework of the French Union. Thus in 1956 the *loi-cadre* (outline law) delineated a new policy: Each French colony received a measure of autonomy, with ministerial government responsible to territorial assemblies elected by universal suffrage. Although France retained control over foreign and military affairs and to a lesser extent over finance and justice, the route to independence was unfolding. The *loi-cadre* was influenced to a great extent by Houphouet-Boigny and reflected his interest in territorial links with France. Senghor and others (federalists) criticized the *loi-cadre* and advocated unity of the territories. In 1957 Sekou Touré, a Guinean trade unionist, formed an interterritorial trade union to unite the workers behind political federation. The federalists believed that "Balkanization" would create too many small, poor units that would be unable to withstand the political and economic pressures of the great powers. In addition to not having the backing of Houphouet-Boigny and his supporters in Paris, the federalists had to solidify their own positions in their respective territories. This necessary involvement in local affairs diverted efforts from the pan-Africanist route enunciated by Touré, Senghor, and others.

Out of general political unrest in France, mainly resulting from the Algerian crisis, Charles de Gaulle regained power in 1958. With the hope of stabilizing developments between France and its colonies, de Gaulle presented another constitution that offered the overseas territories internal self-government within a community (a replacement of the Union), which, with a European French majority, would control foreign affairs, the military, and certain aspects of economic and financial policies; the alternative was immediate and complete independence, which, as clarified in the campaign for the referendum on the new constitution, would risk the loss of French aid and diplomatic support. Only Guinea, led by Touré, opted against the constitution and achieved independence in 1958. Having thus taken that step, Guinea suffered the abrupt and disruptive consequences: withdrawal of French aid and personnel, ejection from the French franc zone, general diplomatic isolation by France and most of its African and Western supporters, and petty destruction of facilities—telephones, elevators, electricity, etc.—in Conakry, Guinea's capital.

But Guinea joined Ghana as the second country in tropical Africa to gain independence from colonial rule, and the temptation was not long resisted in the other territories. Thus, in 1960 the remainder of French West and Equatorial Africa became independent: Cameroon, Central African Republic, Chad, Congo (Brazzaville), Dahomey, Gabon, Ivory Coast, Mali, Mauritania, Niger, Senegal, Togo, Upper Volta; Madagascar also became independent in 1960 as the Malagasy Republic. All of these received the blessings and diplomatic and economic assistance of France and the Western world, but Guinea remained isolated, not only by France but largely by its Western and African allies.

Eastern Africa

Heightened political consciousness in Kenya was manifested in the emergence of several action-oriented organizations during the 1920s, centered around the Kikuyu who, living near the colonial capital of Nairobi, were most affected by land alienation, low wages, and racial discrimination, and could more readily perceive the general political suppression of Africans. Their first political organization was the Kikuyu Association, founded in 1920 to protest land alienation. But in 1921 the more militant East African Association, which included Kikuyus, Buganda, and other Africans living in Nairobi, emerged under the leadership of Jesse Kariuki and Harry Thuku. Thuku, a clerk in the treasury department, also organized the Young Kikuyu Association, while James Beautah formed the Young Kavirondo Association which attracted members of the Luo. These organizations attacked land alienation, tax and labor policies, and the requirement that Africans carry identification cards. When Thuku's program seemed to be appealing to groups outside Nairobi, he was arrested in 1922. This led to the formation of the Kikuyu Central Association (KCA) in 1924; in 1928 Jomo Kenyatta became its secretary-general and editor of its journal. Kenyatta was later sent to London to present grievances to the British government, and while in London he studied at the London School of Economics.

By the 1930s political activism spread beyond Kikuyu borders as the KCA gained favor among other groups. The organization supported the 1939 dock strike in Mombasa; that action coupled with KCA's increasing threat to the status quo led the government to declare the association illegal in 1940. It reportedly continued, however, under the cloak of the Kikuyu Farmers and Traders Association, reflecting the economic motivations involved. World War II delayed the supra-ethnic movement, but its appeal remained not only among the Kikuyu, but also among groups of Luo, Masai, Nandi, and others.

Although official British policy led to the appointment of one African to the legislative council in 1944, a second one in 1947, and the appointment of one to the executive council of twelve in 1952, the European settlers were still determined to maintain their supremacy in Kenya. Consequently, the Kenya Africa Union (KAU) was organized in Nairobi in 1944 by a small group of Africans, including several from the ex-slave community of Freretown. In 1947 Kenyatta became the president and Tom Mbotela (of Freretown) the vice president. The main concern of the KAU was essentially the same as the other groups, but increasing emphasis was placed on African representation on the legislative council and direct elections. When protests failed to secure redress, the KAU gradually moved to strengthen its unity and commitment by the practice of oath-taking. Meanwhile, urban militants also increased their agitation, which led to violence. There was indeed much to precipitate militant political action: rising prices and low wages, unemployment, many acres of unused land in the white highlands while Africans were being evicted and sent to overcrowded reserves, general insult, and the thirst for freedom. Blacks in Kenya thus pursued a course of protest that culminated in the Mau Mau rebellion in which ninety-five Europeans were killed and approximately thirteen thousand Africans lost their lives, including Mbotela. The government declared an emergency in 1952 and it lasted until 1960. Kenyatta and others were arrested. But the important point is that although the resistance was suppressed, the government was forced by it to confront the issues. Some land reform occurred and the franchise for Africans was introduced in 1956.

Although it may be said that Africans were now on the move to independence in Kenya, the only colony-wide body that spoke for them was the Kenya Federation of Labor under Tom Mboya. There soon emerged two political parties, however. The Kenya African National Union (KANU) appeared under the leadership of Kenyatta supporters, including Mboya and Oginga Odinga. Its membership was mostly Kikuyu, Luo, and Kamba, while the other party, the Kenya African Democratic Union (KADU), was headed by Ronald Ngala and appealed mainly to the smaller ethnic groups who feared domination by the larger groups. When KANU won the elections in 1961, the leaders demanded the release of Kenyatta, which occurred later that year. He thus assumed leadership of the party, and when federal status was created in 1963, he became prime minister and led the country to independence in December of that year.

In neighboring Tanganyika the situation was markedly different, partly because no single ethnic group was large enough to dominate the others, and partly because it was a trust territory to which political self-government was promised by the United Nations Charter. But indigenous political activity had an earlier history than that. In 1922 Martin Kayamba, a civil servant, organized the Tanganyika Territory African Civil Service Association, which in 1929 became the Tanganyika African Association (TAA). Although TAA was not a mass organization, it did focus attention on the country as a whole and thus contributed to the foundation of nationalism in the territory.

Other political trends were perceptible in Tanganyika during the 1930s and 1940s. Benevolent societies sprang up in several towns, while the TAA continued to protect the interest of African civil servants. *Kwetu*, the first independent African newspaper in the country, also appeared during the 1930s. Significantly, Swahili, the territorial language encouraged by the government, provided a basis for cross-ethnic, cross-territorial communication and cooperation that occurred as more and more Kenyans and Tanganyikans studied at Makerere College in Uganda. Unity of purpose was not achieved until after World War II, but the foundation for it was laid during the 1930s.

By the end of the war, TAA leadership became largely Makerere-trained and much more oriented to rapid political change. Meanwhile, the appointment of four Africans to the legislative council in 1945 and one in 1951 was part of an official British policy of parity among Africans, Europeans, and Asians. The continuation of that policy would have meant the maintenance of an inferior status for Africans, but this could only be altered by a strong united front by them. It was with the return of Julius Nyerere from a sojourn in England in 1952 that such a step was taken. Nyerere, a teacher, proceeded to make TAA a mass organization, which, in 1954, became the Tanganyika African National Union (TANU). TANU opposed racial parity and sought majority rule. At the same time, the party disavowed racism against settlers. In fact, many Asian and European settlers were attracted to Nyerere's moderate stance and joined TANU. In 1955 and 1956 Nyerere visited the United Nations where he won international status. He proceeded to lead TANU to electoral victories, which resulted in independence in 1961.

Offshore from Tanganyika, the island of Zanzibar witnessed a momentous thrust for independence. After 1945 the Arabs began organizing political groups in the hope of replacing the British. Several of those groups united to form the Zanzibar Nationalist Party (ZNP) in 1956. When a British commission recommended elections for 1957, the Africans and Shirazis formed the Afro-Shirazi Union, later renamed the Afro-Shirazi Party (ASP). Hostilities characterized relations between the two parties as Afro-Shirazis boycotted Arab businesses, and Arabs evicted Afro-Shirazi farmers. This reflected the character of past relations between the privileged Arab landowners and businessmen on the one hand, and the majority—landless Africans—on the other. The ZNP established a coalition with the pro-Arab Zanzibar and Pemba People's Party, and controlled the government at independence in December 1963. But in January 1964, it was displaced by a coup that placed Obeid Karume of the ASP in power. Later that year Tanganyika and Zanzibar joined to form Tanzania with Nyerere as president and Karume as vice president.

Nationalism in the other East African colony, Uganda, was

greatly influenced by Buganda, the wealthiest region in the country and the one in which indirect rule had entrenched a strong commitment to particularism and separatism. Moreover, the kabaka, his ministers, and subordinate rulers were practicing Christians who themselves encouraged their people to accept the faith. In short, British policies and Western influence in general made Buganda a unique region in Uganda and worked against political unity in the colony. The British encouraged local councils, and African politics generally retained a local rather than a colony-wide focus. Consequently, when Britain undertook to develop a unitary government in the 1950s, Kabaka Mutesa II, supported by his lukiko (council), demanded self-government for Buganda. The kabaka thus appeared as a nationalist leader for Buganda and a threat to the colonial government, which deported him in 1953.

The deportation of the kabaka provided another issue around which politically conscious Ugandans could rally. The Uganda National Congress (UNC), which was formed in 1952 with the objective of uniting all Ugandans for independence, capitalized on the deportation issue and helped to force Mutesa's reinstatement. The UNC and other groups also denounced the economic exploitation of Africans by Europeans and Asians. In response to these developments, Britain introduced a ministerial system of colonial government in 1955, and the direct election of Africans to the legislative council in 1958. Britain also conceded special status first to Buganda, and later to the kingdoms of Bunyoro, Toro, Ankole, and Busoga, while the smaller groups were to receive direct administration. In 1961 the UNC under Milton Obote allied with other groups, including the Kabaka Yekka party in Buganda, and formed the Uganda People's Congress, which convened a conference to formulate the constitution that led to independence. By that document Buganda was allowed to appoint its representatives to the national assembly, while other regions elected theirs. These were costly expediencies that, however, did lead to a semblance of unity, and to independence in 1963. The kabaka was elected president and Obote became the prime minister.

Central Africa

The Central African Federation became a catalyst to African nationalism in central Africa. In Nyasaland (Malawi) the African Congress, which was founded in 1944, became more militant as Henry Chipembere and Kanyama Chiume assumed leadership in the 1950s. They sought experience and a broad understanding of Britain and Nyasaland when they persuaded Hastings Banda, who had remained in touch with his country during many years of residence in the United States and Britain, to lead the Congress. Banda returned in 1958 and undertook such a vigorous campaign against the federation that he was arrested and the party was banned in 1959.

The Northern Rhodesian African Congress Party, organized in 1948, lost some popular support after the failure to prevent the inauguration of the Federation, but it proceeded to organize branches throughout much of the country, and during the early 1950s Kenneth Kaunda, Harry Nkumbula, Simon Kapwepwe, and others began a determined approach toward a new nation, Zambia. In 1958, Kaunda, Kapwepwe, and others formed the Zambian African National Congress (ZANC), after having split with the more moderate Nkumbula. In 1959, however, when the government declared an emergency to prevent a "plot" to kill all Europeans, ZANC was banned and its leaders were arrested. The next year the ZANC leaders were released as popular heroes; they then organized the United National Independence Party (UNIP) with Kaunda as president.

At least by 1960 it was obvious that the Federation's continued existence was in serious doubt. (It was finally dissolved in 1963.)

Banda was released from detention and had talks with the Colonial Office; in 1961 his party swept the elections, two years later internal self-government was achieved, and in 1964 independence was proclaimed. In Northern Rhodesia, following elections in 1962, Nkumbula joined Kaunda in forming a coalition government. The 1964 elections, based on a wider franchise, gave Kaunda a clear majority. He then became prime minister with his party in full control of domestic affairs. In October, independence was achieved.

Britain thus chose to dissolve the Federation instead of maintaining it by increased force. But there was still Southern Rhodesia where some whites had opposed the union from the beginning and where, by 1960, an increasing number of whites pressed for complete independence. A major step in that direction occurred in 1962 when the right-wing Rhodesian Front defeated the more liberal United Federal Party. On the African side, repression had already banned the National Congress, which was formed in 1957. But Joshua Nkomo, a trade unionist, and others reorganized in the Zimbabwe African People's Union (ZAPU) in 1962. Unfortunately for the African cause, regional, ethnic, and personal conflicts led to a split of the nationalist ranks and the formation of the Zimbabwe African National Union under Reverend Ndabaningi Sithole in 1963. This split divided African loyalty, seriously weakened the nationalist cause, and enabled the Rhodesian Front more effectively to scrutinize, isolate, and arrest the leaders. The Rhodesian settlers, unlike those in Malawi and Zambia, had been in direct local political control since 1923 and thus had deeper roots in the institutions of their adopted home. Their unilateral declaration of independence in 1965 confirmed this fact by further entrenching their minority racist regime over millions of Zimbabwians in violation of international law and sentiment.

The United Nations voted for economic sanctions against Rhodesia but because several of the powers—notably the United

States, Portugal, and South Africa—refused to comply, the measures failed. However, ZAPU under Nkomo and the Zimbabwe African National Union (ZANU) under Robert Mugabe and their guerrilla armies continued the struggle from bases in neighboring countries.

When Portugal's dictatorship collapsed and its African colonies moved toward independence, Rhodesia lost a valuable ally. South Africa and the United States saw the trend and pressured the Rhodesians into negotiations that led to the country's independence as Zimbabwe under Mugabe in 1980.

In the central African territory of the Congo, Belgian paternalism and censorship pretty effectively prevented the Congolese from being influenced by the nationalist movements in neighboring territories and from developing their own liberation thrust until the late 1950s. However, two important antecedents of Congo nationalism were the ABAKO (Alliance des BaKongo), a cultural society organized in Leopoldville (Kinshasha) by the BaKongo in 1950, and a social group formed in 1953 by Abbé Joseph Malula. The latter group published a journal, *Conscience Africaine,* which in 1956 published a manifesto calling for gradual political participation for the Congolese. This moderate manifesto elicited an impatient response from the ABAKO, which held that freedom should be granted then, 1957. But this was a limited view from only one ethnic group. Moreover, Belgian policy in 1957 began to show signs of serious response to the times. In that year the government inaugurated reforms allowing Africans to participate in urban government and the election of city councillors. These reforms were the immediate stimuli to the growth of political parties and the development of militant nationalism.

ABAKO was transformed into a party under its leader, Joseph Kasavubu; CONAKAT (Confédération des Associations Tribales du Katanga) appeared under Moise Tshombe; and the only trans-ethnic or national party, the MNC (Movement National Congolais), emerged under the leadership of Patrice Lumumba and Cyrille Adoula. (Lumumba's politics were influenced by his experiences and contacts at the All African Peoples' Conference convened by Nkrumah in Ghana in 1958.) Political protest and demonstrations against unemployment and segregation led to riots in Kinshasha in 1959, and were followed by the formation of other parties, most notably the PSA (Parti Solidaire African) under Antoine Gizenga. This accelerated pace of political action caused Belgium to convene a meeting in Brussels in 1960; the Congolese leaders demanded and received a promise of independence in six months.

The unity manifested in Brussels by the Congolese leaders was not maintained in the Congo. Neither national cohesion nor leadership had been allowed to emerge under the Belgians; the institutions that might have met those needs—high schools and universities—were not created until 1955 and 1956. The May elections preceding independence, therefore, were marked by ethnic and regional conflicts, with Lumumba's MNC coming closer to a national party with a plurality of votes, which enabled it to form a coalition government. Independence came in June 1960, with Lumumba as prime minister and Kasavubu as president.

In neighboring Angola, the African quest for freedom led to the formation of the two major political organizations in the 1950s. The Uniao das Populacoes de Angola (UPA) was founded among the BaKongo in 1954, but in 1958 the organization took a more nationalistic approach and sent Holden Roberto to several African countries to establish links with other nationalists. The UPA aim was national liberation of Angola. Almost simultaneously, the Movimento Popular de Libertacao de Angola (MPLA) emerged as a coalescence of several groups in 1956 under Mario de Andrade. The MPLA demanded self-determination and the withdrawal of Portuguese troops from Angola. In 1960 the Portuguese reacted to the intensification of nationalist activities by increasing the number of troops in the colony; later that year several incarcerated nationalists were shot in Luanda. Then in February 1961, several thousand Africans were killed in a rebellion associated with the MPLA. Further disturbances in March resulted from UPA-initiated strikes. These events of 1961 pierced the wall of censorship that for decades largely concealed the injustices and discontent of the Angolans from the outside world.

Portugal's announced reforms—abolition of the *indigenato* system and of forced labor, and in African representation on legislative councils in Portuguese Africa—did not halt the quest for independence. In 1962 the UPA and several other groups formed the Provisional Government of the Republic of Angola with a national liberation army, both headed by Roberto. The UPA and MPLA proceeded to establish headquarters in neighboring Kinshasha, Congo. This enabled both groups to maintain continuous contacts abroad and to funnel aid and guerrillas into Angola. However, after the OAU decided in 1963 to provide funds to the UPA, the MPLA offices were shifted to Brazzaville. These developments underscored the deepening schism in the Angolan nationalist movement, and adversely affected the liberation cause.

Shortly after guerrilla activities broke out in Angola in 1961, the Portuguese reinforced their military forces in Mozambique. At the same time, Mozambique shared in the Portuguese reforms in 1962 and 1963. But the Mozambique nationalists were no more deterred than the Angolan patriots. The Frent de Libertacao Mozambique (FRELIMO), which was formed in 1962 out of the merger of several political groups, spearheaded the movement to unify Mozambicans, develop literacy programs, establish offices and seek aid abroad, and to train cadres to lead the liberation movement. FRELIMO elected for its president Eduardo C. Mondlane, whose background included membership in an African students' organization and education and teaching experience in the United States, where he retained close links with whites and African-Americans. As chief spokesman for Mozambique's nationalist struggle, Mondlane, traveled widely in Europe and the United States to inform the outside world and to seek assistance. In 1963 FRELIMO, like UPA, was promised support by the OAU.

Mozambique was long influenced by its more highly developed neighbors, South Africa and Rhodesia. Lourenco Marques and Beira were popular resorts for white Rhodesians and South Africans; Beira remained an important transit port for Rhodesian goods; and South African mines relied heavily on migrant labor from Mozambique. In addition, the three powers—Portugal, Rhodesia, and South Africa—had economic and military agreements, the implications of which were far-reaching not only because of South Africa's economic and military strength, but also because of Portugal's close ties with the United States and membership in NATO.

As late as the 1970s, when most African countries were independent, the Portuguese colonies still struggled with seemingly no prospect of early liberation. Then in 1974 the revolution in Portugal overthrew the dictatorship there. Thus, already strained economically and militarily and fighting a losing battle in its colonies, Portugal was forced to retrench. Consequently, the first European power to colonize Africa became the last to withdraw.

Portuguese Guinea, the poorest of the colonies and the one that was virtually lost to the guerrillas, obtained its independence in 1973 under Amilcar Cabral. Angola and Mozambique followed in 1975 under Agostinho Neto and Samora Michel respectively.

Ethiopia and Northern Africa

The defeat of the Italians at Adowa in 1896 assured the Ethiopians independence until Mussolini's aggression just prior to World War II. In 1930 Ras Tafari was crowned as Emperor Haile Selassie I, and five years later the Italians avenged their defeat at Adowa by invading Ethiopia. Neither the major countries nor the League of Nations, which Ethiopia had joined in 1923, exerted the pressure necessary to restrain Mussolini, who proclaimed the country's annexation to Italy in 1936. Although the emperor fled and sought support in Europe, the Ethiopians took to the hills and fought a guerrilla war.

There was an international outcry but the League of Nations, although moved by the emperor's appeal for help, did not stem the tide. Descendant Africans abroad rallied around the symbol of their identity. C. L. R. James, a Trinidadian living in London, organized the International Friends of Ethiopia and led protest demonstrations on behalf of Ethiopia. In Washington, D. C., William Leo Hansberry, Ralph Bunche, and William Steen were joined by Hosea Nyabongo of Uganda and Malaku Bayen of Ethiopia to form the Ethiopian Research Council to rally support around and funnel support to the African state. Protest movements also developed in Jamaica, Barbados, St. Kitts, and Trinidad.

A group of Caribbean and United States physicians in New York organized the Medical Committee, which sent medical supplies to Ethiopia, while other groups throughout the country raised money to assist the cause. This was a time of commitment to African identity: A number of African-Americans adopted Ethiopian names and small schools were formed to teach African history and languages. And at least two African-Americans, John Robinson and Hubert Julian, joined the Ethiopian armed forces. But after the emperor's exile, the cause seemed lost. Over the next several years guerrilla attacks were mounted and finally Britain dispatched troops to dislodge the Italians as part of World War II. The emperor thus regained the throne in 1941.

During that struggle Bayen and several African-Americans had founded the Ethiopian World Federation, which became the major pan-African organization in the United States at that time. It had branches throughout much of the country and the

Caribbean. Its newspaper, *The Voice of Ethiopia,* advocated the substitution of black for the term Negro. In fact, a number of African-Americans called themselves Ethiopian. After the return of the emperor to Addis Ababa, the federation was given land on which some of its members settled. Others developed the movement into Rastafarianism in Jamaica. And still others continued to foster pan-African activities.

Several black technicians from the United States and the Caribbean went to Ethiopia as teachers, mechanics, and pilots. They were employed in the government and in schools; some organized a pilots' school, which trained the first Ethiopians to serve in the country's air force and the Ethiopian Air Lines.

The Italo-Ethiopian War revealed the depths of identification blacks around the world felt with Ethiopia and Africa. The pan-African network was thus strengthened by the event.

In 1941, British troops and Ethiopian guerrillas recaptured the country and restored the emperor to his throne. The British troops also evicted the Italians from Eritrea and Italian Somaliland and placed both under military rule. In 1950 the latter became a United Nations trust territory administered for ten years by Italy; in 1960 it was united with British Somaliland to form the independent Somali Republic. In 1952 Eritrea was federated with Ethiopia and ten years later became an integral part of that country, but it won its independence from Ethiopia in 1993. The Italians also lost Libya to the British in 1942, and in 1951, with United Nations assistance, it became independent.

The situation in Egypt and Sudan was much more complicated. Britain had occupied Egypt in 1882, established the Anglo-Egyptian Condominium over Sudan in 1899, and declared a protectorate over Egypt in 1914, when Britain went to war against Turkey, Egypt's nominal ruler. The protectorate was terminated in 1922, but British troops remained in the Suez Canal zone, a fact that became a key target of Egyptian nationalists. But before the problem was resolved, World War II made Suez a vital military

base for the British, and the exigencies of war caused her interference in Egyptian politics to assure the formation of a pro-
British government.

Following the war, Egypt expended considerable energy on
developing the Arab League and resisting Zionism. Charges of
corruption, incompetence, and misdirection of the war against
Israel in 1948 led to the officers' coup d'etat in 1952 and the subsequent emergence of Gamal Abdel Nasser in 1954 as prime minister; in 1956 he became president, thereby marking the end of
monarchical rule in Egypt. Nasser undertook a series of social
and economic reforms, especially agrarian reforms, which won
him widespread popularity among Egyptians. In foreign affairs
his emphasis was to unite the Arab world, which led to the short-
lived federation of Egypt and Syria in the United Arab Republic
(1958), but his vigorous denunciation of imperialism and his
dynamic promises to help liberate the colonized attracted many
African nationalists to Cairo. With Britain's forced evacuation of
Suez in 1956, Nasser's popular image permeated much of Africa
and Asia. His charisma, success in dealing with the great powers,
and assistance to nationalists encouraged and accelerated the
pace of national liberation in many parts of Africa.

Even before Nasser, Egypt was a major influence in Sudanese
politics. The Anglo-Egyptian Condominium provided for equal
responsibility over the Sudan by both England and Egypt, but following a Sudanese rebellion in which Egyptians were implicated
in 1924, the latter were removed from Sudan's administration by
Britain. This action opened more civil service posts (at the junior
level) for the Sudanese. By 1930 Britain began to develop a con-
certed policy for southern Sudan. This reflected a recognition of
basic ethnic, regional, and religious differences between the
northern and southern regions of the country. Thus, the southern
policy encouraged southern indigenous customs to replace Muslim Arab influences. Northern officials were transferred from
southern provinces, local languages and English were encouraged

over Arabic, and Arab dress and names were discouraged by southerners. However, by the 1940s this policy became secondary to World War II, and after the war Britain began to respond to nationalist pressures in Asia and Africa in general, and to northern Sudanese pressures in particular. The concept of unity prevailed over any idea of separate development. Two political parties emerged: the Ashiqqa, which favored union with Egypt; and the Umma, more southern-based, which sought a national state. In 1953 Britain and Egypt decided to let the Sudanese determine their own status in 1956. Riots during the transitional period of 1954 and 1955 highlighted the depth of disunity in Sudan. Although unionists (supporters of union with Egypt) and nationalists, northerners and southerners, Muslims and non-Muslims (which mirror the long and complex history of the Nile Valley) revealed deep division in Sudan, the government in power, the National Union Party (Ashiqqa), passed a resolution in 1955 declaring the country independent. This act further alienated southern groups in Sudan, in particular the Dinka, who spearheaded a separate nationalist movement.

At the western end of northern Africa are Algeria, Morocco, and Tunisia, all former French territories. Algeria, which by World War II had about a million Europeans and eight million Algerians, was regarded as an integral part of France, although most of the indigenous inhabitants did not acquire French citizenship and were not represented in the government. Morocco, with about 400,000 Europeans and over 11 million Moroccans, and Tunisia, with approximately 250,000 Europeans and 4 million Tunisians, were protectorates, ostensibly administered on behalf of the traditional rulers. Although the three territories were ruled in the interest of France, which favored the European settlers, the states of Morocco and Tunisia facilitated a smoother evolution to independence.

French-educated Tunisians formed the Neo-Destour party in 1934 under Habib Bourguiba, whose agitation led to his arrest in

1938. Although he was released during the German occupation of Tunisia, the allied victory reestablished French rule and thus assured a continuation of the liberation struggle. General postwar problems and guerrilla warfare by the Tunisians led to internal self-rule as a transition to independence in 1957, with Bourguiba as president.

Political organization and the nationalist movement solidified in Morocco with the formation of the Istiqlal party in 1944. When it became clear in the early 1950s that Tunisia would become independent, France decided to concentrate on holding its most valuable territory, Algeria, which revolted in 1954. Morocco, which revolted in 1955, thus received its independence in 1956 under the sultan.

The Algerian Front de Libération Nationale (FLN), which led the guerrilla war, was formed in 1954 with the coalescence of several groups opposed to French rule. French settlers in Algeria not only had considerable economic and political stakes in the country, they also had an important influence on metropolitan French politicians. As the guerrilla war continued, the Algerians received the support of Nasser and the Arab world, and nationalists in independent and colonized countries of Africa. But the key support, moral and material, came from Tunisia and Morocco, which bordered Algeria and offered refuge and outside contacts for the guerrillas. This was obviously a conflict that the French increasingly realized they could not win. Thus, under Charles de Gaulle a cease-fire was negotiated and independence was achieved in 1962 with Ahmed Ben Bella as president.

Independence came to Basutoland as LeSotho and Bechuana-land as Botswana in 1966; Swaziland as Swazi, Rio Muni and Fernando Po as Equatorial Guinea in 1968; the Comoro Islands in 1975; Djibuti as Afars and Issas in 1977.

15

The Transformation in Southern Africa: South Africa and Namibia

South Africa

The struggle for self-government by indigenous Africans was so protracted and confronted such inhumane policies and actions in South Africa and Namibia that the region became a symbol for international struggles. The role of the United Nations, especially in regard to Namibia as South Africa's mandate and the blatant racially abusive policies there, aroused the moral indignation of most countries. Few governments could withhold criticism of the situation there, and the issue came to be regarded as central in pan-African relations. The struggles in South Africa and Namibia became larger than individual countries; the South African struggle in particular became a global symbol of struggle for freedom and human rights. For these reasons, they need an extended discussion.

Of all the examples of continued white domination, South Africa was the most striking. While nationalism led to concessions and ultimate independence for most other black states, the white South African government intensified its restrictions against its black inhabitants. There are several reasons for this. Whites have lived longer as settlers in South Africa than in the other territories and had no other place to go; their numerical proportion to Africans—one to four—was higher than elsewhere in Africa; they had direct and internationally recognized political control since 1910; and they controlled a richly endowed economy.

The government's commitment to the concept of black inferiority has a long history that was legalized with the Fish River border proclamation of 1779. Since that time relations between the blacks and whites have remained hostile. White hostility and domination was projected by the Nationalist Party and supported by the South African Dutch Reformed Church. And all of this was reinforced by a fairly well-balanced economy that developed from the exploitation of an enormous supply of gold and substantial supplies of diamonds and other metals. The development of these resources was accomplished by a small number of skilled whites and a large, unskilled African labor force. The key here is that the settlers were able by legislation, custom, and force to create an economy that reserved the best jobs and higher wages for themselves, thereby eliminating black competition and preventing effective political organization. African mobility and political actions were rigorously controlled by pass laws, reserves, police brutality, and a series of other measures and practices. But despite all of this, the African liberation movement in the country survived.

In 1912 Africans formed a national organization, the African National Congress (ANC), and named as president John L. Dube, whose firsthand knowledge of racial injustice included experiences in the United States, which he visited with the help of the African-American Henry M. Turner of the AME Church. The ANC sought to achieve political and civil rights for Africans as equals to whites, and became the most important organizational representative for the Africans.

White domination and the doctrine of apartheid crystallized when the Nationalist Party came to power in 1948. "To keep

South Africa white" became a popular slogan. Laws were adopted for separate residential areas, segregated public accommodations and education, and racial classification. These laws inaugurated official apartheid.

The ANC espoused the philosophy of nonviolence and sought alliances with Asians and whites. This especially characterized the organization under Albert Luthuli, a former Zulu king who became president of the ANC in 1952. Luthuli believed in a non-racial South Africa and sought redress with other races seeking constitutional change. A more radical approach began to gain ground in the mid-1950s when a group of Africans, led by Robert Sobukwe (a lecturer at the University of Witwatersrand), questioned the wisdom of allying with Asians and whites. This group later split from the ANC and in 1959 formed the Pan-Africanist Congress (PAC) with Robert Sobukwe as president. The PAC directed its focus more on rural Africans and through indigenous languages and idioms.

In 1960 the government passed legislation to establish Bantustans, ostensibly to provide Africans with self-government in separate areas of the country for an eventual union, with South Africa as the hub. In point of fact, however, the establishment of Bantustans such as Bophuthatswana, Ciskei, Transkei, and Venda, revealed the government's plan to remove thousands of Africans from the white inhabited urban areas, to create ethnic areas isolated from other blacks in the country, and to control all of them through the South African parliament. Indeed, all Bantustan legislation was subject to government approval, and office holders were appointed and could be removed by the government.

Africans reacted to the Bantustans and general injustices with great indignation. Demonstrations against pass cards occurred in Sharpeville in 1960 and left nearly seventy Africans killed by the police. Luthuli called for a day of mourning, which had the effect of a labor strike. He burned his pass and appealed to others to do likewise. This led to the proclamation of a state of emergency, and both the ANC and PAC were banned. In Pondoland, later in 1960, resentment over some African rulers' acceptance of the Bantustan experiment and the government's appointment of office holders without general consultation led to an additional loss of African life and property. The same year the government held a referendum that led to the establishment of the Republic, but Africans (about 70 percent of the country's population) could not vote. Following this latter occurrence, Nelson Mandela (an alumnus of the University of Fort Hare and law graduate of the University of Witwatersrand) undertook to organize a national strike, but government spies, soldiers, police, and a general show of force foiled that scheme.

By mid-1961 African nationalists decided that they had to meet violence with violence. The ANC and PAC accepted this posture and Umkonto We Sizwe (Spear of the Nation) justified this new course by explaining that all avenues of legal redress were closed to Africans. This new dimension required greater reliance on underground activities and assistance from outside South Africa. Mandela thus attended the PAFMCESA meeting in Addis Ababa in 1962, made a tour of several African countries, and succeeded in receiving various kinds of aid. However, South African authorities arrested him in 1962, and the following year he was sentenced to life in prison. Aid from neither individual countries in Africa or abroad nor the OAU was sufficient for the blacks in South Africa to launch the kind of internal movement necessary to end white domination, although the Black Consciousness Movement continued to lead resistance under the leadership of Steve Biko. South Africans in exile and their supporters thus rose to the challenge.

The United Nations became the major international forum for protest and challenge against the apartheid South African government. It passed resolutions and distributed publications condemning the state, and the General Assembly voted for sanctions, which failed to pass the Security Council where the United States and Britain in particular opposed such moves. However, United Nations members voted to exclude South Africa and provided assistance to liberation movements fighting against apartheid.

During the 1980s in particular, a heightened militant chorus of discontent and condemnation gradually included important followers in Great Britain, France, West Germany, and the United States, all of which were important commercial and political partners of South Africa. Much of that protest in the United States owed a great deal to TransAfrica, the major African-American lobby for African and Caribbean issues.

Founded in 1976, TransAfrica adopted the South African issue as one of its key concerns and in 1984 organized daily demonstrations, which included many prominent persons to underscore the scope and significance of the appeal, in front of the South African Embassy in Washington, D.C. It also coordinated demonstrations against the sale of krugerrands (South African gold coins) and promoted general protest against apartheid. These efforts combined with those of other groups forced President Reagan to change his mind and impose limited economic sanctions in 1986.

What immediately sparked these more recent efforts for sanctions were domestic riots and civil strife in South Africa from 1984, especially the disruption of black South African efforts to commemorate the Soweto confrontation of 1976 when black student demonstrations and riots reached a high point and the police killed over twenty people and wounded over two hundred. That confrontation led to the founding of the Azanian African Peoples' Organization, which intensified the struggle. Thus, Archbishop Desmond Tutu, the Nobel laureate, Reverend Allen Baesak, elected head of the Colored branch of the Dutch Reformed Church in 1986, and Winnie Mandela, wife of the imprisoned organizer, emerged as principal leaders of the demonstrations. By the late 1980s not only had those demonstrations and the militance of all the organizations accelerated, the white community had begun to show signs of greater division.

Although Zulu leader Gatsha Buthelezi opposed apartheid, he collaborated with the government for reform. The ANC retained support in the country and a small but increasingly important pressure for positive change developed among some South African whites, including the Progressive Party and, subsequently, some prominent businessmen. These developments caused a number of companies to become more insistent against apartheid. Groups in the United States and abroad began calling insistently for disinvestment of securities in companies conducting business in the troubled land.

South Africa was able to resist challenges to its policies for several reasons. As the most highly industrialized country in Africa and manufacturer of its own weapons, some of which it exported, it had (and still has) large supplies of the world's most strategic minerals (chrome, manganese, gold, diamonds, antimony, vanadium, platinum, and uranium). The government was in the hands of Afrikaners who were brave and committed advocates of apartheid. Some observers believed that, if necessary to forestall black majority rule, the South African government would unleash unlimited force.

Control of both the government and economy of South Africa was in the hands of descendant Europeans, mainly Dutch and French Huguenots, whose political and economic connections were strong in Western countries. Moreover, South Africa's strong anticommunist stance appealed to the West. The position of the Western countries thus was critical to a solution of the crisis.

Another concern was the fact that the neighboring central and southern African countries depended on South Africa's economy for international transport, food, technical assistance, and employment opportunities, especially in the mines. Those countries also had been invaded when South Africa sought to destroy elements of the African National Congress and other liberation forces on its borders. South Africa took advantage of this dependent relationship to threaten that the effect of any economic sanctions would be passed on to those neighboring countries. But in spite of all of this, the intensified struggle of the blacks in and outside South Africa, the increasing pressure by whites from within the country, and the growing pressure from Western governments and organizations led to momentous changes in the 1990s.

When President Pieter Botha yielded the presidency to F. W. de Klerk in 1989, a new era began. De Klerk led the Nationalist Party to support the unbanning of the African National Congress and other political parties, the release of Nelson Mandela, the repeal of all apartheid laws, and the beginning of negotiations with black leaders to write a new constitution to enfranchise all South Africans. Events moved quickly; elections were held and in 1994 the South African government passed into the hands of the black majority. The long struggle for political independence in Africa had ended.

Namibia

A similar situation existed in Namibia (South-West Africa) which South Africa had administered as a mandate of the League of Nations since 1920. In 1946 the United Nations refused South Africa's request that the mandate be incorporated into its territory. The reasons were that South Africa had exploited African labor, failed to provide educational and social amenities, and pursued a policy of racial discrimination. Although rebuffed by the United Nations, South Africa continued to administer the mandate without international supervision, justifying its action on the ground that the dissolution of the League of Nations terminated legal international obligations. Thus, in effect, Namibia existed under two authorities—the United Nations and South Africa.

In 1960 two former members of the League, Liberia and Ethiopia, initiated proceedings in the International Court of Justice, charging that South Africa had violated provisions of the mandate agreement and the covenant of the League of Nations. The court was specifically asked to uphold an earlier advisory opinion that the United Nations had inherited responsibility for administering South-West Africa. South Africa denied the claim, and in 1966 the court refused to rule on the question.

The determination of South Africa to apply its apartheid policy in the territory, and the failure of the great powers or the United Nations to take strong measures on behalf of Namibians (South-West Africans) placed a heavier responsibility on the principal nationalist organizations, the South-West Africa National Union (SWANU) and the South-West Africa Peoples' Organization (SWAPO), to continue spearheading the liberation movement in Africa, at the United Nations, and elsewhere abroad.

Increasingly the Namibian crisis became entangled with the situation in Angola. When the revolution in Portugal ended the dictatorship in 1974, it hastened the independence of Portuguese colonies. In the case of Angola, the MPLA won independence with substantial assistance from the Soviet Union, including the financing of its ally, Cuba, to send some fifteen thousand Cuban troops that remained to protect the regime from attacks by UNITA, which had the financial backing of the United States and South Africa.

The United States led an unsuccessful effort to deny recognition, but Angola became independent and assumed its position in the United Nations. UNITA, on the other hand, solidified its position in the southern part of the country and continued to receive assistance from the United States and South Africa.

This complex situation led the United States and South Africa to insist that negotiations for Namibia's independence be linked to a withdrawal of the Cubans from neighboring Angola. Although the Angolan government agreed to consider a partial withdrawal, it also insisted that the Cubans were in the country as a result of the government's invitation, a prerogative of an independent state. This argument was supported by the African countries and others as well. Negotiations finally led to the Cuban withdrawal and Namibia became independent in 1990, after over a hundred years of colonial dependency under Germany, the League of Nations/United Nations, and South Africa.

16
The Quest for Unity

The several threads of pan-Africanism culminated in the formation of the Organization of African Unity (OAU) in 1963. The decisive threads in Africa stemmed from the Conference of Independent African States, which Nkrumah and Padmore organized in Ghana in April 1958. Due respect was paid to the pioneer pan-Africanists in the diaspora and a warm welcome was extended to the black delegates in attendance from the United States and the West Indies. The conference then laid the basis for a unity of purpose and action among Africans: The delegates agreed to cooperate for the complete emancipation of Africa, and they recommended the negotiation of trade agreements and cultural exchange. They also decided to establish the African Group at the United Nations to consult and coordinate African policies. In September the Pan-African Freedom Movement of East and Central Africa was launched in Tanganyika with Nyerere as host. It agreed to foster pan-Africanism, coordinate national programs, create a freedom fund, and assist nationalist movements in Africa. In November Ghana and Guinea announced their union, which was later joined by Mali, and declared this as a nucleus of a

United States of Africa. Then in December delegates representing political and labor groups, mostly in colonies, attended the All-African Peoples' Conference in Ghana.

This momentum of solidarity in 1958 became more divisive by 1960. The increasing number of independent nations gave rise to personal conflicts, highlighted national priorities, and revealed different attitudes regarding the civil disorders in the Congo, the question of Algeria's status, and Morocco's claim over Mauritania. Many if not most of those differences no doubt resulted from the historical isolation caused by colonialism, and the resulting languages and perspectives of the colonial powers concerned. In any case, splinter groups emerged: the Brazzaville Group, or African and Malagasy Union (1961), which became the Afro-Malagasy Common Organization (1965), comprised France's former tropical colonies, Guinea excepted; the more militant Casablanca Group (1961) included Ghana, Guinea, Mali, Morocco, the United Arab Republic, and the provisional government of Algeria. Then followed the Monrovia Conference and a subsequent meeting in Lagos, but the Casablanca Group boycotted both.

Seventeen African countries achieved independence in 1960, two in 1961, four in 1962, for a total of thirty-two by 1963, excluding South Africa. Also by that time, Algeria was independent, the Congo crisis was temporarily resolved, and the white supremacist regimes in southern Africa became the primary target of the newly independent nations. The time now seemed ripe for another dimension of pan-Africanism. Thus, the venerable Emperor Haile Selassie I seized the initiative and convened in Addis Ababa a conference of African state delegations, which founded the OAU in May 1963. While the charter of the organization recognizes the sovereign equality of member nations, it emerged in "response to the aspiration of our peoples for brotherhood and solidarity in a large unity transcending ethnic and national differences."

The OAU was founded at a time when the spirit of pan-Africanism pervaded Africa. Nkrumah's vision of a United States of Africa excited many Africans and non-Africans alike. And although he, Nasser, and a few other heads of state did not carry the day for a strong, centralized body, the signing of the charter establishing the OAU was itself a momentous event.

Despite the jubilation of the moment, serious and complex problems have faced the OAU from its inception. Organizationally, it has been an assembly of heads of state designed to provide a forum for international issues, to seek solidarity on matters of common concern, and to mediate intra-African conflicts.

All the member states are artificial creations, with boundaries inherited from the colonial powers. Rather than face endless problems of trying to untangle the impossible, the OAU accepted the principle of maintaining existing borders. In addition, it adopted the principle of noninterference in the affairs of other countries. These two basic principles were designed to minimize intra-African conflicts and lead to greater cooperation.

When the OAU was founded, nearly twenty states were still colonies and several were involved in armed struggles for independence. The OAU thus established what became one of its most important organs, the Liberation Committee. When in 1964 the African Development Bank (not part of the OAU) was established, prospects for the future of Africa looked bright.

The extent to which the OAU has been a vital force in Africa may be revealed through an examination of how and with what results the body has responded to its basic principles. With respect to the principle of maintaining the territorial boundaries, the body took a firm stand. Such a stand during Biafra's efforts to secede from Nigeria is credited with preventing the major powers from stepping in and playing an effective part, even though Tanzania and a few other states expressed support for Biafra.

The OAU's rejection of the establishment of the Bantustans also deterred recognition of these entities by other nations and helped assume territorial integrity for the new South Africa. The powers of the world did not want to risk enmity of African states by ignoring their continental organization. The body also continued to try mediation in the situation of breakaway efforts in the Horn of Africa. These few examples confirm that the OAU originally held to its principle on boundaries and thus was a factor in keeping the lid on territorial integrity. How much longer this would last became a matter of debate, because secessionist movements regarded their grievances as legitimate and have widespread local support.

The policy of the United States was cause for some concern. The U.S. government decided in 1986 to resume support to UNITA in its struggle to overthrow the official Angolan government of the MPLA. This conflict threatened the tenure and unity of the MPLA regime and the country. This issue dated back to 1975 when the United States sought unsuccessfully to prevent recognition of the MPLA at independence. The OAU held firm and won the day.

On the issue of noninterference in the affairs of other states, the results are uneven. Angola also fits this discussion, for not only the United States but also Zaire sought to destabilize the MPLA. And while the several states refrained from direct involvement in the Nigeria-Biafra crisis, other cases show the opposite. Tanzania clearly violated the principle when it sent troops into Uganda to assist in the overthrow of Amin and Libya disregarded the principle when it occupied part of northern Chad. South Africa was not a member of the OAU and disregarded its principles at will, especially when it wanted to invade neighboring countries to attack African National Congress supporters.

The high level of political instability evidenced by numerous coups in the 1970s and early 1980s was exacerbated by the long years of drought, and resulted in serious refugee problems. Host states assumed a large responsibility for social services and unrest as a result of refugee communities. Many of those refugees initiated and continued armed struggles against their home regimes. These problems as well as others like the armed clash between Egypt and Libya in 1977, ongoing internal conflicts like that between northern and southern Sudan, within Ethiopia, etc., severely taxed the individual states and the OAU's Commission on Mediation, Conciliation and Arbitration.

During the early years of the OAU, Nkrumah, Nasser, and Selassie dominated the scene as influential figures in Africa. They often sought to resolve intra-African crises. Indeed, the emperor played a key role in the 1972 peace settlement between northern and southern Sudan. Julius Nyerere emerged as an influential figure especially in the early 1970s. But by the mid-1970s Nigeria began to assert its influence.

Having consolidated itself after years of civil strife in the 1960s, Nigeria rose to international prominence as a major oil-producing country. During the 1974–75 Arab oil embargo, for example, Nigeria became the primary supplier of crude oil to the United States; afterward its position became second to Saudi Arabia, and the United States became its major trading partner.

As a member of OPEC (Organization of Petroleum Exporting Countries) Nigeria received impressive international exposure. Its spokesmen therefore commanded world attention. It was thus significant when Nigeria asserted its support to recognize the MPLA regime over United States opposition in 1975.

Nigeria has not backed away from admonishing African states. It denounced executions for corruption by Ghana's Jerry Rawlings, and executions as revenge against the Tolbert regime by Liberia's Sergeant Doe; and it criticized Tanzania's invasion of Uganda to help in the overthrow of Idi Amin. At the 1980 OAU meeting Nigeria interceded to prevent a crisis among member states over the question of recognition of the Saharan Arab Democratic Republic. Nigeria also tried to mediate the crisis between Chad and Libya. But Nigeria's effectiveness has been diminished by its continued political instability and change of presidents, regional, ethnic, religious, and class conflicts, as well as economic crises, oil notwithstanding.

In the final analysis the president of the OAU is the acknowledged spokesman and leader of Africa. He travels frequently to member states and abroad to consult on various matters. He automatically becomes involved when intra- or inter-African crises develop. But not only does the position have little real executive power, the OAU itself has no standing army and must rely primarily on funds from member states, most of which are usually in arrears.

To be effective, therefore, the president must establish a dynamic presence to gain meaningful continental and world influence. Unfortunately, Idi Amin's term did not bring respect to the office, and Qaddafy's tenure aroused considerable controversy because of his strong anti-Western stance and interference in the affairs of Chad. The situation improved with the election of Abdou Diouf of Senegal, a moderate and respected head of state. But Diouf's term was full of crises, not the least of which was the drought. In addition, the growing recession in the world and diminished interest in African affairs following the earlier nation-building years combined to make influential leadership difficult.

As Africa's national leaders seem to be focusing more attention on internal structures and means of employing resources more effectively, so too is the case with the OAU. At its summit a number of reforms continued to be discussed, including some structural changes and the establishment of an Assembly for Development Cooperation to facilitate coordinated economic planning. These and other reforms embodied in the Turkson Report (1977) are still under consideration.

A critical problem the OAU faces is the tension between nationalism and continentalism. Having won national power, too few leaders are prepared to concede authority to a higher order. This is also a national vs. continental problem for other continent-wide groups such as the trade unions: All-African Trade Union

Federation, African Trade Union Confederation, and the Organization of African Trade Union Unity. These unions must be careful not to run afoul of national governments.

As seen in previous chapters, regional groupings have had some short-lived success. Most of them, however, have been oriented toward economic issues. Although the East African Federation, which facilitated economic and cultural cooperation, broke up over complaints that Kenya benefited more than did Uganda and Tanzania, there is talk of reviving a similar organization. Several such groupings exist in West Africa: the Mano River Union of Liberia, Sierra Leone and Guinea; the Economic Community of African States (fifteen). Senegal and Gambia formed the Senegambian Confederation, following the earlier model of Tanzania that combined Tanganyika and Zanzibar. Somalia emerged as a combination of both British and Italian Somalilands.

A little discussed problem of the OAU is the membership of several of its members in non-African organizations whose activities sometimes conflict with the OAU. The Arab League, for example, requires divided loyalty on the part of eight African states. And associate membership in the European Economic Community places some constraint on affected OAU members. Such dual or even multi-memberships may be inevitable and thus need to be closely monitored to prevent serious conflicts of interest.

The Organization of African Unity's policies of respecting the borders inherited from the colonial powers and the nonintervention in the affairs of other countries have caused havoc in a number of countries and regions and fueled secessionist movements. The policy of nonintervention was seriously challenged by Amin in the 1970s. Even then, one head of state, Julius Nyerere of Tanzania, who did not subscribe to the policy, invaded Uganda in 1979 in an effort that led to the overthrow of Amin. During the 1980s and early 1990s dozens of conflicts occurred without intervention, including the 1994 slaying of a reported half a million Tutsis in Rwanda. That incident caused a tremendous migration into neighboring countries and created a serious refugee problem.

In the past the UN stepped in in a major way, as was the case in Somalia and Liberia. But the UN rejected intervention in Burundi and that forced action upon the OAU, which encouraged some of its members to act. Once again Nyerere emerged as senior statesman to lead negotiations in Central Africa to resolve the serious problems confronting the Hutus and Tutsis. Significantly, Tanzania, Kenya, Uganda, Ethiopia, Zaire, and Rwanda initiated sanctions against Burundi. The lingering conflict in Liberia is another example of a challenge to the policy of nonintervention. In this case, Nigeria led a military contingent to restore stability there and, more recently, in Sierra Leone as well. However, the Nigerian government of General Sani Abacha came to power after having incarcerated Mashood Abiola who appeared to have won the election as president in 1994. But it will be years before the problem of nonintervention will be resolved and there are other areas with similar flashpoints.

The other policy of maintaining colonial-era borders is closely related to the problem of ethnic conflict. No borders are free from contestation in Africa. Thus, conflict is virtually inevitable. That of course is the reason for ignoring the issue, for to confront it risks turmoil all over the continent. The fact that Eritrea succeeded in declaring its independence from Ethiopia could set a precedent in two regards. First, borders in Africa are not sacrosanct; and second, negotiations remain a route for settlement, although in this case, resolution followed many years of war. Still, negotiations finally brought what seems now to be a peaceful solution.

However, effective unity eludes most world and regional bodies; Africa is no exception.

17

Africa and Contemporary Issues

The preceding chapters have clearly demonstrated that Africa is heterogeneous. It has over fifty independent countries with an approximate population of more than five to eight hundred million people speaking hundreds of different languages and practicing indigenous religions alongside Islam and Christianity. The countries vary greatly in size and density of population. Some are arid and others receive heavy rainfall; most are coastal but several are landlocked. These factors have greatly influenced Africa's history and helped to shape its present condition.

As diverse as African countries are, there exist commonalities. They are ethnically diverse; have vulnerable, basically agrarian societies, with a few engaged in significant mineral extraction; have high birth and death rates; and are heavily dependent on foreign assistance. In addition, all African governments face the challenge of developing and implementing policies directly and indirectly affecting traditional practices regarding gender, courtship, marriage, family, labor roles, health care, legal procedures, religion, etc. Although committed to resolving this myriad of problems, leaders in contemporary Africa must also build on their indigenous heritage.

No attempt is made here to discuss in detail any particular country, leader, or event; rather, the focus is placed on key issues and trends perceived in Africa as a whole. Vital cultural and social issues will receive particular attention. The reader is thus challenged not only to relate these contemporary developments to the historical continuum but to pursue additional investigation in the recommended sources and elsewhere.

Economic Issues

Until about 1500, when international trade consisted essentially of luxury goods and items in demand by the aristocracies in different, primarily European countries, African societies were subsistence economies either excluded from or highly peripheral to that trade. The industrial revolution of the eighteenth century prompted the industrial capitalist countries, notably Great Britain, to link overseas territories to the metropolitan states for raw materials, markets, and investments. Africa was thus brought closer into the international economy.

As France, Germany, and other European countries, and the United States, gradually challenged Britain's commercial supremacy, the scramble for African colonies intensified, partition occurred, and European migration to the continent increased, with white settlements springing up principally in the highlands of eastern, central, and southern Africa. These developments accelerated the trend toward greater political and economic planning by Europeans to assure beneficial structural arrangements between the imperial power and its colonies.

Although still peripheral and more dependent, African countries were brought into a closer relationship with the major powers in international trade and provided certain cash crops: timber, coffee, tea, sugar, cocoa, meat, and minerals—gold, copper, diamonds, bauxite, etc. The processing of these products occurred in the imperial countries. The critical point here is that from the late eighteenth century and especially during the nineteenth century, Africa increasingly became a dependent partner in the expanding world economy.

At the same time, a growing number of Africans became socialized in European culture as missionaries, teachers, clerks, lawyers, physicians, and business persons. It was primarily from these classes that the leaders of the nationalist movements and first heads of state emerged. Understandably, therefore, the socioeconomic system these early leaders knew best was the one in which they had been schooled and gained their political experience and power. The message of most of them at the time of independence seems to have been for control over, not destruction of, the existing systems. They no doubt honestly wanted to modify the systems for the greater benefit of Africans generally, but seem not to have fully perceived the enormity of the task. They very likely realized, however, that the elimination of the existing system would have destroyed not only their and their colleagues' hoped-for economic and political bases, but would have seriously delayed the chances of fulfilling the material aspirations of their people.

Given this situation and the fact that the colonial powers, on recognizing that independence was inevitable, sought to transfer power to the most sympathetic leaders, one is not surprised that several political and economic agreements favorable to both the imperial power and the new leaders were consummated. These agreements extended political, economic, and cultural links with the former colonial powers. For example, to help ease the situation in Kenya, since white settlers feared retribution after independence, Britain agreed to make subsidized payments so that the new government could purchase land from the white settlers. In this way the government had more land to distribute to Africans for use, the settlers received payments for their land, and Britain strengthened its ties with the government of Kenya. But the arrangement made Kenya more dependent on Britain.

Many other examples illustrate not only how the colonial system socialized many Africans into the Western mode but also how specific agreements riveted the former colonies to the excolonial power. Perhaps the best examples are those of the former French colonies, which, except for Guinea, initially agreed to remain in the French community and thus continue to have strong ties to France rather than complete independence. The former British colonies were admitted into the Commonwealth in which they receive preferential treatment. Both blocs of countries thus became more integral parts of the international economic order by virtue of their dependent relationship on the major Western powers that determined world economic policies and controlled their implementation.

Even when Africans nationalized expatriate firms, the problems of skilled manpower, spare parts, access to capital, shipping concessions, fluctuation of prices, scientific research, product substitutes, international advertisements, and so forth posed insurmountable obstacles. In addition, protective measures against imports by foreign countries, and competition with other countries in Africa and elsewhere have severely crippled African economies. In the final analysis many African leaders have had to appeal to the world bodies and former colonial powers to provide relief in the form of grants, loans, and other kinds of assistance.

Africa is dependent on foreign exchange for development. Consequently, it continues to promote the production of cash crops and minerals for foreign markets and relies heavily on foreign firms for basic imports, including food. But agricultural and mining output have declined over the last decade or so. Part of this resulted from the oil crisis of the 1970s and the escalation of energy costs, which caused a rise in prices for other products. The Arab oil-producing countries did not provide the amount of assistance they had led Africans to expect as a result of the latter's support of them in the Arab-Israeli conflict.

But some oil-producing countries in Africa benefited from the crisis. Nigeria, Libya, and Gabon, for example, were able to garner a part of the world market. Nigeria is a good example. It became the principal supplier of crude oil to the United States during the Arab oil embargo of 1974–75, and subsequently ranked the second major supplier after Saudi Arabia. The United States became Nigeria's major trading partner for oil. However, the mid-1980s witnessed a depression of oil prices and these African countries suffered dramatic setbacks along with other world oil-producing states.

These several problems have made African states heavily dependent on foreign aid arrangements. Thus the external debt for the continent has reached over an estimated $315 billion, with about $79 billion to service that debt. This situation encourages inflation and additional borrowing, discourages investments, deepens dependency, and contributes to political instability.

Although some of these difficulties have resulted from the colonial period, a lack of experience and expertise, failure of domestic policies, corruption, natural disasters such as the drought, and so forth, share responsibility. During the 1970s and 1980s the Sahelian countries, Ethiopia, the Sudan, and parts of eastern Africa were severely affected by the drought. Several million people died as a result, while millions of others suffered malnutrition, deformation, and disease. It is of course impossible to calculate the impact of this calamity on the ecological, demographic, political, economic, health, and psychological future of Africa and its people.

There have been some brighter spots during independence. Note has been taken of the breakthrough for African oil producers. Important economic growth occurred in Botswana, Cameroon, Ivory Coast, Kenya, and Malawi. Cameroon deserves a special word. It is located at a crossroad of great linguistic and ethnic diversity and yet has had reasonable stability over the last generation. That helped to facilitate a bilingual (English and French) policy and the development of an agricultural, mineral, and oil economy based on French backing. Largely because of these factors, President Ahmadou Ahijo was able to effect a peaceful transition of power when he stepped aside and became one of a few African heads of state to voluntarily vacate the office. Presidents Senghor of Senegal and Julius Nyerere of Tanzania are others.

An especially significant trend is the growing recognition on the part of African leaders of the following: deficiencies in aspects of domestic policies and their implementation; more emphasis necessary for efficiency and honesty in government and the private sector; closer scrutiny of problems before committing public funds; that modernization will be a slow and difficult process; and the contribution of traditional experiences can contribute to the process. In short, there is a growing consensus that African leaders must face these realities if development is to occur.

These were prominent factors in the minds of the several African heads of state when in 1980 they signed the Lagos Plan of Action as a blueprint for an Economic Community of Africa. Follow-up statements by those leaders at the OAU summit in 1985 show that they placed a high priority on these concerns. Noteworthy also is the fact that the World Bank has outlined a Joint Program of Action that calls for collaborative efforts between African governments and international donors. The design of this program would be agriculture and policy reform.

This may well be the kind of convergence that will mark Africa's accelerated move from the economic periphery toward the center.

Socio-political Issues

Having achieved independence, African leaders and their followers faced the complex task of establishing a national identity as a basis for national unity. Within their artificial boundaries, and at the outset of independence, all African governments sought to balance ethnic loyalty with an emphasis on national identity. President Sekou Touré, for example, called on his Guinean compatriots to regard themselves primarily as Guineans and secondly as Susu, Fula, Malinke, etc. But in fact, ethnicity remains a dominant element of life throughout Africa, especially when it becomes necessary to mobilize grassroots support for political purposes. Ethnicity, therefore, is at the root of the political process in Africa.

This process is also rooted in class interests. Although class consolidation varies from country to country and region to region and even though communal or ethnic affiliation frequently transcends class, there exists in parts of Africa a small landed gentry, a Western- and a Muslim-oriented elite in business and government. The military also constitutes a class interest, and there are religious interests as well. Indeed, the principal political and economic leaders emerged from these interest groups that formed part of the struggle for independence. Independence was nationtime, a period when Africans united seemed on the verge of controlling their own destiny and of deciding and implementing policies of their own choice, based on their own values and aspirations.

That was indeed an era of great excitement, enthusiasm, and optimism throughout Africa and much of the world where many people and several governments, for various reasons, hoped to join in the building of new nations and the development of viable economies. But by the end of the 1960s the euphoria had to be tempered, and by the 1980s serious questions arose about the prospects for African development.

This course of events stemmed from the fact that African independence afforded an opportunity for change and experimentation. What indeed surfaced early across the continent reflected the determination to establish a system that would serve the people equitably, and the formula most frequently cited was African socialism, which essentially meant a basis in African traditions of communalism coupled with consensus democracy or democratic centralism. There had to be, it was argued, a central force to galvanize a consensus that would be implemented. Thus, the one-party system became a model for many countries. But whether the one-party or multi-party system was adopted, African socialism was the central ingredient.

This context was ideal for Ghana's Kwame Nkrumah, the charismatic leader of the continent's first independent black country, which had a comfortable national budget based on cocoa. He was well-educated and experienced in the United States and England where he became acquainted with several brands of socialism. The "African Personality" became his creed as he promoted the path of African socialism for Ghana and the rest of Africa, and as he insisted, "Ghana would not be free until all of Africa was free." His appeal in Africa was enormous.

Julius Nyerere of Tanzania also charted a route of African socialism, with a one-party system. Nyerere aimed for self-reliance and equity with concentration on the *ujamma* (Swahili term for community), where the peasants would gain control over production. Development was to come without massive foreign aid.

The free enterprise or capitalist system also had its proponents. The Ivory Coast was a leading example of this approach. President Houphouet-Boigny and his colleagues established a single party and decided to pursue the route laid out by France, supported by French aid. And although Kenya's leaders joined the chorus on African socialism, they also pursued the capitalist route. In reality, to varying degrees the several countries implemented a mixed system of state control and private enterprise.

Although the trend has been toward the one-party state, several countries pursued the multi-party route: Botswana, Ghana, Kenya, and Nigeria, for example. But neither form of government has escaped instability, with coups and attempted coups. Indeed, by 1974 the following countries had experienced at least one military coup: Algeria, Benin, Burkina Faso, Burundi, Central African Republic, Congo, Egypt, Ethiopia, Ghana, Libya, Mali, Niger, Nigeria, Sierra Leone, Somalia, Sudan, Togo, Uganda, and Zaire. Of all of these, the several coups in Nigeria and the secessionist attempt by Biafra were supremely illustrative of the price of national unity.

There have been various kinds of coups and results. Perhaps the most disastrous and notorious examples occurred in the Central African Republic and Uganda. In the former case, Jean-Bedel Bokassa, who had a secondary education and military service as a noncommissioned officer, benefited from a policy of Africanization and was promoted to the position of chief of staff, which provided him with the base from which he seized power in 1966. After his meteoric ascendancy to power Bokassa demonstrated a lack of understanding of the magnitude of the national problems and how to deal with them. Although he became a patron of schools and the university was named after him, Bokassa's greatest legacy is one of pomposity, extravagance, massive torture and murder, and economic and political strife.

Uganda was a special case. Idi Amin rose to power from the non-commissioned ranks to chief of staff as a result of an Africanization policy. He is reported to have been functionally illiterate but a good soldier. He remained suspicious and resentful of intellectuals, many of whom he ordered murdered while others simply disappeared.

Asians became Amin's early target after he became president in 1971. Since the colonial era Asians had for the most part owned the big plantations and dominated the import-export business as well as the wholesale and retail sectors of the economy. In addition, like many expatriates, large numbers of them had retained British passports and had not sought Ugandan citizenship, a sore spot for Ugandans. In fact, Amin accused the Asians of exploiting the people and preventing African advancement. Thus in 1972 he gave non-citizen Asians three months to leave the country.

Those with British passports were taken in by Britain and Commonwealth countries; a few went to India and Pakistan; others went into general exile. An estimated forty thousand to sixty thousand departed.

At the time, the expulsion of Asians seemed popular not only in Uganda but in other countries where Asians and Europeans retained economic advantage without taking out citizenship. Many critics regarded this as a lack of confidence in and commitment to African governments at a time when they were under pressure to Africanize.

Amin, his cohorts, and a number of businessmen appropriated Asian property. How much was turned into productive pursuits for the people instead of serving selfish desires is debatable. In the longer run, however, the expulsion left a major void of expertise, capital, and confidence among foreign investors. It remained one of the factors feeding the long years of civil strife, torture and murder, low morale, and psychological malaise related to the Amin regime. Milton Obote, who succeeded Amin, oversaw continued economic and political deterioration. Political reconciliation and economic reconstruction resumed after Yoweri Museveni assumed power in 1986.

Another kind of coup occurred in 1965 when Joseph Mobutu gained control over the government of Congo-Kinshasha after a period of violent clashes between rival forces with foreign backing. Mobutu, also from the noncommissioned ranks, was welcomed as hope for stability after the days of Katanga's secession and Lumumba's assassination. The early years of Mobutu's regime were marked especially by efforts to Africanize. He adopted the name Sese Seko instead of Joseph and changed the name of the country to Zaire. He urged his compatriots to follow his example. However, his reliance on the capitalist system led to heavy investments by Western powers, which in turn led to large scale corruption, with rumors that he became one of the richest persons in the world.

By the late 1970s Mobutu had established an authoritarian system against which a number of resistance groups emerged. But the Western powers, the United States in particular, supported him mainly as a counter to perceived communist influence and a possible loss of economic advantage. The economy, however, was allowed to decline as the government tightened its hold. Increasingly isolated from the people, Mobutu's regime resorted to the tactics of brutality, torture, and murder. He finally was overthrown in 1997 and Laurent Kabila became head of state.

The record of military coups in Africa is mixed. Some led to economic advancement and greater political openness than others. Gamal Abdel Nasser's 1952 overthrow of King Farouk of Egypt was followed by political and economic advancement and influence in the world. The early regimes following the overthrow of Nkrumah pursued policies that addressed economic problems, lessened corruption, and organized free elections that reinstalled civilian rule, which later strayed as a result of economic extravagance, political restrictions, and resistance from the Western powers. Becoming head of state following a coup in Ghana, Jerry Rawlings, in spite of some human rights abuses, set his country on the road to economic advancement and stability. The coup by General Omar al-Bashir in Sudan in 1989 failed to end the fighting between the largely Arabized and Islamized northerners and mostly non-Muslim southerners. Rather, repression deepened and the economy deteriorated significantly. The coup led by General Ibrahim Babangida in Nigeria in 1985 was regarded as having been a positive move to reverse the course of economic disaster; but his regime became increasingly authoritarian; and his refusal to accept the 1994 election of Mashood Abiola led to the assumption of power by General Sani Abacha, with internal and world protests and limited sanctions by the United States supported by TransAfrica.[1]

---

[1] For the first time a major African-American organization publicly protested against an African government.

In the case of Libya, whatever one might say about Qaddafy, he did launch that country toward economic transformation with increased agricultural productivity in previously arid lands. Of course the oil boom greatly accelerated the country's development. Libya is one of the few countries able to provide economic and military assistance to neighboring countries. On the other hand, Qaddafy's aggressive stance, occupation of Chad, and support for international revolutionary movements and terrorism create anxiety and fear among a number of African as well as non-African countries.

The Ethiopian case differs from all the others. Following his triumphant return to the throne in 1941, Emperor Haile Selassie began a series of reforms and attracted foreign investments as a way to modernize. As a symbol of African struggle and liberation and its revered place in history, Ethiopia was chosen as the headquarters for the Organization of African Unity, which brought additional prestige and visibility to the emperor, Ethiopians, and the country. These several factors and the rising tide of anticolonialism brought Ethiopians into closer touch with momentous changes taking place throughout Africa and elsewhere. A result was that a number of groups expressed disappointment about the country's unfavorable infrastructure, general lack of development and political responsiveness compared with neighboring ex-colonies. These concerns led to protests that sparked attempted coups that failed.

In 1974, however, Colonel Haile Mengistu Mariam and his colleagues succeeded in overthrowing the emperor and established a Marxist regime with Soviet backing. In 1977 when Somalia, a former Soviet ally, invaded the Ogaden as part of its plan to reunite all Somalis, the Russians provided Ethiopia, a former United States ally, with technical advisers, equipment, and support from some eighteen thousand Cuban troops. With this aid the Ethiopian government not only decisively defeated the Somalis, it also mounted strong attacks against Eritrean, Oromo, and Tigray resistance.

The Ethiopian regime continued to develop a communist state, while facing a number of internal resistance movements. Peace on its borders with Somalia and Sudan was precarious, and its economy was in straits. All of this was complicated by the disastrous drought over several years. Finally, Mengistu was overthrown in 1991 and replaced by Meles Zenawi, whose government later endorsed a constitution that supports political decentralization and the possibility of secession for its ethnic groups. In fact, Eritrea won its independence from Ethiopia in 1991 as the Zenawi forces gained control. It is worthy of note that recognition of the right of secession in Ethiopia departs from the earlier commitment of OAU members to the inviolability of established borders. This could become a significant precedent for other states.

Much of the political instability during Africa's first generation of independence stemmed from inexperience and a weak base for parliamentary democracy and party politics. In addition to ethnic rivalries, insufficient resources, and unrealistic aspirations, foreign involvement complicated the situation. Indeed, the deep involvement of the former colonial powers, the United States, the Soviet Union, and, to a lesser extent, the Republic of China has been an integral part of independent Africa's experience. This reflects Africa's political and economic fragility; it also reveals African diplomatic agility in maneuvering to maintain nonalignment, the status proclaimed by most African countries during the Cold War.

Several examples will suffice. For the first twenty-five years or so after independence, the following countries switched ties, when the pressure became great, between the United States and the Soviet Union: Egypt, Sudan, Somalia, and Ethiopia. Moreover, although the emergence of a number of Marxist-oriented governments in Africa—Angola, Benin, Congo, Ethiopia, Mozambique, and Zimbabwe—and significant arms sales to Algeria and Libya demonstrated the Soviet Union's determination to cultivate influence on the continent, to challenge United

States and Western European influence, the African states themselves seemed committed to nonalignment. The Congo, for instance, proclaimed its Marxist ideology and received military and economic aid from the Soviet Union, but refused to permit Soviet bases in the country and maintained close ties with France. In short, African states were not satellite countries but were pragmatic in their struggle for independent survival.

The situation with China was different. It had the advantage of being non-Western, non-white, underdeveloped, critical of both the United States and the Soviet Union, and virulently anticolonial, anti-imperial, and antiracist in its pronouncements. China thus identified strongly with Africa and the Third World generally.

During those early decades of African independence, China demonstrated significant economic development without reliance on foreign aid and represented a potential model for African states. And although it had only limited resources available for export, China made a few dramatic accomplishments on the continent. The construction of Tanzam, the 1,200-mile railroad link between Lusaka, Zambia, and Dar es Salaam, Tanzania, was hailed at the time as a capital achievement; and the building of the highway in mountainous Rwanda is regarded as a well-engineered feat. Moreover, the Chinese established a consistent reputation of being hard workers, doing quality work, being efficient, and maintaining good relations with the indigenous workers. Still, Chinese involvement in Africa was very limited and they, like the other major powers, were charged with racial incidents against African students in their country.

Democratization

For the 1990s, the issue of democratization has dominated discussions about Africa's political future. One-party states and authoritarian leaders, so popular in the first decades of independence, by the 1980s in particular came under great pressure by the Western powers and international financial organizations like the World Bank and the International Monetary Fund. Those pressures increased significantly as governments and private organizations around the world were aroused by the fragmentation and population displacement, accompanied by some major human rights abuses, involved in the collapse of the Soviet Union in 1991, which signaled the demise of the Cold War and the emergence of the United States as the single superpower; the several cases of ethnic conflict, for example, in Ethiopia, Eritrea, Burundi, Rwanda, Somalia, Liberia, and Sierra Leone also added to world anxiety about democracy, stability, and economic development in Africa. These concerns reinforced longer-standing grievances of the African masses who reacted against corruption, dictatorial rule, human rights violations, gender inequity, and economic and infrastructural deterioration.

During the 1980s and 1990s some Western leaders saw the expansion of an assertive Islam in Algeria, Sudan, and elsewhere as a threat to democratic institutions and secularism in Africa. This issue remains and demonstrates the lack of consensus about the meaning and process for the establishment and maintenance of democracy in Africa.

For Westerners, periodic, free, and open elections between and among political parties, and respect for freedom of thought, expression, and assembly are necessary ingredients of a democratic society, whereas the current African political systems were inherited from European colonialists who excluded Africans, violated basic rights of expression and assembly, detained Africans without due process, and governed in an authoritarian manner. Moreover, precolonial African states generally were characterized by centralization and strong, frequently authoritarian leadership. Colonial rule reinforced and entrenched this state of affairs by bringing many ethnic groups under the authority of a single imperial power, often governing indirectly. In short, African states have a significantly different political heritage, indigenous and colonial, from that of the West and not surprisingly have great difficulty adopting the Western mode of democratization.

This process has been aggravated by the fact that not only did the great powers ignore human rights violations during the imposition of colonial rule, they handsomely rewarded undemocratic regimes that supported Western national interests during the Cold War. With the end of the Cold War and thus little or no opportunity to play one power against another for major financial gains, a new era of African development emerged; and with it a new generation of African leaders is assuming power and seems more committed to greater concentration on African resources for development. Most of them are products of their countries since independence and have been educated in national schools, socialized by national institutions, and evince a confidence in Africa's future. They are committed to local values and seem to be prepared to rely on relevant internal solutions. Unencumbered by training and experience in a colonial society and not overly constrained by contracts, promises, agreements, or convictions about European models, this new generation should find greater freedom to experiment with bold solutions for the challenges they must face in the twenty-first century.

Bibliographical Notes

General

These bibliographical notes are primarily intended to suggest some additional readings for each chapter. The suggestions are not exhaustive, and the reader is advised to consult the bibliographies of each work. In general, articles have been included only when they are of particular note or when there are few works in book form. In many cases, of course, works other than the ones cited could also suffice; time, space, and a sometimes arbitrary choice also had to be determinants of selections.

Before presenting the chapter notes, it is appropriate to refer to a few general and standard works that are not referred to in the chapter notes. There are three multi-volume collections that cover the history of the entire continent from the earliest times to the present. UNESCO's *General History of Africa,* which appears in English, French, Arabic, and several African languages, as well as prospective versions in German, Russian, Portuguese, Spanish, and Chinese, is the most ambitious. The drafting committee was two-thirds African, each volume's editor is African, and the chapters are written by experts from around the world. The eight volumes have been well received internationally. The three-volume *Encyclopedia of Africa* (Charles Scribner's Sons, 1997), produced under an international editorial board, is also a valuable resource.

The other multi-volume work is the *Cambridge History of Africa,* which is already established as a valuable source. Its editorial board is primarily European and so are most of its authors; some Africans and others are chapter authors.

The *Encyclopedia Africana Dictionary of African Biography*, published by Reference Publications, is the project initiated by W. E. B. DuBois many years ago and nourished by a number of scholars with major sponsorship by the government of Ghana. Twenty volumes are planned.

Roland Oliver, *The African Middle Ages, 1400–1800* and Oliver and Anthony Atmore, *Africa Since 1800* (Cambridge University Press, 1981) are useful shorter versions; Jack Goody, *Technology, Tradition and the State in Africa* (Oxford University Press, 1971) is a stimulating account.

Arnold Temu and Bonaventure Swai, *Historians and Africanist History: A Critique* (Zed Press, 1981) remains a penetrating analysis of post-colonial historiography.

Chapter 1   A Tradition of Myths and Stereotypes

Africana is replete with demeaning comments about Africans and their descendants, from Herodotus to the present time. But only a few systematic studies of this subject and its impact on African history have appeared. Three books that do relate to the problem but reach more moderate conclusions than this chapter does are: Philip Curtin, *The Image of Africa: British Ideas and Action 1780–1850* (Madison, Wis., 1964); Frank Snowden, *Blacks in Antiquity: Ethiopians in the Greco-Roman Experience* (Cambridge, Mass., 1970); and the first two sections of Robin Hallett, *The Penetration of Africa* (New York, 1965). For an African's interpretation of the American image, consult Felix N. Okoye, *The American Image of Africa: Myth and Reality* (Buffalo, N.Y., 1971).

In addition to works mentioned in the text of this chapter, the following ascribe achievements in African history to foreign influences: Hermann Junker, "The First Appearance of the Negroes in History," *Journal of Egyptian Archaeology*, VII (1921), pp. 121–32; D. B. MacIver, *Mediaeval Rhodesia* (New York, 1906); W. C. Willoughby, *Race Problem in New Africa* (Oxford, 1923); A. J. Arkell, *History of the Sudan* (London, 1961); J. Scott Keltie, *Partition of Africa* (London, 1895); and C. H. Stigand, *The Land of Zinj* (London, 1913). It is virtually impossible to list all such books, but one should note that the popular *Short History of Africa* by Oliver and Fage also speculates about the impact of Southwest Asian influences on "Sudanic" civilization.

Two good articles that helped to reinforce this author's opinions are in the *Journal of African History:* Wyatt MacGaffey, "Concepts of Race in the Historiography of Northeast Africa," vol. VII, no. 1 (1966), pp. 1–17; and Edith R. Sanders, "The Hamitic Hypothesis; Its Origins and Functions in Time Perspective," vol. X, no. 4 (1969), pp. 521–32. A third useful article is John Markakis, "African Nationalism and the History of Africa," *African Forum,* vol. III, no. 2, Fall 1967–Winter 1968.

The following are relevant recent works: Molefi Kete Asante, *Kemet: Afrocentricity and Knowledge* (Trenton, N.J., 1990); Martin Bernal, *Black Athena: The Afro-Asian Roots of Classical Civilization* (London, 1987); Cheikh Anta Diop, *The Cultural Unity of Black Africa* (Chicago, 1978); and Kwame Anthony Appiah, *In My Father's House: Africa in the Philosophy Culture* (Oxford, 1992).

The point should be made that the appearance of conscious or unconscious racially biased propositions does not mean those books should not be read; indeed, they should be read with an awareness of that perspective. The most significant study of this subject is St. Clair Drake's two-volumed *Black Folk Here and There* (Los Angeles, 1986, 1990), which surveys and analyzes the origins, development, and impact of color prejudice since antiquity and is rich in copious bibliographical notes and seminal ideas.

Chapter 2   The Evolution of Early African Societies

Very significant advances have been made in the understanding of Africa's prehistory. A valuable synthesis of the subject is by J. D. Clark, "The Prehistoric Origins of African Culture," *Journal of African History,* vol. V, no. 2 (1964). Recent views of Dr. Leakey and others are summarized in "Man in Africa," *Tarikh,* vol. I, no. 3 (1966). The standard books include: Sonia Cole, *The Prehistory of East Africa* (New York, 1965); J. D. Clark, *The Prehistory of Southern Africa* (New York, 1959); C. B. M. McBurney, *The Stone Age of Northern Africa* (New York, 1960); H. Alimen, *Préhistoire de l'Afrique* (Paris, 1955) and translated as *The Prehistory of Africa* in 1957; and George Murdoch, *Africa: Its People and Their Culture History* (New York, 1959). Also recommended are: V. G. Childe, *New Light on the Most Ancient East* (London, 1954); A. J. Arkell, *History of the Sudan from the Earliest Times to 1821* (London and New York, 1961); Merrick Posnansky, *Prelude to East African History* (London, 1966). Joseph H. Greenberg's

Studies in African Linguistics (New Haven, Conn., 1955) is also recommended. A good synthesis of Africa in the Iron Age is Basil Davidson's *Old Africa Rediscovered* (London, 1965), also published as *Lost Cities of Africa* (Boston, 1959).

The following are recommended: David Phillipson, *African Archaeology* (Cambridge, Mass., 1985) is good for current themes in the field; Christopher Ehret and Merrick Posnansky, *The Archaeological and Linguistic Reconstruction of African History* (Berkeley, London, and Los Angeles, 1983) is perhaps the best on its subject; Richard Leakey, *People of the Lake* (New York, 1978) updates the Leakey works; J. Desmond Clark and Steven A. Brandt, *From Hunters to Farmers* (Berkeley, London, and Los Angeles, 1984); and Andrew M. Watson, *Agricultural Innovation in the Early Islamic World. The Diffusion of Crops and Farming Techniques, 700–1100* (Cambridge, Mass., 1983) are highly recommended. Also recommended are: Martin Hall, *Settlement Patterns in the Iron Age of Zululand* (London, 1981); James Currey, *Archaeology Africa: Writing the Past* (Oxford, 1996); Marianne Convin, *Archeologie Africaise* (Paris, 1993); Peter R. Schmidt, *Historical Archaeology: A Structural Approach in African Culture* (Westport, Conn., 1978); and Roland Oliver and Briand M. Fagan, *Africa in the Iron Age* (Cambridge, Mass., 1975).

Chapter 3   Early Kingdoms and City-States

An excellent account of Africa in ancient times is L. A. Thompson and J. Ferguson (eds.), *Africa in Classical Antiquity* (Ibadan, 1969). For early Egypt, Kush, Axum, and Nubia, the following are recommended: Walter A. Fairservis, *The Ancient Kingdoms of the Nile* (New York, 1962); A. J. Arkell, *A History of the Sudan from the Earliest Times to 1821;* P. L. Shinnie, *Meroë* (London, 1967); Basil Davidson, *Lost Cities and Old Africa* (Boston, Mass., 1970); A. Kammerer, *Essai sur l'Histoire Antique d'Abyssinie* (Paris, 1926); Jean Doresse, *L'Empire du Prete-Jean* (Paris, 1957); Ernest Budge, *A History of Ethiopia* (New York, 1966); and various issues of the periodicals *Kush* and *Annales d'Ethiopes.* See also Richard Pankhurst, *The Ethiopian Royal Chronicles* (Addis Ababa and London, 1967).

Information pertaining to northern Africa and the western and central Sudan is abundant. Good recommendations include: B. H. Warmington, *Carthage* (Penguin, 1964); H. A. R. Gibb, *Ibn Battuta* (New York,

1958); J. D. Fage, *Ghana* (Madison, Wis., 1961); E. W. Bovill, *Caravans of the Old Sahara* (London, 1933) and *The Golden Trade of the Moors* (London, 1958); R. Mauny, *Tableau Geographique de l'Ouest Africain au Moyen Age* (Dakar, 1961); J. Rouch, *Contribution à l'Histoire des Songhay* (Dakar, 1953); H. R. Palmer, *Sudanese Memoires* (Lagos, 1928); Y. Urvoy, *Histoire de l'Empire du Bornu* (Paris, 1949); Leo Africanus, *The History and Description of Africa* (London, 1896); D. T. Niane, *Sundiata: An Epic of Old Mali* (New York, 1965); Nehemia Levtzion, *Muslims and Chiefs in West Africa* (Oxford, 1968); J. S. Trimingham, *A History of Islam in West Africa* (London, 1962) and *Islam in West Africa* (Oxford, 1959); Robert Smith, *Kingdoms of the Yoruba* (London, 1969); and Samuel Johnson, *The History of the Yorubas* (Lagos, 1937).

The first eleven chapters of B. A. Ogot and J. A. Kieran, *Zamani: A Survey of East African History* (New York, 1968) are most valuable for this chapter, while *History of East Africa* (London, 1963), vol. I, by Roland Oliver and Gervase Mathew is also recommended reading. G. P. S. Freeman-Grenville, *The Medieval History of the Coast of Tanganyika* (London, 1962) and *The East African Coast* (Oxford, 1962), deal credibly with those subjects. The dated account by Reginald Coupland, *East Africa and Its Invaders* (Oxford, 1938), is still useful. John Gray, *History of Zanzibar* (London, 1962), and Justus Standes, *The Portuguese Period in East Africa* (Nairobi, 1961), are valuable works. J. S. Trimingham's *Islam in the Sudan* (London, 1965) and *Islam in Ethiopia* (London and New York, 1965) are authoritative accounts. Trimingham's *Islam in East Africa* (Oxford, 1964) and I. M. Lewis, *Islam in Tropical Africa* (Oxford, 1966) deal effectively with Islam's impact on Africa and, to some extent, vice versa.

Note also Mordecai Abir, *Ethiopia and the Red Sea: The Rise and Decline of the Solomonic Dynasty and Muslim-European Rivalry in the Region* (London, 1980); Yusuf Fadl Hasan, *The Arabs and The Sudan* (Khartoum, Sudan, 1973); Aziz A. Batran, *Islam and Revolution in Africa* (Brattleboro, Vt., 1984); Elias N. Saad, *Social History of Timbuktu: The Role of Muslim Scholars and Notables, 1400–1900* (Cambridge, Mass., 1983); D. T. Niané, *Recherches sur l'Empire du Mali au Moyen Age* (Paris, 1975); and Sekéné Mody Cissoko, *Tombouctou et L'Empire Songhay* (Dakar, Abidjan, 1975).

Chapter 4   Africa and the World, 1400–1850

Several works examine the expansion of European contacts with Africans during the fifteenth century and the development of the Atlantic slave trade. A good introduction to the subject can be obtained in J. W. Blake, *Europeans in West Africa* (London, 1942); J. H. Parry, *Europe and a Wider World, 1415–1715* (London and New York, 1949); Eric Axelson, *The Portuguese in South-East Africa, 1600–1700* (Johannesburg, 1960); and James Duffy, *Portuguese Africa* (Cambridge, Mass., 1959).

For a direct focus on the Atlantic slave trade, a good survey is Basil Davidson, *Black Mother* (New York, 1968). Philip D. Curtin, *The Atlantic Slave Trade: A Census* (Madison, Wis., 1969), is an excellent synthesis of the literature on the subject as well as a valuable statistical study. An especially good documentary work is Elizabeth Donnan's four volumes, *Documents Illustrative of the History of the Slave Trade to America* (Washington, D.C., 1930–1939). Eric Williams, *Capitalism and Slavery* (Chapel Hill, 1944), is a good analysis of the slave trade's relation to world trade. Walter Rodney's pamphlet, *West Africa and the Atlantic Slave-Trade* (Nairobi, 1967), is a valuable summary. James Duffy, *A Question of Slavery* (Cambridge, Mass., 1967), examines slavery in Portuguese Africa and British protectorates. W. E. B. DuBois, *The Suppression of the African Slave Trade in the United States* (Cambridge, Mass., 1896), is a classic on that subject. Walter Rodney, *A History of the Upper Guinea Coast, 1545–1800* (Oxford, 1970), is also available.

The Indian Ocean slave trade has not been as thoroughly studied as the Atlantic trade. Edward Alpers' pamphlet, *The East African Slave Trade* (Nairobi, 1967), is a good introduction. Reginald Coupland's *East Africa and Its Invaders* (Oxford, 1938) and *The Exploitation of East Africa* (1939; reprint ed., Evanston, Ill., 1967) are dated but still contain useful information. Valuable data are also dispersed in B. A. Ogot and J. A. Kieran, *Zamani: A Survey of East African History* (New York, 1968); Roland Oliver and Gervase Mathew, *History of East Africa* (London, 1963), vol. I; and J. B. Kelly, *Britain and the Persian Gulf, 1795–1880* (Oxford, 1968). E. A. Loftus, *Elton and the East African Coast Slave Trade* (London, 1952), is a helpful account of a British consul's observations and views. C. S. Nicolls, *The Swahili Coast* (London, 1971), has some very relevant data. Also recommended is Joseph E. Harris, *The African Presence in Asia: Consequences of the East African Slave Trade* (Evanston, Ill., 1971).

The following are highly recommended: Claude Meillasoux, *The Anthropology of Slavery: The Womb of Iron and Gold* (Chicago, 1991) and *L'Esclavage en Afrique Précoloniale* (Paris, 1975); Paul Lovejoy, *The Ideology of Slavery in Africa* (London, 1981); *The African Slave Trade from the Fifteenth to the Nineteenth Century* (UNESCO, 1979); John Grace, *Domestic Slavery in West Africa* (London, 1975); Joseph Inikori, *Forced Migration* (New York, 1982); Patrick Manning, *Slavery, Colonialism and Economic Growth in Dahomey, 1640–1960* (Cambridge, Mass, 1982); Robert Ross, *Cape of Torments: Slavery and Resistance in South Africa* (London, 1983); Robert Louis Stein, *The French Slave Trade in the Eighteenth Century* (Madison, Wis., 1979); Claire C. Robertson, *Women in Slavery in Africa* (Madison, Wis., 1983); R. W. Beachey, *The Slave Trade of East Africa* (New York, 1976); Suzanne Miers and Igor Kopytoff, *Slavery in Africa* (Madison, Wis., 1977); Edward A. Alpers, *Ivory and Slaves* (Berkeley, Los Angeles, 1975); Frederick Cooper, *Plantation Slavery on the East Coast of Africa* (New Haven, Conn., and London, 1977); Elizabeth A. Eldredge and Fred Morton, ed., *Slavery in South Africa: Captive Labor on the Dutch Frontier* (Boulder, Colo., 1994); Elizabeth Savage, ed., *The Human Commodity: Perspectives on the Trans-Saharan Slave Trades* (London, 1992); Joseph Miller, *Way of Death: Merchant Capitalism and the Angolan Slave Trade* (Madison, Wis., 1988); Frederick Cooper, *From Slaves to Squatters: Plantation Labor and Agriculture in Zanzibar and Coastal Kenya, 1890–1925* (New Haven, Conn., 1980); and John Ralph Willis, *Slaves and Slavery in Muslim Africa* (Frank Cass, 1985).

Chapter 5   The Expansion of Africa

The dispersion and settlement of Africans abroad have been studied primarily in individual countries, principally the United States. Some of the Caribbean countries have received attention and so has England. But even those generally have ignored the African relationship. The following are sources that examine aspects of that relationship: Joseph E. Harris, *Global Dimensions of the African Diaspora* (Washington, D.C., 1982) focuses on concept, methodology, and case studies; St. Clair Drake, *Black Folk Here and There* (Los Angeles, 1986 and 1990), a two-volume study covering different parts of the diaspora across a wide time span; Drake, "Black Religion and the Redemption of Africa" (Chicago, 1971) is a stimulating monograph; Roger Bastide, *African Civilizations in the New World* (New York, 1972) remains a pioneering work, as does C. L. R. James, *The Black Jacobins: Toussaint L'Ouverture and San Domingo Revolution* (New York, 1963). Ibrahima B. Kaké, *Les Noirs de la Diaspora* (Libreville, Gabon, 1978) is a good study, and so is Leslie Rout, *The African Experience in Spanish America* (Cambridge, Mass., 1976). A unique and stimulating study is Robert Farris Thompson, *Flask of the Spirit* (New York, 1984). So also are: Okon Uyu, *Black Brotherhood: African-Americans and Africa* (Lexington, Mass., 1971); Folarin O. Shyllon, *Black People in Britain* (Oxford, 1977); James Walvin, *Black and White: The Negro and the English Society, 1555–1945* (London, 1973) and his *Black Personalities in the Era of the Slave Trade* (Baton Rouge, La., 1983). Manuela Carneiro da Cunha, *From Slave Quarters to Town House* (Sao Paulo, Brazil, 1985) also in Portuguese, *Negros. estrangeiros* (Sao Paulo, Brazil, 1985), and Gaston-Martin, *Nantes au Xville Siècle: L'ève des négviers (1714–1774)*, new edition (Paris, 1993), are good studies; and so is Decio Freitas, *Palmares* (Porto Alegra, Brazil, 1984); and *Quince Duncan, El Negro en Costa Rica* (San Jose, 1981). Still valuable is George Shepperson, "The African Abroad or the African Diaspora," *Emerging Themes of African History,* T. O. Ranger, ed., East African Publishing House, 1968; and "Notes on Negro American Influences on the Emergence of African Nationalism," *Journal of African History,* vol. I, no. 2, 1960.

Chapter 6   Repatriation and the Development of a Pan-Africanist Tradition

The literature on which the thrust of this chapter is based is limited, but there are a few very significant works. The antislavery activities leading to abolition in England and the founding and development of Sierra Leone are authoritatively covered by: Christopher Fyfe, *A History of Sierra Leone* (London, 1962); Arthur T. Porter, *Creoledom: A Study of the Development of the Freetown Society* (New York, 1963); and John Peterson, *Province of Freedom: A History of Sierra Leone* (Evanston, Ill., 1969). For a valuable account of Liberia's founding and development, see: Raymond L. Buell, *Liberia: A Century of Survival, 1847–1947* (Philadelphia, 1947); Merran Fraenkel, *Tribe and Class in Monrovia* (New York, 1964); and C. L. Simpson, *The Symbol of Liberia* (London, 1961). Studies that reveal various pan-African developments in the nineteenth century are: Hollis R. Lynch, *Edward Wilmot Blyden:*

Pan Negro Patriot (London, 1967); Jean H. Kopytoff, *A Preface to Modern Nigeria* (Madison, Wis., 1965), which examines the role of Sierra Leoneans in Nigeria; and Robert W. July, *The Origins of Modern African Thought* (New York, 1967), which deals very effectively with intellectual currents. Joseph E. Harris, *The African Presence in Asia* (Evanston, Ill., 1971), considers some of the relationships between East Africa and Asia. José Honorio Rodrigues, *Brazil and Africa* (Berkeley, 1965), covers the period from 1500 to the 1960s and is the best study of that subject.

Several of the sources listed under chapters 4 and 5 are also relevant for this chapter. In addition, the following are recommended: Hollis Lynch, *Black Spokesman: Selected Published Writings of Edward Wilmot Blyden* (London, 1971); Manuela Carneiro da Cunha, *From Slave Quarters to Town House* (Sao Paulo, Brazil, 1985); Tom Shick, *Behold the Promised Land: A History of African-American Settler Society in Nineteenth Century Liberia* (Baltimore, Md., 1980).

Chapter 7   Politics and State-Building I: The Guinea Coast and Forest Regions

There are several good studies of centralized and segmented societies on the Guinea coast and its forest region. Very specialized attention is provided in several chapters of Darylle Forde and P. M. Kaberry, *West African Kingdoms in the Nineteenth Century* (London, 1967). Works on the Niger area include: J. F. A. Ajayi and Robert Smith, *Yoruba Warfare in the Nineteenth Century* (Cambridge, Mass., 1969); J. C. Anene, *Southern Nigeria in Transition, 1885–1906* (Cambridge, Mass., 1966); E. Alago, *Small Brave City-State* (Madison, Wis., 1964); Saburi O. Biobaku, *The Egba and Their Neighbors* (New York, 1957); R. E. Bradbury, *The Benin Kingdom* (London, 1957); J. Egharevba, *Short History of Benin* (Ibadan, 1960); Kenneth Dike, *Trade and Politics in the Niger Delta* (New York, 1956); M. M. Green, *Ibo Village Affairs* (New York, 1964); G. I. Jones, *The Trading States of the Oil Rivers* (Oxford, 1956); Samuel Johnson, *The History of the Yorubas* (Lagos, 1937); and Robert Smith, *Kingdoms of the Yorubas* (London, 1969).

For Dahomey, see: I. A. Akinjobin, *Dahomey and Its Neighbors, 1708–1818* (Cambridge, Mass., 1967); Richard Burton (C. W. Newbury, ed.), *A Mission to Gelele, King of Dahomey* (New York, 1966); and Melville Herskovits, *Dahomey* (New York, 1938; Evanston, Ill., 1967).

For the Gold Coast: Kofi Busia, *The Position of the Chief in the Modern Political System of Ashanti* (London, 1951); W. W. Claridge, *A History of the Gold Coast and Ashanti* (London and New York, 1964); J. D. Fage, *Ghana* (Madison, Wis., 1959); R. S. Rattray, *Ashanti Law and Constitution* (London, 1929); William Tordoff, *Ashanti Under the Prempehs* (New York, 1965); Ivor Wilks, *The Northern Factor in Ashanti History* (Legon, Ghana, 1961); Freda Wolfson, *Pageant of Ghana* (Oxford, 1958); and T. C. McCaskie, *State and Society in Pre-Colonial Asante* (Cambridge, Mass., 1995).

Four general histories on the subject are: Michael Crowder, *Story of Nigeria* (London, 1962); David Kimble, *Political History of Ghana* (New York, 1963); C. Newbury, *The Western Slave Coast and Its Rulers* (Oxford, 1961); and W. E. F. Ward, *A History of Ghana* (London, 1958).

The following are recommended: A. G. Hopkins, *An Economic History of West Africa* (Cambridge, Mass., and New York, 1973); Mervyn Hiskett, *The Development of Islam in West Africa* (London, 1984); Joseph Cuoq, *Histoire de l'Islamisation de l'Afrique de l'Ouest* (Paris); J. K. Flynn, *Ashanti and Its Neighbors* (London, 1971); John Ralph Willis, *Studies in West African Islamic History* (London, 1979); S. A. Akintoye, *Revolution and Power Politics in Yorubaland, 1840–1893* (London, 1971); and Elizabeth Isichei, *A History of the Ibo People* (London, 1976).

Chapter 8   Politics and State-Building II: The Sudan

For this chapter one would want to examine the following: Adu A. Boahen, *Britain, the Sahara, and the Western Sudan* (Oxford, 1964); Thomas Hodgkin, *Nigerian Perspectives* (London, 1960); several chapters in Darylle Forde and P. M. Kaberry, *West African Kingdoms in the Nineteenth Century* (London, 1967); S. J. Hogben and A. H. M. Kirk-Green, *The Emirates of Northern Nigeria* (London, 1966); M. Last, *The Sokoto Caliphate* (New York, 1967); H. A. S. Johnston, *The Fulani Empire of Sokoto* (London, 1967); and Elliott P. Skinner, *The Mossi of the Upper Volta* (Stanford, 1964). A. Hampate Ba and J. Daget, *L'Empire Peul du Macina, 1818–1853* (Bamako, Mali, 1955); Paul Marty, *L'Islam en Guinea* (Paris, 1921); Louis Tauxier, *Moeurs et Histoire des Peuls* (Paris, 1937); Y. Urvoy, *Histoire de l'Empire du Bornu* (Paris, 1949); David Robinson, *The Holy War of Urmar Tall: The Western Sudan in the Mid-Nineteenth Century* (Oxford, 1985); and George E.

Brooks, *Landlords and Strangers: Ecology, Society and Trade in Western Africa,* 1000–1630 (Boulder, Colo., 1994).

Readings for the eastern Sudan include: Richard Gray, *A History of the Southern Sudan, 1839–1889* (London, 1961); Robert Collins, *The Southern Sudan, 1883–1898* (New Haven, Conn., 1962); P. M. Holt, *The Mahdist State in the Sudan* (Oxford, 1958); J. S. Trimingham, *Islam in the Sudan* (London and New York, 1965); and Neil McHugh, *Holymen of the Blue Nile: The Making of an Arab-Islamic Community in the Nilotic Sudan, 1500–1850* (Evanston, Ill., 1994). Jean-Loup Amselle, *Les Negociants de le Savane, Histoire et Organisation Sociale des Korroko* (Paris, 1977) describes Mali in precolonial and colonial times. See also Philip D. Curtin, *Economic Change in Pre-Colonial Africa; Senegambia in the Era of the Slave Trade* (Madison, Wis., 1975). See also notes for chapter 3.

Chapter 9 Politics and State-Building III: Central and Southern Africa

A good general account of precolonial central Africa is Jan Vansina, *Kingdoms of the Savanna* (Madison, Wis., 1966). Also useful is A. J. Wills, *An Introduction to the History of Central Africa* (Oxford, 1967). T. O. Ranger, ed., *Aspects of Central African History* (London, 1968), includes accounts of Congo, Malawi, Zambia, and Southern Rhodesia. Lloyd Fallers, *Bantu Bureaucracy* (Chicago and London, 1965), is very good for its subject. Other valuable studies on individual territories include: L. Jadin, *L'Ancien Congo* (Brussels, 1954); Roger F. H. Summers, *Zimbabwe* (Johannesburg, 1963); and D. P. Abraham, "Ethno-History of the Empire of Mutapa," *The Historian in Tropical Africa,* eds., Jan Vansina and others (Oxford, 1964). L. H. Gann, *A History of Northern Rhodesia* (London, 1964) and *A Short History of Zambia* (Oxford, 1966), are useful, but deal more with colonial and European matters, while Richard Hall, *Zambia* (London, 1965), focuses more on African politics, though concerning itself mainly with the twentieth century. E. T. Stokes and R. Brown, *The Zambesian Past* (Manchester, 1966), and Brian Fagan, *A Short History of Zambia* (Oxford, 1966), are also recommended. Racial matters receive special focus in Philip Mason, *The Birth of a Dilemma* (London, 1958), and Richard Gray, *The Two Nations: Aspects of the Development of Race Relations in the Rhodesias and Nyasaland* (London, 1960).

There are several valuable works on southern Africa for this period.

Absolam Vilakazi, *Zulu Transformations* (Natal, 1962), should be read. Monica Wilson and Leonard Thompson, *The Oxford History of South Africa* (Oxford, 1969), vol. I, covers the period to 1870 and is the best focus on African activities for that time. J. D. Omer-Cooper, *The Zulu Aftermath* (London, 1966), is an excellent study of the nineteenth-century Zulus. For accounts focusing on European contacts and relations with southern Africans, see: Eric Axelson, *South East Africa, 1488–1530* (London, 1940) and *South African Explorers* (London, 1954); and David Livingstone, *Narrative of an Expedition to the Zambezi and Its Tributaries* (New York, 1866). Other recommended books on the subject are: C. W. De Kiewiet, *A History of South Africa, Social and Economic* (London and New York, 1941) and *British Colonial Policy and the South African Republics, 1848–1872* (London, 1929), and W. M. MacMillan, *Bantu, Boer and Briton* (Oxford, 1964). E. A. Walker, *A History of Southern Africa* (London, 1959), is a standard European-focused work.

The following are helpful sources: H. H. Bhila, *Trade and Politics in a Shona Kingdom* (London, 1982); Jeff Guy, *The Destruction of the Zulu Kingdom* (London, 1979); and John K. Thornton, *The Kingdom of Kongo: Civil War and Transition, 1641–1718* (Madison, Wis., 1983); Catherine Coquery-Vidrovitch, *Le Congo français au temps de grandes compagnies concessionnaires, 1898–1930* (Paris and The Hague, 1972); W. G. Clarence-Smith, *Slaves, Peasants and Capitalists in Southern Angola, 1840–1926* (Cambridge, Mass., 1979); B. Pachai, *The Early History of Malawi* (London, 1972); K. David Patterson, *The Northern Gabon Coast to 1875* (Oxford, 1975); René Pélissier, *Les guerres grises: résistance et révoltés en Angola (1845–1941)* (Orgeval, 1977); Andrew D. Roberts, *A History of the Bemba: Political Growth and Change in Northeastern Zambia Before 1900* (Madison, Wis., 1974); Eric Stokes and R. Brown, *The Zambezian Past: Studies in Central African History* (Manchester, 1966); and Douglas Wheeler and René Pélissier, *Angola* (New York, 1971).

Chapter 10   Politics and Trade in East Africa

Recommended works for this chapter include several relevant chapters in B. A. Ogot and J. A. Kieran, eds., *Zamani: A Survey of East African History* (Nairobi, 1968); and Roland Oliver and Gervase Mathew, eds., *History of East Africa* (Oxford, 1962), vol. I. James

Duffy, *Portugal in Africa* (Penguin, 1962), is good for that subject. Somewhat outdated, but still useful are Reginald Coupland, *East Africa and Its Invaders* (Oxford, 1938), and *The Exploitation of East Africa, 1856–1890* (London, 1939, and Evanston, Ill., 1967). C. S. Nicholls, *The Swahili Coast* (London, 1971), is a good study of its subject. G. P. A. Freeman-Grenville, *The Medieval History of the Coast of Tanganyika* (London, 1962) and *The East African Coast* (Oxford, 1962), are highly recommended. For accounts of certain local societies in the area, see: Andrew Roberts, ed., *Tanzania Before 1900* (Nairobi, 1968); B. A. Ogot, *History of the Southern Luo* (Nairobi, 1967); Jomo Kenyatta, *Facing Mount Kenya* (New York, 1962); J. S. Mangat, *A History of the Asians in East Africa, 1886–1945* (Oxford, 1969); Isaria N. Kimambo, *A Political History of the Pare of Tanzania* (Nairobi, 1969); and R. G. Abrahams, *The Political Organization of Unyamwezi* (Cambridge, Mass., 1967). George Bennett, *Kenya: A Political History* (London, 1963), is a good survey, as is Janet J. Ewald, *Soldiers, Traders and Slaves: State Formation and Economic Transformation in the Greater Nile Valley, 1700–1885* (Madison, Wis., 1990). For useful materials on Ethiopia and other parts of the eastern coast, refer to the bibliographical notes for chapter 3. The following are three accounts of fascinating African personalities in the region: Norman Bennett, *Mirambo of Tanzania* (London and New York, 1971); J. B. Webster, "Mirambo and Nyamwezi Unification," *Tarikh*, vol. I, no. 1; and S. J. S. Cookey, "Tippu Tib and the Decline of the Congo Arabs," *Tarikh*, vol. I, no. 2.

The following sources are also recommended: Robert Gregory, *India and East Africa* (London, 1971); Derek Nurse and Thomas Spear, *The Swahili* (Philadelphia, 1985); Norman Robert Bennett, *Mirambo of Tanzania* (London, 1971); Hyder Kindy, *Life and Politics in Mombasa* (Nairobi, 1972); August Nimtz, *Islam and Politics in East Africa* (Minneapolis, 1980); Allen Isaacman and Barbara Isaacman, *The Tradition of Resistance in Mozambique: The Zambezi Valley, 1850–1921* (London, 1976).

Chapter 11 *The Scramble and Partition*

The "scramble and partition" are covered from various perspectives by several writers too numerous even to name. For the objectives and diplomacy of the European powers, the following selections are suggested: Ronald Robinson and John Gallagher, *Africa and the Victorians* (London, 1961); William Langer, *The Diplomacy of Imperialism* (New

York, 1951); Henri Brunschwig, *L'Avenement de l'Afrique Noire* (Paris, 1963); and relevant essays in L. H. Gann and Peter Duignan, *Colonialism in Africa, 1870–1914* (Cambridge, Mass., 1969), vol. I. Mary E. Townsend, *The Rise and Fall of Germany's Colonial Empire* (New York, 1930), and P. Gifford and W. R. Louis, *Britain and Germany in Africa* (New Haven, Conn., 1967), are also useful works. Sybil E. Crowe, *The Berlin West African Conference, 1884–1885* (London, 1942), remains standard for its subject. Two important regional studies are John Hargreaves, *Prelude to the Partition of West Africa* (London and New York, 1963), and G. N. Sanderson, *England, Europe and the Upper Nile* (Edinburgh, 1965). Two excellent articles in the *Journal of African History*, vol. III, no. 3 (1962), are: J. Stengers, "L'Impérialisme Colonial de la Fin du XIXe Siècle: Mythe ou Réalité," and C. W. Newbury, "Victorians, Republicans, and the Partition of West Africa."

Three important books on European penetration of Africa are: A. A. Boahen, *Britain, the Sahara, and the Western Sudan, 1788–1861* (Oxford, 1964); A. S. Kanya-Forstner, *The Conquest of the Western Sudan: A Study in French Military Imperialism* (Cambridge, Mass., 1969); and Robin Hallett, *The Penetration of Africa: European Exploration in North and West Africa to 1815* (New York, 1965).

The following are significant biographical and area studies: Basil Williams, *Cecil Rhodes* (New York, 1921); Margery Perham, *Lugard* (London, 1956, and New York, 1960); Roland Oliver, *Sir Harry Johnstone and the Scramble for Africa* (London, 1959); John Flint, *Sir George Goldie and the Making of Nigeria* (London, 1960); Ruth Slade, *King Leopold's Congo* (London, 1962); and Robert O. Collins, *King Leopold, England, and the Upper Nile, 1899–1909* (New Haven, Conn., 1968).

Highly recommended works for this chapter are: A. I. Asiwaju, *Partitioned Africans: Ethnic Relations Across Africa's International Boundaries, 1884–1984* (New York, 1985); Godfrey Uzoigwe, *Britain and the Conquest of Africa: The Age of Salisbury* (Ann Arbor, Mich., 1974); William R. Louis, *Imperialism: The Robinson and Gallagher Controversy* (New York, 1976); and Julia A. Clancy-Smith, *Rebel and Saint* (Berkeley, Calif., 1994).

Chapter 12 African Diplomacy, Resistance, and Rebellion

The subject of African resistance to the European introduction of colonial rule and the subsequent rebellion against it is gaining increased attention. This is best affirmed by Robert I. Rotberg and Ali A. Mazrui, eds., *Protest and Power in Black Africa* (Oxford, 1970), which surveys several different kinds of African protest and resistance movements, and has an extensive bibliography. A shorter work containing selections from *Protest and Power in Black Africa* is Robert Rotberg, ed., *Rebellion in Black Africa* (Oxford, 1971). Terence Ranger, ed., *Aspects of Central African History* (London, 1968), has several excellent chapters on African reactions to colonial rule; Ranger has also authored *Revolt in Southern Rhodesia, 1896–7: A Study in African Resistance* (Evanston, Ill., 1967), and a two-part article in the *Journal of African History* (1968): "Connections Between 'Primary Resistance' Movements and Modern Mass Nationalism in East and Central Africa," vol. IX, nos. 3 and 4. Also recommended is Ian Henderson, "Lobengula: Achievement and Tragedy," *Tarikh,* vol. II., no. 2.

The authoritative account for Malawi is George Shepperson and Thomas Price, *Independent African: John Chilembwe and the Origins . . . Significance of the Nyasaland Rising* (Edinburgh, 1958). The Maji Maji rebellion receives a good analysis by John Iliffe, "The Organization of the Maji Maji Rebellion," *Journal of African History,* vol. VIII, no. 3 (1967), and also Iliffe, *Tanganyika and German Rule, 1905–1912* (Cambridge, Mass., 1969). For the Zulu, see J. D Omer-Cooper, *The Zulu Aftermath* (London, 1966). The Ethiopian defeat of the Italians in 1896 is well examined by Richard Pankhurst, "The Battle of Adowa," *Ethiopia Observer,* vol. I, no. 12 (November, 1957), and Pankhurst's articles on Theodore and Menelik, *Tarikh,* vol. I, nos. 1 and 4. See also the general works of Ethiopia cited for chapter 3.

West African resistance has not received as much specialized attention as other regions, but useful data may be found in: J. D. Hargreaves, *Prelude to the Partition of West Africa* (London and New York, 1963); W. Tordorff, *Ashanti Under the Prempehs, 1888–1935* (London, 1965); and other listings for chapter 10. There are some valuable articles: Martin Legassick, "Firearms, Horses, and Samorian Army Organization, 1870–1898," *Journal of African History,* vol. VII, no. 1 (1966); Amadou Kouroubari, "Histoire de l'Iman Samori," *Bulletin de l'IFAN,* Parts 3 and 4 (1959); Mamadou Suleymane Diem, "Un Document Authentique sur Samory," *Notes Africaines*, LXXIV (April, 1957); R. Griffeth, "Samori Toure," *Tarikh*, vol. II, no. 4 (1967); and Joseph E. Harris, "Protest and Resistance to the French in Fouta Diallon," *Genève Afrique*, vol. VIII, no. 1 (1969).

Several articles cited in these notes and others have been reprinted in *The Africa Reader: Colonial Africa* (New York, 1970), eds., Wilfred Cartey and Martin Kilson.

Additional helpful sources are: Lamin Sanneh, *West African Christianity: The Religious Impact* (London, 1983); Ian Linden, *Catholics, Peasants, and Chewa Resistance in Nyasaland, 1889–1939* (Berkeley and Los Angeles, 1974); and Cynthia Brantley, *The Giriama and Colonial Resistance in Kenya, 1800–1920* (Berkeley, 1981).

Chapter 13 *The European Colonizers*

Chapter 14 *The Struggle for Independence*

There are several general works on colonial policies and practices. Lord Hailey's *African Survey* (London, 1938, 1945, 1957) is a massive study of European activities south of the Sahara. A bit dated but still useful is Raymond L. Buell, *The Native Problem in Africa* (London, 1926 and 1965), 2 vols. Frederick D. Lugard, *The Dual Mandate in British Tropical Africa* (London, 1922 and 1965), is good on British colonial administration. For French policies see: Robert Delavignette, *Freedom and Authority in French West Africa* (Oxford, 1950, and New York, 1968); Stephen H. Roberts, *A History of French Colonial Policy, 1870–1925* (Oxford, 1963); J. Suret-Canale, *Afrique Noire, Occidentale et Central: L'Ere Coloniale, 1900–1945* (Paris, 1964). Michael Crowder's *Senegal: A Study in French Assimilation Policy* (London and New York, 1967) is the best account of that subject in English; see also his *West Africa Under Colonial Rule* (London, 1968). Henri Brunschwig, *French Colonialism, 1871–1914* (New York, 1966), is also valuable. John Marlowe, *Anglo-Egyptian Relations, 1800–1953* (London, 1954), covers that subject; and James Duffy, *Portuguese Africa* (Cambridge, Mass., 1959), covers that area.

The best survey of the concept and development of the colonial state is Crawford Young, *The African Colonial State in Comparative Perspectives* (New Haven, Conn., 1994). Other good recent studies include:

Michael Havinden and David Meredith, *Colonialism and Development: Britain and Its Tropical Colonies, 1850–1960* (New York, 1993); John Kent, *The Internationalization of Colonialism: Britain, France and Black Africa, 1939–56* (Oxford, 1992); W. O. Henderson, *The German Colonial Empire, 1884–1919* (London, 1991); and Tiyambe Zeleza, *A Modern Economic History of Africa,* vol. 1: *The Nineteenth Century* (Dakar, 1993).

The ex–Belgian Congo is examined in the following: Roger Anstey, *King Leopold's Legacy* (London, 1966); Alan Merriam, *Congo: Background to Conflict* (Evanston, Ill., 1961); René Lemarchand, *Political Awakening in the Belgian Congo* (Berkeley, 1964); Crawford Young, *Politics in the Congo* (Princeton, N.J., 1965); and Ruth Slade, *The Belgian Congo* (London, 1961). Frantz Fanon, *The Wretched of the Earth* (New York, 1966), is a stimulating analysis of national revolutions in Africa, and his *Black Skin, White Masks* (New York, 1968) is recommended for the racial factor in the colonial and nationalist situations. Racial politics in central Africa are discussed in Patrick Keatley, *The Politics of Partnership* (Penguin, 1963), and Elspeth Huxley, *White Man's Country* (London, 1935, and New York, 1968).

In order to best understand the influence of either Islam or Christianity on Africans, one should gain some knowledge of traditional African thought, which is deeply embedded in religious concepts. Valuable works for this are: John S. Mbiti, *African Religions and Philosophies* (New York, 1970); Pauline J. Hountondji, *African Philosophy: Myth and Reality* (Bloomington, Ill., 1983); Y. Mudimbe, *The Invention of Africa: Gnosis, Philosophy, and the Order of Knowledge* (Bloomington, Ill., 1988) and *The Idea of Africa* (Bloomington, Ill., 1994); and Kwesi Wiredu, *Philosophy and an African Culture* (Cambridge, Mass., 1980). Various aspects of Christianity in Africa are covered by: C. P. Groves, *The Planting of Christianity in Africa* (London, 1964) I (to 1840), II (1840–1878), III (1878–1914), IV (1914–1954); C. G. Baeta, ed., *Christianity in Tropical Africa* (Oxford, 1968); N. Goodall, *A History of the London Missionary Factor in East Africa* (London, 1952); I. Schapera, ed., *Livingstone's Missionary Correspondence, 1841–1856* (London, 1967); Robert Rotberg, *Christian Missionaries and the Creation of Northern Rhodesia, 1880–1924* (Princeton, N.J., 1965); J. F. A. Ajayi, *Christian Missions in Nigeria, 1841–1891* (London and Evanston, Ill., 1965); E. A. Ayandele, *The Missionary Impact on Modern Nigeria, 1842–1914* (London, 1966, and New York, 1967); and F. L.

Bartels, *The Roots of Ghana Methodism* (Cambridge, Mass., 1965). James Bertin Webster, *The African Churches Among the Yoruba, 1888–1922* (Oxford, 1964), and Marie-Louise Martin, *Kimbangu: An African Prophet and His Church* (Oxford, 1975), deal with those churches established by African Christians in revolt against foreign missionaries. The classic study of separatist churches, however, is B. G. M. Sundkler, *Bantu Prophets in South Africa* (Oxford, 1964). F. B. Welbourn, *East African Rebels* (London, 1961), is also a valuable account.

Several of the works above contain valuable data on African nationalism. The literature is rather extensive, and the choice here highly selective. Thomas Hodgkin's *Nationalism in Colonial Africa* (London, 1956, and New York, 1957) remains very informative, and so is his *African Political Parties* (Penguin, 1961). The edited work by Gwendolen Carter, *National Unity and Regionalism in Eight African States* (Ithaca, N.Y., 1966), crosses from colonial to independence politics. Immanuel Wallerstein, *Africa: The Politics of Independence* (New York, 1961), is a good, readable study. James S. Coleman and Carl G. Rosberg, eds., *Political Parties and National Integration in Tropical Africa* (Berkeley and Los Angeles, 1964), is a very able study.

For the French areas, consult: Virginia Thompson and Richard Adloff, *French West Africa* (London, 1958) and *The Emerging States of French Equatorial Africa* (Stanford, 1960), and Ruth. S. Morgenthau, *Political Parties in French-Speaking West Africa* (Oxford, 1964).

From the many accounts of nationalism in individual countries, the following samples are recommended: Mohamed O. Beshir, *The Southern Sudan, Background to Conflict* (London and New York, 1968); James S. Coleman, *Nigeria* (Berkeley and Los Angeles, 1958); Dennis Austin, *Politics in Ghana, 1946–1960* (London, 1964); Martin Kilson, *Political Change in a West African State: A Study of Modernization in Sierra Leone* (Cambridge, Mass., 1966); Aristide Zolberg, *One-Party Government in Ivory Coast* (Princeton, N.J., 1964); Willard Johnson, *The Cameroon Federation* (Princeton, N.J., 1970); David Apter, *The Political Kingdom in Uganda* (Princeton, N.J., 1961); Carl Rosberg and John Nottingham, *The Myth of "Mau Mau": Nationalism in Kenya* (New York, 1966); Colin Legum, *Congo Disaster* (Penguin, 1961); Michael F. Lofchie, *Zanzibar* (Princeton, N.J., 1965); I. N. Kimambu and A. J. Temu, *A History of Tanzania* (Nairobi, 1969); Nathan Shamuyarira, *Crisis in Rhodesia* (New York, 1965); and Robert Rotberg, *The Rise of Nationalism in Central Africa* (Cambridge, Mass., 1965).

L. Gray Cowan, *The Dilemmas of African Independence* (New York, 1968), briefly considers post-independence problems and includes a reference section of valuable data. Some other good sources are: *Angola: A Symposium* (London, 1962); D. M. Abshire and M.A. Samuels, eds., *Portuguese Africa: A Handbook* (New York, 1969); R. J. Hammond, *Portugal and Africa* (Stanford, 1967); and John Marcum, *The Angolan Revolution* (Cambridge, Mass., 1969). Amilcar Cabral (tr., Richard Handyside), *Revolution in Guinea* (London, 1969), contains speeches by the nationalist leader in Guinea. Gerard Chaliard, *Armed Struggle in Africa* (New York, 1969), is an eyewitness's account of the revolt in Guinea.

Essays from several of the works cited above are included in L. H. Gann and Peter Duignan, *Colonialism in Africa, 1870–1960* (Cambridge, Mass., 1969), vols. 1 and 2, and Victor Turner (1971), vol. 3. These are important volumes, though the general editors' views overemphasize the advantages of the colonial era.

The pan-African dimension is ably discussed in George Padmore's *Pan Africanism or Communism* (London, 1956); see also his *The Gold Coast Revolution* (London, 1953). Another good study is Vincent Bakpetu Thompson, *Africa and Unity* (Humanities Press, 1969). For African-American sentiments on Africa, Adelaide Hill and Martin Kilson, eds., *Apropos of Africa* (London, 1969), is very useful. James R. Hooker, *Black Revolutionary* (London and New York, 1967), is a valuable biography of Padmore. W. E. B. DuBois, *The World and Africa* (New York, 1947), and his *Autobiography* (New York, 1968), should also be consulted. C. L. R. James, *A History of Pan-African Revolt* (Washington, D.C., 1969), is another useful account by a participant. See also: K. A. B. Jones-Quartey, *A Life of Azikiwe* (Penguin, 1965); AMSAC, *Pan Africanism Reconsidered* (Berkeley, 1962); and the complete issues of *African Forum,* vol. I, nos. 1 and 2 (1965). Ali Mazrui, *Towards a Pax Africana* (London and Chicago, 1967), is recommended. For cultural pan-Africanism, or negritude, see various issues of *Présence Africaine* and *African Forum;* and Mercer Cook and Stephen E. Henderson, *The Militant Black Writer in Africa and the United States* (Madison, Wis., 1969). Important studies of practical steps toward unity include: Albert Tevoedjre, *Pan Africanism in Action* (Cambridge, Mass., 1965); Richard Cox, *Pan Africanism in Practice* (London, 1964); William Foltz, *From French West Africa to the Mali Federation* (New Haven, Conn., 1965); Joseph S. Nye, *Pan Africanism and East African Integration* (Cambridge, Mass., 1965); and Claude Welch, *Dream of Unity* (Ithaca, N.Y., 1966). Joseph E. Harris, *African-American Reactions to War in Ethiopia 1936–1941* (Louisiana 1994), examines the impact of war on nationalism and pan-Africanism.

Nationalism and pan-Africanism have received serious and creditable treatment by a number of African leaders. The following are a few selections of informative and stimulating works by Africa's most prolific political writer, Kwame Nkrumah: *Ghana: An Autobiography* (Edinburgh, 1959); *I Speak Freedom* (London and New York, 1961); *Africa Must Unite* (London and New York, 1963); and *Neo-Colonialism: The Last Stage of Imperialism* (London and New York, 1965). Recommendations by other African nationalists include: *Awo: The Autobiography of Chief Obafemi Awolowo* (Cambridge, Mass., 1960); Ahmadu Bello, *My Life* (Cambridge, Mass., 1962); K. A. Busia, *The Challenge of Africa* (New York, 1962); Patrice Lumumba, *La Pensée Politique de Patrice Lumumba* (Paris, 1963) and *Congo My Country* (New York, 1962); Kenneth Kaunda, *Zambia Shall Be Free: An Autobiography* (London, 1962); Julius Nyerere, *Education For Self-Reliance* (Dar es Salaam, 1967) and *Freedom and Socialism, Uhuru na Ujamaa* (New York and Oxford, 1969); Tom Mboya, *Freedom and After* (London and Boston, 1963); Oginga Odinga, *Not Yet Uhuru; an Autobiography* (London, 1967); Alex Quaison-Sackey, *Africa Unbound* (New York, 1963); N. Sithole, *African Nationalism* (London, 1969); Leopold Senghor (translated by Mercer Cook), *On African Socialism* (New York, 1964); Janet G. Vaillant, *Black, French, and African: A Life of Leopold Sedar Senghor* (Cambridge, Mass., 1990); Sekou Touré, *Expérience Guinéene et Unité Africaine* (Paris, 1961); and *A Selection from the Speeches of Nnamdi Azikiwe* (Cambridge, Mass., 1961). Some of these and other African leaders have essays in Wilfred Cartey and Martin Kilson, *The Africa Reader: Independent Africa* (New York, 1970), and several issues of *African Forum*.

Good recent studies are E. A. Brett, *Colonialism and Underdevelopment in East Africa* (New York, 1973); Robert Ross, *Racism and Colonialism: Essays on Ideology and Social Structure* (The Hague, 1982); A. I. Asiwaju, *Western Yorubaland Under European Rule, 1889–1945* (London, 1976); J. Forbes Munro, *Colonial Rule and the Kamba* (Oxford, 1975); John Galbraith, *Mackinnon and East Africa, 1878–1895* (Cambridge, Mass., 1972); J. Gus Liebenow, *Colonial Life and Political Development in Tanzania* (Evanston, Ill., 1971); Robert O. Collins,

Shadows in the Grass: Britain in the Southern Sudan, 1918–1956 (New Haven, Conn., and London, 1983); B. E. Kipkorir, *Biographical Essays on Imperialism and Collaboration in Colonial Kenya* (Nairobi, 1980); Sharon Stichter, *Migrant Labour in Kenya* (London, 1982); Joseph E. Harris, *Repatriates and Refugees in a Colonial Society* (Washington, D.C., 1987); Brian Weinstein, *Eboué* (New York, 1972); Rita Cruse O'Brian, *White Society in Black Africa: The French of Senegal* (Faber, 1972); Henri Brunschwig, *Noirs et blancs dans l'Afrique noire française, ou comment le colonisé devient colonisateur* (Paris, 1983); Allen and Barbara Isaacman, *Mozambique: From Colonialism to Revolution: 1900–1982* (Boulder, Colo., 1983); Malyn Newitt, *Portugal in Africa: The Last Hundred Years* (London, 1981); Gerald Bender, *Angola Under the Portuguese: The Myth and the Reality* (London, 1978); Eduardo de Soussa Ferreira, *Portuguese Colonialism in Africa: The End of an Era* (Paris, 1974); Luis B. Serapiao, *Mozambique in the Twentieth Century: From Colonialism to Independence* (Washington, D.C., 1979); L. H. Gann and Peter Duignan, *The Rulers of German Africa, 1884–1914* (Stanford, 1977); and Opoku Agyeman, *Nkrumah's Ghana or East Africa: Pan-Africanism and African Interstate Relations* (Rutherford, N.J., 1992).

Recent studies recommended for individual countries are: Allen F. Isaacman, *The Tradition of Resistance in Mozambique* (Berkeley and Los Angeles, 1976); Anthony Clayton, *The Zanzibar Revolution and Its Aftermath* (London, 1981); Abdallah Laroui, *Les origines sociales et culturelle du nationalisme marocain* (Paris, 1977); and Donald L. Barnett and Karari Njama, *Mau Mau from Within* (New York and London, 1966). For pan-Africanism see: J. Ayodele Langley, *Pan-Africanism and Nationalism in West Africa, 1900–1945* (London, 1980), and Robert A. Hill, *The Marcus Garvey and Universal Negro Improvement Association Papers,* vols. 1–4 (Berkeley and Los Angeles, 1983–). For African leaders see *Harry Thuku: An Autobiography* (Lusaka, Dar es Salaam, Addis Ababa, 1970), and Harold Marcus, *Haile Sellassie I: The Formative Years, 1892–1936* (Berkeley, 1987). Also recommended are Prosser Gifford and William Roger Louis, *The Transfer of Power in Africa: Decolonization, 1940–1960* (New Haven, Conn., and London, 1982); O. Olusanya, *The West African Students' Union and the Politics of Decolonization, 1925–1958* (Ibadan, Nigeria, 1982); UNESCO, *The Role of African Student Movements in the Political and Social Evolution of Africa from 1900 to 1975* (Paris, 1994); Ras Makonnen, *Pan-Africanism from Within* (Nairobi, London, New York, 1973); and Kenneth James King, *Pan-Africanism and Education* (London, 1971).

Chapter 15   The Transformation in Southern Africa: South Africa and Namibia

In addition to previous references on South Africa (chapters 9, 11–13), the following are suggested for this chapter: Albert Luthuli, *Let My People Go* (London, 1962); Bloke Modisane, *Blame Me on History* (New York, 1963); and Peter Abrahams, *Tell Freedom* (New York, 1969), are illuminating accounts by black South Africans. Other highly recommended works include: Mary Benson, *South Africa: The Struggle for a Birthright* (New York, 1971); Gwendolen Carter, *The Politics of Inequality* (New York, 1959); E. S. Munger, *Afrikaner and African Nationalism* (London, 1967); Brian Bunting, *The Rise of the South African Reich* (Penguin, 1964); "South Africa and Her Neighbors Within," *African Forum*, vol. II, no. 2 (1966) (complete issue); Ruth First, *South-West Africa* (Penguin, 1963); and Jack Halpern, *South Africa's Hostages* (Penguin, 1965), deal with South Africa in relation to Botswana, Lesotho, Swazi, and South West Africa (Namibia).

Several pieces by nationalist leaders still struggling against European rule are contained in Wilfred Cartey and Martin Kilson, eds., *The Africa Reader: Independent Africa* (New York, 1970), and John A. Davis and James W. Baker, eds., *Southern Africa in Transition* (New York, 1966).

From among the many recent works relevant for this chapter, the following provide stimulating and substantive perspectives: For racism and apartheid see UNESCO, *Racism and Apartheid in Southern Africa: South Africa and Namibia* (Paris, 1974); and Marion O'Callaghan, *Namibia: The Effects of Apartheid on Culture and Education* (UNESCO, Paris, 1977). For resistance see: Nelson Mandela, *The Struggle Is My Life* (New York, 1986), and Tom Lodge, *Black Politics in South Africa Since 1945* (London and New York, 1983). Cherryl Walker, *Women and Resistance in South Africa* (London, 1982), focuses on multiracial resistance among women. For labor issues see: Norman Levy, *The Foundations of the South African Cheap Labor System* (London, 1982), and Marian Lacey, *Working for Boroko: The Origins of a Coercive Labor System in South Africa* (Johannesburg, 1981). Three highly recommended comparative studies are: George M. Frederickson, *White Supremacy: A Comparative Study in American and South African His-*

tory (Oxford, 1981); John W. Cell, *The Highest Stage of White Supremacy: The Origins of Segregation in South Africa and the American South* (Cambridge, Mass., 1982); and Howard Lamar and Leonard Thompson, *The Frontier in History: North America and South Africa Compared* (New Haven, Conn., and London, 1981). For multinationals see Ann and Neva Seidman, *South Africa and U.S. Multinational Corporations* (Westport, Conn., 1977). Significant recent works are: John A. Williams, *From the South African Past: Narratives, Documents, and Debates* (New York, 1997); Lynn Berat, *Walvis Bay: Decolonization and International Law* (New Haven, Conn., and London, 1990); Joshua Brown, Patrick Manning, Karin Shapiro, Jon Wiener, eds., *History from South Africa* (Philadelphia, 1991); Millard Arnold, ed., *The Testimony of Steve Biko* (London, 1979); Nelson Mandela, *Long Walk to Freedom: The Autobiography of Nelson Mandela* (Boston, 1994); and Ronald Dreyer, *Namibia and Southern Africa: Regional Dynamics of Decolonization 1945–1990* (New York, 1994). Written accounts of more recent developments, since 1994, have appeared in several journals. A readily available one is the *Journal of Modern African Studies.*

Chapter 16   The Quest for Unity

The OAU is discussed by its former secretary-general, Diallo Telli, in "The Organization of African Unity in Historical Perspective," *African Forum* (1965), vol. I, no. 2. See also: Zdenek Cervenka, *The Organization of African Unity* (New York, 1969), and V. Bakpetu Thompson, *Africa and Unity* (New York, 1969). I. William Zartman, *International Relations in the New Africa* (Englewood Cliffs, N. J., 1966), examines foreign relations among states in northern and western Africa between 1956 and 1965.

Of the comparatively few recent books published on this subject, the following are recommended: Zdenek Cervenka, *The Unfinished Quest for Unity: Africa and the OAU* (New York, 1977); Michael Wolfers, *Politics in the Organization of African Unity* (London, 1976); and Organization of African Unity (OAU), *Lagos Plan of Action for the Economic Development of Africa, 1980–2000* (Geneva, 1981). Timely and perceptive articles appear in a number of issues of the *Journal of Modern African Studies.*

Chapter 17   Africa and Contemporary Issues

The political economy of the continent is examined well in C. W. Gutkind and Emmanuel Wallerstein, *The Political Economy of Contemporary Africa* (Beverly Hills and London, 1976); Claude Ake, *A Political Economy of Africa* (Harlow and New York, 1982); and Richard Harris, *The Political Economy of Africa* (New York and London, 1975). Stimulating perspectives are provided by Nzongola Ntalaja, *Class Struggles and National Liberation in Africa: Essays on the Political Economy of Neo-Colonialism* (Roxbury, Mass., 1982); John W. Harbeson, Donald Rothchild, and Naomi Chazan, eds., *Civil Society and the State in Africa* (London, 1994), and John O. Hunwick, ed., *Religion and National Integration in Africa: Islam, Christianity and Politics in the Sudan and Nigeria* (Evanston, Ill., 1992). The theme is also approached from the perspective of individual countries: Guy Gran, *Zaire: The Political Economy of Underdevelopment* (New York, 1979); Gavin Kitching, *Class and Economic Change in Kenya* (New Haven, Conn., and London, 1980); and Colin Leys, *Underdevelopment in Kenya* (Berkeley and Los Angeles, 1974). Economic and cultural issues are viewed by younger scholars in Pearle T. Robinson and Elliott P. Skinner, *Transformation and Resiliency* (Washington, D.C., 1983). A stimulating and global historical approach is J. Forbes Munro, *Africa and the International Economy, 1800–1960* (London, 1976).

Also recommended are: Organization of African Unity, *Lagos Plan of Action for the Economic Development of Africa, 1980–2000* (Geneva, 1981), and Robert Cummings and Robert S. Browne, *The Lagos Plan of Action vs. the Berg Report, Contemporary Issues in African Economic Development* (Lawrenceville, Va., 1985).

Questions of identity are addressed in the following: Sulayman S. Nyang, *Islam, Christianity and African Identity* (Brattleboro, Vt., 1985); Cheikh Anta Diop, *Black Africa: The Economic and Cultural Basis for a Federated State* (Westport, Conn., 1978); Tukumbi Lumumba-Kasongo, *Political Re-Mapping of Africa: Transnational Ideology and the Redefinition of Africa in World Politics* (New York, 1994); O. A. Masolo, *African Philosophy in Search of Identity* (Bloomington; Ill., 1994); and Richard P. Werbner and Terrance Ranger, eds., *Post-Colonial Identities in Africa* (London, 1996).

Foreign policy issues are examined in: F. Chidozie Ogene, *Interest Groups and the Shaping of Foreign Policy: Four Case Studies of United States African Policy* (Lagos, 1983); Henry F. Jackson, *From the Congo to Soweto: U.S. Foreign Policy Toward Africa Since 1960* (New York, 1984); Harold Marcus, *Ethiopia, Great Britain, and the United States, 1941–1974* (Berkeley, Los Angeles, and London, 1983); Holis Lynch, *Black American Radicals and the Liberation of Africa: The Council on African Affairs, 1937–1955* (Ithaca, N.Y., 1978); Robert Legvold, *Soviet Policy in West Africa* (Cambridge, Mass., 1970); Richard P. Stevens and Abdelwahab M. Elmessiri, *Israel and South Africa* (New York, 1976); Peter Duignan and L. H. Gann, *The United States and Africa* (Cambridge, Mass., and New York, 1984); Sondra Hale, *Gender Politics in Sudan: Islamism, Socialism and the State* (Westview, 1996); Claude Ake, *Democracy and Development in Africa* (The Brookings Institution, 1996); Denis Dwyer and David Drakakis-Smith, eds., *Ethnicity and Development: Geographical Perspectives* (Chichester, 1996); Claude Emerson Welch, *Protecting Human Rights in Africa: Strategies and Roles of Nongovernmental Organizations* (Philadelphia, 1995); Harold Marcus, *Ethiopia, Great Britain and the United States, 1941–1974* (Berkeley, 1983); and Elliott P. Skinner, *African Americans and U.S. Policy Toward Africa, 1850–1924* (Washington, D.C., 1992).

From among the growing body of literature on women in Africa, the following are recommended: Christine Obbo, *African Women: Their Struggle for Economic Independence* (London, 1980); Nina Emma Mba, *Nigerian Women Mobilized: Women's Political Activity in Southern Nigeria, 1900–1965* (Berkeley, 1982); Nancy J. Hafkin and Edna G. Bay, *Women in Africa* (Stanford, 1976); Marjorie Wall Bingham and Susan Hill Gross, *Women in Africa of the Sub-Sahara*, vol. 1. (Hudson, Wis., 1982); and David Sweetman, *Women Leaders in African History* (London, Ibadan, Nairobi, 1984). Valuable recent books include: Stanlie M. James and Abena P. A. Busia, eds., *Theorizing Black Feminisms: The Visionary Pragmatism of Black Women*, (New York, 1993), and Catherine Coquery-Vidrovitch, *Les Africaines: Histoires des Femmes d'Afrique Noises du XIXe An Xxe Siècle* (Paris, 1994).

Books on selected countries include: T. V. Sathyamurthy, *The Political Development of Uganda, 1900–86* (Aldershot, 1991); Phares Mutibwa, *Uganda Since Independence: A Story of Unfulfilled Hopes* (Kampala, 1992); David Burringham, *Frontline Nationalism in Angola and Mozambique* (London, 1992); John Mumpanga Mwanakatwa, *End of Kaunda Era* (Lusaka, 1994); Bealwell Chisala, *The Downfall of President Kaunda* (Lusaka, 1994); Akol Ruay, *The Politics of Two Sudans: The South and the North, 1821–1969* (Uppsala, 1994); Bahru Zewde, *A*

History of Modern Ethiopia, 1885–1974, (Athens and Addis Ababa, 1991); John H. Spencer, *Ethiopia at Bay: A Personal Account of the Haile Selassie Years* (Algonac, Mich., 1984); Teshome G. Wagaw, *The Development of Higher Education and Social Change: An Ethiopian Experience* (East Lansing, Mich., 1990); Anthony Sillery, *Botswana: A Short Political History* (London, 1974); Thomas Tlou and Alec Campbell, *History of Botswana* (Gaborone and Basingstoke, 1984); Dunstan Wai, *The Southern Sudan* (London, 1973); John Iliffe, *A Modern History of Tanganyika* (Cambridge, Mass., 1979) and *Modern Tanzanians* (Dar es Salaam, 1973); Ali A. Mazrui, *Soldiers and Kinsmen in Uganda* (Beverly Hills and London, 1975); Roderick J. Macdonald, *From Nyasaland to Malawi* (Nairobi, 1972); Skyne R. Uku, *The Pan-African Movement and the Nigerian Civil War* (New York, 1978); Sheldon Gellar, *Senegal: An African Nation Between Islam and the West* (Boulder, Colo., 1982); Barry Munslow, *Mozambique: The Revolution and Its Origins* (London, 1983); Patrick Chabal, *Amilcar Cabral, Revolutionary Leadership and People's War* (Cambridge, Mass., 1983); and Sylvester Cohen, Jr., *Frontline Nationalism in Angola and Mozambique* (Trenton, N.J., 1992). Two standard works on urbanization are: Marc Howard Ross, *Grass Roots in an African City: Political Behavior in Nairobi* (Cambridge, Mass., 1975); and Elliott P. Skinner, *The Transformation of Ouagadougou* (Princeton, N.J., 1974). For the conflict in the Horn of Africa see: Bereket Hapte Selassie, *Conflict and Intervention in the Horn of Africa* (New York and London, 1982); Basil Davidson, Lionel Cliffe, and Bereket Selassie, *Behind the War in Eritrea* (Nottingham, 1980); and Amrit Wilson, *The Challenge Road: Women and the Eritrean Revolution* (London, 1991). Olusegun Obasanjo and Hans D'Orville, *Challenges of Leadership in African Development* (New York and London: Crane Russak, 1990) provides insightful analyses on contemporary leadership and developments; Lionel Cliffe et al., *The Transition to Independence in Namibia* (Boulder and London: Lynne Riennen 1994) analyzes the decolonization process; R. Osoro, *The African Society in Crisis* (Hudsonville, M.I.: Bayana, 1993) relates the issue of identity to development of African societies.

Index